Foundational Theology

Foundational Theology

Neil Ormerod and
Christiaan Jacobs-Vandegeer

Fortress Press
Minneapolis

FOUNDATIONAL THEOLOGY
A New Approach to Catholic Fundamental Theology

Cover image: Mosaic from apex of apse arch: Christ. Location: S. Apollinare in Classe, Ravenna, Italy. Photo Credit: Scala / Art Resource, NY

Cover design: Tory Herman

Library of Congress Cataloging-in-Publication Data
Print ISBN: 978-1-4514-8041-2
eBook ISBN: 978-1-5064-0188-1

The paper used in this publication meets the minimum requirements of American National Standard for Information Sciences — Permanence of Paper for Printed Library Materials, ANSI Z329.48-1984.

Manufactured in the U.S.A.

This book was produced using Pressbooks.com, and PDF rendering was done by PrinceXML.

Contents

Preface

Gerald O'Collins, SJ

Neil Ormerod recalls precisely the meal at which I suggested to him the value of writing a book on fundamental theology from the perspective of Bernard Lonergan. I had just published *Rethinking Fundamental Theology: Toward a New Fundamental Theology*,[1] which ended with three questions, the last question being: "How might Lonergan's method and, in particular, his reflections on 'foundations' reshape the whole discipline of fundamental theology in the third millennium?" (343). I did not myself presume to "wrap it all up" by attempting to answer this and two other questions, which concerned, respectively, a debate on historical interpretation between Hans-Georg Gadamer and Jürgen Habermas and debates over the founding of the church.

Reading this joint work of Neil and his colleague, Christiaan Jacobs-Vandegeer, I have found it a significant contribution not only to Lonergan studies but also to the development of fundamental

---

1. Gerard O'Collins, *Rethinking Fundamental Theology: Toward a New Fundamental Theology* (Oxford: Oxford University Press, 2011).

theology. It has grown out of the conviction that conversion, in its various forms, is the foundational reality of theology.

The book puts into sharp focus for fundamental theology not only what Lonergan proposed about religious, moral, and intellectual conversion but also what Robert Doran later added about psychic conversion and the aesthetic concerns of Hans Urs von Balthasar. Such a fourfold conversion will enable theologians to see with the eyes of religious love. Unconverted theologians remain theologians who will never fulfill their mission. As the foreword to this book puts it, they resemble "an empty gong booming, full of sound and fury, but lacking the one thing essential." Converted theologians, however, are "the foundation from which all sound theology emerges," as our two authors state below.

If I were to name my favorite chapter in this work, which Neil and Christiaan have coauthored, I would pick chapter 5, "Psychic Conversion and the Question of Beauty." Through the experience of beauty, the splendor of meaning, truth, and value can capture and hold our attention. What Doran has proposed about psychic conversion and von Balthasar has developed at length about the claims of beauty should shape deeply the practice of fundamental theology.

Our two authors appreciate the way in which fundamental theologians, even more than other theologians, need to share in debates that concern foundational questions. They offer their readers help in navigating the way "through the competing claims of various theological camps." Neil and Christiaan provide such help for those facing debates triggered by René Girard's mimesis theory, by John Milbank's Radical Orthodoxy, and by what various writers have argued about experience and, in particular, mysticism in the religions of the world.

In elaborating a foundational theology from a Lonergan

perspective, our two authors have aimed to illustrate basic issues rather than provide a "comprehensive" treatment. They do not, for instance, tackle the question of the nature of scriptural inspiration and the truth to which the Scriptures witness. But they show us how to attend to foundational questions about God, the divine self-revelation, human faith, and so forth. They point to ways in which the study of foundations can anticipate something of what systematic theology elaborates about the Trinity, the incarnation, and the church.

All in all, I was delighted to discover not only that Neil and Christiaan approved of my proposal about the need to develop a fundamental theology in the light of Bernard Lonergan's achievement, but also how competently they have carried out this project. I hope that their book will be widely and positively received; I feel privileged to be associated with what they have done.

Gerald O'Collins, SJ
Australian Catholic University and the University of Divinity (Melbourne)

Foreword

While the initial seeds for this work go back to my own doctoral thesis,[1] the more proximate cause for the project was a celebratory dinner in which I happened to be sitting next to the eminent Australian theologian, and recognized authority on fundamental theology, Gerald O'Collins. Though we were both aware of one another's work (who could not be aware of his work!), it was the first time we had met, and Gerald began talking about his recently published book on fundamental theology, *Rethinking Fundamental Theology*. He noted that in this book he mentions Lonergan at the beginning and end of the work, but nowhere in between.[2] Knowing my interest in Lonergan he looked me in the eye and said something like, "What we really need is a book on fundamental theology from a Lonergan perspective." This was enough to revive my enthusiasm for the project. My thought turned to possible collaborators and I quickly identified Christiaan Jacobs-Vandegeer, a young Lonergan scholar and colleague at Australian Catholic University, as my partner.

Writing a book on fundamental theology from a Lonergan

---

1. Published in less than polished form as Neil Ormerod, *Method, Meaning and Revelation: the Meaning and Function of Revelation in Bernard Lonergan's* Method in Theology (Lanham, MD: University Press of America, 2000).
2. The two substantial mentions of Lonergan occur on pages 16–17 and 340–44.

perspective might seem like a redundant task. To some extent, the first four chapters of *Method in Theology* are themselves a short course in fundamental theology, and it is tempting to say to people, "Read *Method*."[3] However, that work was not conceived as a work in fundamental theology but in theological method, and so the ordering of topics may not be optimal, and the lack of linkages to traditional topics in fundamental theology means that a reader needs to make the connections herself. So our project is not entirely redundant.

Moreover, it is not a matter of us simply repeating what Lonergan said, and certainly not saying everything that he said, in his book. *Method* is a rich and complex work and some of that complexity has been shorn from the present work so as not to overload the reader with all Lonergan's distinctions. Also, there have been advances since Lonergan, in particular Robert Doran's notion of psychic conversion and its relation to the aesthetic concerns of Hans Urs von Balthasar that needed our attention.[4] More generally, we have sought to make the needed connection between our discussion of theological foundations and various theological debates that help illustrate the significance and usefulness of the foundations we develop. These debates are of course ongoing, with new theological positions being proposed on a regular basis. This only highlights the ongoing need for sound foundations in order to equip theologians with the means to navigate their way through the competing claims of various theological camps.

One such accommodation to the present climate was the decision to begin our discussion of foundations with the topic of religious experience and conversion. This decision helps locate our project within contemporary debates raised by Balthasar and Radical

3. Bernard J. F. Lonergan, *Method in Theology* (London: Dartman, Longman, and Todd, 1972).
4. See Robert M. Doran, *Theology and the Dialectics of History* (Toronto: University of Toronto Press, 1990).

Orthodoxy of the primacy of religious foundations for theology. The theologian herself, as religiously converted, is the basic foundation for theology. Such conversion evokes further conversions, moral, intellectual, and psychic, which fill out that foundational reality, but a theologian without religious conversion is like an empty gong booming, full of sound and fury, but lacking the one thing that is essential. However, the road to theological authenticity does not end with religious conversion. A theologian who is unfamiliar with the issues of moral, intellectual, and, increasingly, psychic conversion, will not be adequate to the challenges theology currently faces.

The book has four sections. The first argues for the need of foundations in the light of ongoing and interminable theological disputation on a variety of fronts. Given these difficulties (which arise in what Lonergan refers to as "dialectics") we argue for an approach that will assist the theologian in navigating the divergences through an appeal to the various conversions, religious, moral, intellectual, and psychic, as a sound foundation for theological reflection. The second part spells out in more detail the meaning of these foundations and the categories that arise in relation to them. In each case, we then illustrate how these foundations relate to specific theological debates and provide a way forward toward their resolution. The third part relates our foundations to more traditional theological themes and concerns, God, revelation, apologetics, and our present context. Our aim has not been to be comprehensive, but more illustrative. And we have operated under the constraint, imposed by Lonergan, that foundations prescind from doctrinal and systematic engagement. A final section then seeks to locate the work of foundations within Lonergan's overall schema of theological method, as one of eight distinct functional specializations within the overall task of theology.

As with some other book projects I have undertaken, this one was conceived from the beginning as a collaborative project.[5] Christiaan is an accomplished Lonergan scholar in his own right.[6] We had initially planned a third collaborator, but that did not eventuate. Working collaboratively brings a different energy, a new set of insights, and a deeper set of background knowledge to a project such as this, leading, we hope, to a better text in the end. Lonergan always spoke of theology as a collaborative venture, and it has been fruitful to see what it concretely entails. While each of us took responsibility to provide an initial draft of different chapters, multiple editing of one another's text should have smoothed out the stylistic differences between us. Hopefully the reader will find it a relatively seamless work.

We would like to thank friends, colleagues and students who commented on the book or individual chapters of this work: Gerald O'Collins, Dominic Doyle, Robert Doran, Cynthia Crysdale, Cristina Vanin, and Celeste Kumar. For whatever remaining faults and shortcomings, we take responsibility, but we are very grateful for their assistance. Both Christiaan and I have drunk deeply from the well of Bernard Lonergan's thought and we hope this present work contributes to the further dissemination of his ideas among the theological community. Finally we would like to thank Michael Gibson and the team at Fortress Press for their interest and support in bringing this work to a wider theological audience.

Neil Ormerod

5. Neil Ormerod and Shane Clifton, *Globalization and the Mission of the Church*, ed. Gerard Mannion, Ecclesiological Investigations (London: T&T Clark, 2009); Neil Ormerod and Cynthia S. W. Crysdale, *Creator God, Evolving World* (Minneapolis, MN: Fortress Press, 2013).
6. His article Christiaan Jacobs-Vandegeer, "Sanctifying Grace in a 'Methodical Theology," in *Theological Studies* 68 (2007): 52–76 is highly regarded among Lonergan scholars. Subsequent papers have maintained this high standard.

1

Why Theological Foundations?

This book endeavors to develop sound foundations for undertaking theological study and research. More precisely, we seek foundations for the doctrinal, systematic, and communicative work of theology—its normative phase, wherein the theologian is seeking to hand on the tradition in all its revealed authority and depth. This phase differs from theology's historical or positive phase, wherein the theologian is seeking to recover from the past just what it is that has been revealed within that tradition. The book's final chapter (chapter 10) explains how these two phases fit together in a comprehensive theological method. Prior to the emergence of historical consciousness, the doctrinal and systematic work of theology would have been considered the most proper meaning of the term *theology*. Today, these tasks struggle to find their place within the vast array of positive historical theological studies; that is, the theological work of placing the documents and events of the past in increasingly enriched social and cultural contexts often remains somewhat unconnected to sound doctrinal and systematic theologies. By focusing on the normative elements of the theological project, we are not suggesting that the positive phase is unimportant, but more seeking to reestablish some direction and purpose to the normative phase where, one might argue, considerable confusion is present. Following Bernard Lonergan then, and adopting the terminology of his theological method, "we are seeking the foundations, not of the whole of theology, but of the three last specialties, doctrines, systematics, and communications."[1]

Now, anyone with even a passing familiarity with current theological culture will know how rich and diverse theological literature is: from the theo-dramatics of Hans Urs von Balthasar[2] to the dense theological prose of Karl Rahner;[3] from biblical theologies to those who seek to revive the work of Thomas Aquinas;[4] from the postcolonial approaches of feminist[5] and liberationist theologies[6] to the postsecular perspective of Radical Orthodoxy, which seeks to promote a return to some form of Christendom.[7] Yet, despite this diversity, we can all recognize that these approaches are engaged in some fashion in "doing theology." There are appeals to authoritative sources, the Scriptures, Church Fathers, officially declared teachings, and recognized theological giants from the past and present; there is a common desire to clarify, to understand, to apply reasoning to push the tradition further in certain areas, or to explore the meaning of what has been handed down in as coherent a way as possible.

1. Bernard J. F. Lonergan, *Method in Theology* (London: Darton, Longman, and Todd, 1972), 267.
2. For instance, the first volume of his multivolume work on theological aesthetics, Hans Urs von Balthasar, *Seeing the Form*, trans. Erasmo Leiva-Merikakis, vol. 1, *The Glory of the Lord: A Theological Aesthetics*, 7 vols. (San Francisco: Ignatius Press, 1983).
3. Perhaps his most accessible work would be Karl Rahner, *Foundations of Christian Faith: An Introduction to the Idea of Christianity*, trans. William V. Dych (New York: Crossroad, 1982).
4. For one of the better examples of neo-Scholasticism, see Gilles Emery, trans. Matthew Levering, *Trinity in Aquinas* (Ypsilanti, MI: Sapientia Press, 2003).
5. See the classical feminist study Elisabeth Schüssler Fiorenza, *In Memory of Her: A Feminist Theological Reconstruction of Christian Origins*, 10th anniversary ed. (New York: Crossroad, 1994).
6. See the seminal work in liberation theology, Gustavo Gutiérrez, *A Theology of Liberation: History, Politics, and Salvation*, trans. Sister Caridad Inda and John Eagleson (Maryknoll, NY: Orbis Books, 1973).
7. For example, John Milbank, *Theology and Social Theory: Beyond Secular Reason* (Cambridge, MA: Blackwell, 1991).

Further, there is a desire to communicate the results of this work, so that the Christian community as a whole might benefit from theological labors. These many tasks belong to the specialties of doctrines, systematics, and communications identified above.

However, even given this commonality among many different theologies, it might be difficult to grasp what holds this entire theological endeavor together. In particular, why do various theologians arrive at such diverse results? Could there be such diversity that different approaches no longer recognize one another as actually engaged in the same process? And how do we deal with the fact that these diverse approaches can lead to such diverse outcomes, even to outright conflict, over a range of theological issues such as the Trinity, Christology, sacramental theology, and so on?

As conceived in this present work, the two major tasks of foundations arise in relation to two aspects of this theological diversity. The first is the question of theological language. How should we talk theologically? Should we be restricted to words or concepts from the Bible, or can we deploy metaphysical notions, and if so which ones? Can we incorporate sociological insights and language into theology where appropriate? What roles then do philosophy, the social and natural sciences, and history have in theology? One goal of the present work is to provide well-grounded categories for undertaking the tasks of doctrines, systematics, and communications. These categories shape theological language. And the grounds for their selection are unclear unless we can systematically account for them in relation to the diverse fields of human inquiry and knowledge.

And so our second question concerns theological outcomes and the conflicts that arise when theologians have significant disagreements. What are the origins of these disagreements and how might they be resolved? Is it just a matter of being clearer, more precise, more rigorous in our thinking, or is there something more fundamental at stake, a shift in perspective that no argument alone can resolve or produce (such as religious faith)? Here the concern is not just with the categories we use but also with the horizons within which we operate. Radically different horizons lead to significantly different theological outcomes. In the terms we shall use in this work, these two matters are questions, not unrelated, of categories and of conversion.

In the first instance then, one way of approaching the question of Why foundations? is to seek to move beyond the present diversity in theological language and outcomes and to set forth a theological horizon broad enough to encompass that diversity and resolve disagreements in a constructive and theologically responsible manner.

What Sort of Foundations?

The concept of foundations elicits different images for different people. When we build a house we set foundations in the earth that are strong enough to support the weight of the building, and stable enough to withstand the normal forces of wind and earth movement that might otherwise damage it. So theological foundations might sound like something solid and stable enough to support a theological edifice that will not be blown around by intellectual fads and passing disruptions.

For some, the concept of foundations refers to attempts in various disciplines (such as mathematics) to identify fundamental starting points, indubitable propositions or axioms, from which we can deduce all other truths. And so Euclid deployed a small number of axioms from which he could deduce the whole of geometry, or so he thought. It was later shown that one of his axioms need not be true, so that other forms of geometry—non-Euclidean geometries for example—were possible. René Descartes sought to do something similar to Euclid in philosophy by identifying the foundations of knowledge in basic truths that remain invulnerable to doubt.[8] Later philosophers would suggest that Descartes's foundations were little more than assertions requiring further justification. Last century, two mathematicians, Bertrand Russell and Alfred Whitehead, sought to provide foundations for the whole of mathematics by developing a rigorous account of set theory. Their major work, *Principia Mathematica*, took nearly four hundred pages to establish that the proposition "1+1=2" is true.[9] Unfortunately, another mathematician, Kurt Gödel, demonstrated in 1931 how futile such foundational attempts were, when in a few pages he proved that any system complex enough to provide foundations for arithmetic was either inconsistent, leading to internal contradictions, or incomplete; that is, there are true statements in arithmetic which cannot be proved by means of arithmetic alone.[10]

So if we talk about foundations for theology we do not mean something like an axiomatic system from which all theological truths can be deduced. This type of project is largely discredited. Still, we find traces of it when theologians think that theological issues can be resolved simply by reference to one's theological sources. Indeed, there can be a tendency to use Scripture or Church dogmas as if they provide the starting axioms for theological deductions. Whatever can be deduced from these "axioms" using the usual rules of deduction must then be true. While there are many problems with

8. It's not clear whether the foundation for knowledge is the *cogito* ("I think therefore I am") or God. See Richard J. Bernstein, *Beyond Objectivism and Relativism: Science, Hermeneutics, and Praxis* (Philadelphia: University of Pennsylvania, 1983), 16.

9. Alfred North Whitehead and Bertrand Russell, *Principia Mathematica* (Cambridge: University Press, 1910), 379.

10. It is possible they could be proved in a more complex system, but that larger system would suffer from the same problem of either being inconsistent or incomplete. For an account of Gödel's theorem and its implications see http://plato.stanford.edu/entries/goedel-incompleteness/.

such an approach, one significant problem is its failure to attend to the historical contexts of both the Scriptures and Church dogmas, to grasp their meanings within that context, and so to be able to distinguish between what is being proposed for belief as a truth revealed by God and what is merely an unquestioned cultural assumption of the author, or a consequence of a literary form of expression. For example, Scripture might tell us that Jesus sits at the "right hand of the Father," but we cannot deduce from this that God the Father has a left and a right hand. The authors of Scripture and various Church dogmas were not always seeking to define universal and necessary truth, but were responding to particular situations and contexts that we need to understand before we can grasp what it is they are saying.

Of course, this does not mean we should abandon logic, any more than mathematics did in light of Gödel's work. Logic has its place and is particularly useful in clarifying issues and pushing boundaries within a particular system. But where does the system come from in the first place, and what happens when a system becomes sterile and unproductive, so that we need to consider a major expansion or shift in our system? Some would argue that the system known as neo-Scholasticism, drawn from a particular approach to the writings of Thomas Aquinas and later commentators of his work, had in the nineteenth and early twentieth centuries become sterile and unproductive, no longer able to face the challenges posed by modern critical historical studies, contemporary philosophical approaches and scientific advances. More than logic was needed to transform this system.

What then do we mean by foundations? The approach we adopt here is that the converted theologian herself is the foundation from which all sound theology emerges.[11] The theologian is the one who must decide when the application of logic is called for; when and how one must come to an understanding of the particular contexts of Scripture and dogmas; and the one who with creativity and fidelity must work to create new theological systems when existing systems are no longer productive or credible. The theologian must decide which authorities demand her allegiance and with whom she should collaborate and from whom to draw inspiration, because the theological task is not a solitary or individual project, but rather a culturally collaborative enterprise spanning generations, and each theologian has a contribution to make.[12]

In all these tasks, the theologian has a fundamental orientation toward diligently attending to the sources, intelligently understanding their meaning, reasonably affirming their truth, and responsibly committing to their goodness. This orientation is evident in the diligent attention given to what are often viewed as theological foundations such as Scripture and tradition; the theological demand that the meaning of Scripture and Church dogmas be understood within a certain historical and cultural context; in the theological affirmation of truth as revealed by God who can neither be deceived nor deceive; and in a theological commitment to the good of the theological enterprise itself as a contribution to the life of the Christian community. Moreover, theologically we may affirm these orientations as orientations to the divine, a restlessness of the heart that can never rest until it rests with God.[13] Still, such a statement is a

11. Lonergan, *Method*, 267: "Foundational reality, as distinct from its expression, is conversion: religious, moral, and intellectual. Normally it is intellectual conversion as the fruit of both religious and moral conversion; it is moral conversion as the fruit of religious conversion; and it is religious conversion as the fruit of God's gift of his grace." Following Robert Doran we shall add psychic conversion to the foundations of theology. See Robert M. Doran, *Theology and the Dialectics of History* (Toronto: University of Toronto Press, 1990).

12. At the simplest level this is evident in the theologians one chooses to read and thus influence the topics which draws one's interest, the authorities one accepts, and the style of theology one writes.

13. Paraphrasing Augustine: "You have made us and drawn us to yourself, and our heart is unquiet until it rests in you." Augustine, *The Confessions*, trans. Maria Boulding (New York: Vintage Books, 1998), 39.

theological conclusion, not a premise; it is something that we need to justify in light of other aspects of our investigation into foundations. Nonetheless, these orientations serve performatively as the starting point for theological foundations.

Simply to identify these orientations as foundational is not to grasp their full significance. We must unpack and explore their significance, and to this task we turn in Part 2 of the present work where we take up the questions of conversion and categories relevant to theology (chapters 2–5). It is through conversion that the theologian comes into a fuller self-possession of herself as oriented to beauty, meaning, truth, and goodness, and within the horizon established by conversion that categories find their proper meaning. In Part 3 we explore the foundational significance of these orientations and correlated conversions in relation to various theological topics often addressed in a course on fundamental theology (chapters 6–9).[14] We conclude with some overall comments on the theological method underpinning our approach in chapter 10.

The Question of Theological Language

The question of what is the proper language for theology is hardly a new one. As early as the third century, Tertullian asked the question, "What indeed has Athens to do with Jerusalem?" implying that philosophical language has no place in the church.[15] Still, this did not prevent him from introducing the categories of person/*persona* and substance/*substantia* into Trinitarian theology. Centuries later,

---

14. See, for example, the range of topics explored in Gerald O'Collins, *Rethinking Fundamental Theology*.

15. Tertullian, *On Prescription Against Heretics* 7, trans. Peter Holmes, *The Anti-Nicene Fathers: Translations of the Writings of the Fathers Down to A.D. 325*, 10 volumes (Buffalo: Christian Literature, 1888) 3: 246. Tertullian also introduced "Trinitas" into Trinitarian theology, see Gerald O'Collins, *The Tripersonal God: Understanding and Interpreting the Trinity* (New York: Paulist, 1999), 105.

Thomas Aquinas responded to those who said we should use only categories drawn from the Scriptures, by noting that if such were the case we should only do theology in Hebrew and Greek, the language of the Scriptures.[16] More recently, Bernard Lonergan has argued that theology mediates between a religion and its cultural matrix.[17] The more complex and variegated the culture, the more theology needs to draw upon a variety of resources to perform such a mediating function. In particular, the cultural expansions occasioned by critical history, together with the emergence of the natural and human sciences, have made the theological task more complex and pluralistic than for previous generations.

Of course, all theologians might accept that language drawn from Scripture is used legitimately in some respect in theological discourse. However, when we examine biblical language closely we find that many terms take on religious significance because of their reference to God and realities related strictly to God. Let us consider three words of theological importance drawn from Scripture: grace, forgiveness, and mediation. Paul uses the language of grace to speak of God's gift to us in Jesus Christ, poured out through the Holy Spirit (Rom. 5:5). However, the Greek word we translate as grace, *charis*, means simply gift. What makes it a religious term is the giver of the gift and the nature of what is given. Forgiveness, too, is central to many of the Gospel parables, and Jesus often offers people forgiveness for their sins. But forgiveness may simply be between two people, a matter of forgiving a financial debt, with no religious significance at all. What makes forgiveness a religious term is the nature of the one who forgives, and the kind of "debt" forgiven. Finally, the New Testament speaks of Jesus as the mediator between God and humanity (1 Tim. 2:5). But a mediator is simply one who is a go-

16. See Thomas Aquinas, *Summa Theologiae* 1.29.3 ad1.
17. Lonergan, *Method*, xi.

between for two parties. What makes this a religious term is that one of the parties involved is God.

And so much of what we take as religious language draws in its own way from more general terms that take on a religious significance in their specific context. In any religious tradition, we find a wide variety of such terms, which are constituted as religious by their referent, the reality to which they relate. Much of the language we take as religious from the Bible falls into this category. There are, however, other terms that theologians draw from sources other than the Bible, but which they use in hopes of clarifying the realities to which the Bible refers. A good example of this is the use of the category of *substance*, which Tertullian first used in Trinitarian theology to identify what is common between God the Father and God the Son. The Nicene Creed then speaks of the Father and Son as "consubstantial" or "of one substance." The term has no profound biblical meaning (if any biblical meaning at all).[18] It may take on a technical meaning in philosophy, but it might also express the commonsense meaning of "stuff." Its use in the Creed creates a new situation. Why should we use such nonscriptural language to express our beliefs? Is this the corruption of the pure spirit of the Gospel by Greek philosophy, as suggested by Adolf von Harnack,[19] or the successful inculturation of the Gospel in a more philosophically literate culture? Foundations must allow us to address such questions.

The Middle Ages witnessed a rapid expansion of the use of philosophical categories in theological discourse. It reached its summit in the work of Thomas Aquinas, who used and transformed Aristotle's philosophical categories to create a remarkable Christian synthesis of faith and reason. Aquinas's use of Aristotle provided

18. The Greek term *hypostasis* occurs once in the New Testament in Heb. 11:1. It is doubtful that it has a technical meaning there.
19. Adolf von Harnack, *Outlines of the History of Dogma*, trans. Edwin Mitchell (London: Hodder and Stoughton, 1893).

a framework of systematic meaning that he could then deploy to investigate within a single view a wide variety of theological questions, such as the Trinity, the Incarnation, the relationship between grace and freedom, the place of human virtues in the life of grace, and so on. Despite the power of this synthesis, it slid into decadence and was eventually rejected by the Reformers, who wanted a return to the "plain" language of the Bible.

The question of the proper use of nonreligious, or what we shall call "general," categories has become more pressing in recent centuries with the emergence of a range of new disciplines such as sociology, psychology, economics, critical history, and so on. These have greatly enriched human culture, but often those who developed these new accounts of human existence did so with an explicitly antireligious agenda.[20] They sought to develop a new science of human existence that would sidestep the endless controversies of the theologians and philosophers. Thus, Emile Durkheim (often referred to as the "Father of Sociology") states of the discipline: "Sociology does not need to choose between the great hypotheses which divide metaphysicians."[21] Does this agnosticism preclude these disciplines from the possibility of dialogue with theologians, or exclude theologians from the fruitful use of such insights as these disciplines may contain? Some theologians reject their use as contrary to the proper task of theology; others suggest that, properly reoriented, such disciplines may fruitfully assist in the theological task of understanding faith.[22]

Our purpose at this stage is not to resolve such issues, but to

---

20. Milbank, *Theology and Social Theory*, provides a genealogical account of the origins of the human sciences. While valuable to address, it does not resolve the issue of the relationship between these human sciences and theology.

21. Emile Durkheim, *The Rules of Sociological Method*, ed. George E. G. Catlin, trans. Sarah A. Solovay and John H. Mueller, 8th ed. (Chicago: The University of Chicago Press, 1938), 141.

22. More fully, Neil Ormerod, "A Dialectic Engagement with the Social Sciences in an Ecclesiological Context," *Theological Studies* 66, no. 4 (2005): 815–40.

note that the question of theological language is complex and needs further work, some of which we shall develop in later chapters. In the meantime, two additional issues in relation to theological language require our attention: the problem of the control of meaning and the possibility of explanatory or systematic meaning in theology.

A perennial problem in theology is the question of the control of meaning. Theologians use a variety of terms, a few of which we noted above. But how can we control the meaning of our basic terms? How can we speak precisely and clearly about the realities of faith? In mathematics, this is done through a strict axiomatic system where basic terms and their relations are mutually defining. In theology, things are more difficult. We already noted the introduction of the term *substance* in theological discourse through the teaching of Nicaea on the Trinity. It has a variety of possible meanings. In common language, we speak, for example, of chemical substances, or perhaps we imagine some type of gooey "stuff" as our meaning of the term; but we use the term in other ways as well. We might say that someone is a person of substance. The meaning then is very different. Or a lawyer might say, "the substance of my argument is . . ." to indicate the key insight she is trying to convey. When we say that the Father and the Son are of one substance (consubstantial), which of these meanings are meant? Do we mean the Father and the Son are made of the same "stuff" or do we mean that to correctly understand the Father, is to correctly understand the Son? This latter meaning is certainly the meaning given in the rule of Athanasius—that "what is true of the Father is true of the Son, except the Father is not the Son, nor the Son the Father." On the other hand, a theologian who is not even aware of the need for controlling the meaning of such terms is likely to adopt a commonsense position, and fail to attend to the nuances of meaning involved. What results will not be good theology.

A problem that is related to the question of the control of meaning is the possibility of systematic meaning in theology. Many theologians claim that all religious and theological language is metaphorical.[23] If such a claim were true a strict control of theological language would be impossible and with it any possibility of systematic or explanatory meaning. Metaphor is by its nature polyvalent and evocative. It seeks to say more than can be said, while systematic, explanatory meaning seeks to exclude possibilities by bringing precise meaning to as sharp a focus as possible.

Of course, it is difficult to know how one might establish the claim that all religious language is metaphorical; indeed, it would be very difficult to establish such a claim unless one adopted some systematic, explanatory framework to do so. Mostly, such a claim is simply asserted. This is not to say that some, if not the majority of, religious language is metaphorical, but the theological task is to move beyond descriptive and metaphorical categories to enter into systematic and explanatory meaning.[24] Without this movement, theology becomes simply an exercise in rhetoric. We then become content with a satisfying flow of image and affect rather than achieving genuine understanding. In other words, metaphor and other types of analogy are useful, if not necessary, tools for theology, but they require explanatory control if they should move beyond descriptive associations and contribute to solving theological problems (for example, Aquinas's use of Augustine's psychological analogy for understanding relations within God).

One could argue, for example, that in the work of Thomas Aquinas terms like *grace* move from being descriptive, operating in a commonsense way, to becoming technical with a precise control of

---

23. See, for example, Sallie McFague, *Metaphorical Theology: Models of God in Religious Language* (Philadelphia: Fortress Press, 1982).

24. Keeping in mind, however, that the modes of such systematic and explanatory meaning may still be thought of in traditional terms such as the ways of negation, eminence, and analogy.

meaning. This precision allowed him to resolve a number of the pressing issues of his day regarding the question of grace and its relationship to free will. More recently there has been considerable debate on whether Vatican II is in strict continuity with the tradition or whether there are elements of discontinuity. Such a problem cannot be resolved unless one knows what it is that is supposed to be continuous or discontinuous and how possible discontinuity might be measured. Unless one can achieve this, the debate will go on interminably and possibly even meaninglessly.[25] If one wants to make significant theological progress on a range of such matters, one needs to operate within some type of systematic framework that allows for a relatively precise control of meaning. And this goal is not the task of the individual theologian, but of a collaborative community of theologians working in concert for decades or even centuries.

Sound theological foundations need to address the issues associated with theological language and categories. However, the discussion also indicates some of the potential sources of disagreement and conflict that arise in theology. To this issue we now turn.

The Problem of Theological Conflict and Disagreement

As we can see above, there are many possible sources of disagreement and conflict in theology. People may disagree over the meanings of various theological terms. This disagreement might arise because one person uses a term metaphorically, while another seeks a systematic and explanatory meaning. Science, for example, moves from descriptive terms, like *hot* and *cold*, to explanatory terms like *temperature* and *latent energy*. Theology, on the other hand, tends to use the same term both descriptively and systematically. For example,

---

25. See, for example, Neil Ormerod, "Vatican II—Continuity or Discontinuity? Toward an Ontology of Meaning," *Theological Studies* 71, no. 3 (2010): 609–36.

the New Testament uses the term *grace* in a more descriptive manner, as does Augustine, but in Aquinas the use of the term is explanatory and systematically controlled. And so one source of disagreement and conflict is the failure to note this distinction. Such a failure leads to theologians speaking at cross-purposes, where one takes a descriptive account as systematic, or treats a systematic account as merely descriptive.

It may seem that different systems of thought, or forms of theological language, disagree quite significantly. But theologians must take great care in ascertaining whether the disagreement is real or only apparent. Scientists, for example, can formulate quantum mechanics in more than one way. However, each of the ways is equivalent to the others; the different formulations lead to the same results. So too, different theological languages might be saying the same thing in different ways. How can we tell? Can we map one language into the other?[26] An interesting historical example here is the conflict over the question of justification by faith, which arose at the time of the Reformation. Catholic theologians tended to express their position in the scholastic language of metaphysics; the reformers expressed the Lutheran position in the terms of a more interior and biblical language of the heart. Could these different forms of expression really be saying the same thing in a different language, or was there a genuine conflict here? Recent Catholic-Lutheran dialogues suggest that perhaps the difference was not as great as was felt to be the case at the time.[27]

This is not to say that there cannot be genuine conflict between

26. See, for example, Kathryn Tanner, *God and Creation in Christian Theology: Tyranny and Empowerment?* (Minneapolis, MN: Fortress Press, 2004). Her notion of a noncompetitive relationship between Creator and creature successfully maps classical metaphysical language of primary and secondary causation.

27. See Avery Dulles, "Two languages of Salvation: The Lutheran-Catholic joint declaration," *First Things* 98 (December 1999): 25–30, for an analysis of the recent dialogue documents and their outcomes.

different theological positions. A classic example is to be found in the meaning of John 1:1: "In the beginning was the Word and the Word was with God and the Word was God." In the early church, some argued that the claims that "the Word was God" should not be taken at face value but should be taken to mean that the Word was "divine," having its origin in God, but not fully God in the sense in which God is God.[28] The problem then could be stated: either the Word is God in every sense in which God is God; that is, the Word is fully divine or it is not. There is no middle ground. What is called for is a judgment between one position and the other. Either one is true, or the other is true, but both cannot be true. Such a difference is dialectical, an irreducible difference which can only be resolved in one direction or the other. How such matters are to be resolved is another issue, one which goes beyond a directly foundational concern and into questions of structures of ecclesial authority.[29]

On the other hand, not all theological differences are necessarily of this type. Both sides of a dispute may accept a given belief as true, but they may differ on the best way to understand the truth of the belief. If the belief truly belongs to the divine mystery, then we cannot attain full understanding in this life, and different approaches may assist, complement, or include one another. We need not insist on one approach to the exclusion of all others. Of course, theologians can and often should debate as to whether one approach is "better" or more adequate than another, but always with the understanding that divine mystery surpasses all of our efforts at comprehension. Here one can recognize the possibility of genuine theological pluralism.[30]

28. This position was known as subordinationism, in which the Son/Word is in some sense subordinate to the Father. The most extreme form is Arianism, which claims that the Son/Word is a creature. It was the debate over Arianism that led to the convocation of the Council of Nicaea in 325 CE.
29. Of course, one might avoid the dialectic by asserting that the language used here is metaphorical, but this would need to be proved, not just asserted in each case.
30. For a detailed discussion of theological pluralism, see Bernard J. F. Lonergan, "Doctrinal

The task of foundations in this matter is to assist the theologian in understanding disagreements and conflicts, to get to their sources as quickly as possible with an eye to either alleviating the tension or resolving the dispute. Such a process may require a development of or shift in the horizon of the theologian herself. If the differences are indeed dialectical, the theologian might need to decide where she stands on the matter in question. Long held beliefs might be called into question or may require a renewed affirmation in a new context. The theologian is not a disinterested observer in such matters, seeking to resolve problems in a detached manner. Good theology draws on the fullness of our religious, moral, intellectual, and psychological development, the authenticity of which we can never take for granted.[31]

Examples of Theological Conflict and Disagreement

There are countless examples of theological conflict and disagreement, but the ones we have chosen here for further engagement reflect specific dimensions of conflict that illustrate key points relevant to our later discussions on conversion. They also typify the kinds of conflicts and disagreements that regularly occur in current theological debates.

The Quest for the Historical Jesus

Walk into any theological bookstore and you will find a huge range of works purporting to present a "real" account of the historical Jesus. There is an endless fascination about the topic of Jesus, about

Pluralism," in *Philosophical and Theological Papers: 1965–1980*, ed. Robert Croken and R. M. Doran, *Collected Works of Bernard Lonergan*, 25 volumes (Toronto: University of Toronto Press, 2004), 17:70–106.

31. As Lonergan notes, "So human authenticity is never some pure and serene and secure possession. It is ever a withdrawal from unauthenticity, and every successful withdrawal only brings to light the need for still further withdrawals" (Lonergan, *Method*, 110).

what he was really like and how we might understand him within the historical context of his day. This fascination has given rise to a vast amount of literature on the topic, a literature that exhibits constant disagreement among authors about the various outcomes of this research. Among the present day literature one might distinguish three broad approaches:

1. The approach of the Jesus seminar authors such as Dominic John Crossan[32] and Marcus Borg[33] utilizes various sociological and historical categories in ways that seek to emphasize discontinuity between the historical Jesus and the community of the emerging church of the first century.

2. A critical historical methodology that seeks objectivity in terms of a cross-denominational scholarly consensus between competing perspectives, as found in the work of John Meier.[34] Meier conceives of his outcomes as the product of an imaginatively constructed "unpapal conclave" of Catholic, Protestant, and Jewish exegetes. While this does not set Jesus in opposition to the early church, its claims about Jesus are moderated in such a way as to avoid confessional "biases."

3. An approach described by its proponents as "critical realist," which recognizes both the Gospels and the rest of the New Testament literature as products of the early church itself, and so posits a much greater continuity between the historical Jesus and the early church. We find this approach in authors such as Ben Meyer, James Dunn, and N. T. Wright.[35]

32. See, for example, Dominic John Crossan, *The Historical Jesus: the Life of a Mediterranean Jewish Peasant*, 1st ed. (San Francisco: HarperSanFrancisco, 1992).

33. See, for example, Marcus J. Borg, *Jesus, a New Vision: Spirit, Culture, and the Life of Discipleship*, 1st ed. (San Francisco: Harper & Row, 1987).

34. See his massive four-volume work, John P. Meier, *A Marginal Jew: Rethinking the Historical Jesus*, 3 vols. (New York: Doubleday, 1994), specifically vol. 2.

35. Ben F. Meyer, *The Aims of Jesus* (London: SCM Press, 1979); James D. G. Dunn, *Jesus*

Each of these authors draws from the same basic sources (such as the New Testament and various other extrabiblical sources), and uses quite similar methodological criteria, but they differ in the weighting and significance they give to each source. The weighting and significance given often depends on the author's prior commitment to a particular view of the world and how God relates to it.

These differences were perhaps more stark in the first quest for the historical Jesus, a quest initiated in the eighteenth century when theologians first used the methods of critical history to investigate the historical reliability of the Gospels and their account of Jesus. The early questers into the historical Jesus brought with them the presuppositions of the Enlightenment, which rejected the authority of religious tradition and restricted God's activity in the world to at most an initial act of creation.[36] When the questers read the Gospels, they rejected all elements of the supernatural and claims to divine authority regarding Jesus; they read these elements as creations of the early church, a community more interested in justifying its own claims to divine origins than in presenting an accurate account of Jesus' life. The questers then developed an account of the historical Jesus that opposed the claims of the church and Christian tradition. The community of theologians cannot resolve diverging presuppositions by reference to the text alone, because the divergence raises the question of how we ought to read the text, whether through a basic stance of suspecting (a hermeneutic of suspicion) the early church of distorting the data about Jesus, or through trusting

---

Remembered (Grand Rapids: Eerdmans, 2003); N. T. Wright, *Jesus and the Victory of God* (Minneapolis: Fortress Press, 1996). Meyer adopts the notion of critical realism from Lonergan; subsequently both Dunn and Wright adopt the term from Meyer.

36. For an excellent analysis of the origins and presuppositions of the initial quest, see Meyer, *The Aims of Jesus*, 25–59.

the early church's interpretations of Jesus' intentions and the significance of his life and death.

In chapter 2, we indicate how at least some of these differences might reside in the presence or absence of what we call "religious conversion." The presence of this conversion makes the theologian "adequate" to the theological object, much as one might attune one's aesthetic sensibilities to good art. The lack of such a conversion can render one "deaf" to hearing the religious qualities of a text under investigation, and so seek other explanations for its meaning.

The Preferential Option for the Poor in Theology

The second half of the twentieth century witnessed the emergence of a new type of theologizing, which went by the name of liberation theology. This style of theologizing sought to write theology from the perspective of the poor, viewing history from the underside, from the side of history's victims. One of the central doctrines of liberation theology became known as the "preferential option for the poor."[37] This "option" has two aspects, firstly that the poor have the first call on the resources of the church, and secondly that theology must be written from the underside of history. This program of theologizing was built upon a pastoral strategy of base Christian communities, small ecclesial gatherings that read the Scriptures in light of their experiences of poverty and oppression, and vice versa. As its proponents saw it, liberation theology was not simply a new topic among the many existing theological topics, but a new way of doing all theology.[38]

One of the more controversial aspects of liberation theology was its use of the social sciences and in particular Marxist accounts of

---

37. See the classic text, Gutiérrez, *A Theology of Liberation*, 156.
38. For a brief introduction to liberation theology, see Leonardo Boff and Clodovis Boff, *Introducing Liberation Theology* (Maryknoll, NY: Orbis Books, 1987).

economic inequality in society in the development of its theological position. Some people viewed the use of Marx in Catholic theology as opening the door to communist influences in Latin America, a move that raised concern in the Vatican (and elsewhere). The Congregation for the Doctrine of the Faith issued two documents seeking to correct what it saw as weaknesses in the approach of liberation theology; they focused in particular on the use of Marxist categories.[39]

Liberation theology raises a number of interesting issues that elicit theological disagreement and conflict. The first is the place of the poor in theology. Liberation theology insists that theologians consider their social location. It requires theology to confront the issue of the privileged outlook of Western and generally male theologians in a world of massive poverty (especially of women) and oppression. The second concerns the use of Marxist categories in theology, especially given the Marxist critique and rejection of religion as the opium of the people. Is it possible to use Marxism as a "scientific" account of society without buying into its atheistic underpinnings? The Congregation for the Doctrine of the Faith raised this question as a matter of critical concern. The third is the questionable validity of using any form of social scientific analysis at all in theology. Here, John Milbank and the school of Radical Orthodoxy have been particularly scathing of liberation theology and others who have adopted social scientific categories in developing their theologies.[40]

This issue touches on a number of points raised above, in particular

39. Congregation for the Doctrine of the Faith, "Instruction on Certain Aspects of the Theology of Liberation" accessed August 4, 2015, http:// www.vatican.va/ roman_curia / congregations / cfaith / documents / rc_con_cfaith_doc_19840806_theology-liberation_en.html (published in 1984), and idem, "Instruction on Christian Freedom and Liberation," accessed August 4, 2015, http:// www.vatican.va / roman_curia / congregations / cfaith / documents / rc_con_cfaith_doc_19860322_freedom-liberation_en.html (published in 1986).
40. In particular, see Milbank, *Theology and Social Theory*.

the forms of theological language and the role of the social sciences in theology. Different theologians can take quite radically different approaches on these questions, and with little clear indication of a resolution. In chapter 3, we explain how a phenomenology of "moral conversion" allows us to address the use of the social sciences in theology and some of the other concerns raised by liberation theology.

The Real Presence of Christ in the Eucharist

The Christian practice of blessing and breaking bread and blessing wine to be shared in a sacred meal goes back to the origins of the church, indeed many would say, to Jesus himself, who asked his followers to "do this in memory of me."[41] For centuries, the church followed Jesus' command unhindered by any controversy over what the words *This is my body* means. There was a simple acceptance that somehow Jesus was present in the Eucharist, present as a gift to the church to enrich and feed Christian believers. Controversy initially arose as people began to ask, how is Jesus present? What happens to the bread and wine? People spoke of Jesus as "real presence" in the Eucharist, which arose from a change in the substance of bread and wine into the substance of Jesus' body and blood (transubstantiation). Some believers thought in terms of an exaggerated realism that expected the broken host once consecrated to bleed, and the wine to change in color through consecration to that of blood.[42] When Thomas Aquinas sought to explain the real presence of Jesus in

---

41. Meyer, *The Aims of Jesus*, 219. Of course, the command to continue the Eucharistic act in remembrance is only found in Luke and 1 Corinthians, but Meyer argues strongly for its historicity—see 311n133. Even the claim that the practice goes back to Jesus himself is contentious to some.

42. Francis Clark, "'Bleeding Hosts' and Eucharistic Theology," *The Heythrop Journal* 1, no. 3 (1960): 214–28.

terms of transubstantiation, one of his aims was to dampen such exaggerated realism.

Controversy arose again at the time of the Reformation. The reformers were more suspicious of the metaphysical categories utilized by Aquinas and noted the strong connection between sacramental realism and the sacerdotal nature of church ministry. Their emphasis on the priesthood of all believers diminished the focus on the real presence of Jesus in the Eucharist, a presence that many viewed as more symbolic or spiritual. These differences continue to create ecumenical tensions on questions of the Eucharist:

> Many churches believe that by the words of Jesus and by the power of the Holy Spirit, the bread and wine of the eucharist become, in a real though mysterious manner, the body and blood of the risen Christ, that is, of the living Christ present in all his fullness. Under the signs of bread and wine, the deepest reality is the total being of Christ who comes to us in order to feed us and transform our entire being. Some other churches, while affirming a real presence of Christ at the Eucharist, do not link that presence so definitely with the signs of bread and wine. The decision remains for the churches whether this difference can be accommodated within the convergence formulated in the text itself.[43]

Of course, all these different positions accept in some sense Jesus' words recorded in the New Testament, *This is my body*. There is a common acceptance that in some sense the Eucharist makes Jesus present to the believer. So the source of the divergences lies not in the text, but in grasping the significance of what it means for that presence to be "real." For this divergence to be overcome one must examine what it means to say something is real or that something is not real. This inevitably involves philosophical discussion on the

---

43. *Baptism, Eucharist and Ministry—Faith and Order Paper No. 111*, accessed August 4, 2015, http://www.oikoumene.org/en/resources/documents/commissions/faith-and-order/i-unity-the-church-and-its-mission/baptism-eucharist-and-ministry-faith-and-order-paper-no-111-the-lima-text.

nature of reality, and in a way that moves beyond the category of substance. As we saw above, "substance" is subject to the same confusions and conflicts as "real." Until we resolve such prior confusions and conflicts, we cannot resolve questions of the real presence of Christ in the Eucharist. More recently, some theologians suggest that rather than speak of a change of substance we should speak of a change of meaning or significance, a "transsignification."[44] Others object that such a presence would not be "real" or "objective," but merely "subjective." In chapter 4, we return to this example in light of the question of "intellectual conversion," which clarifies the meanings of terms such as real, existence, substance, and objectivity.

The Saving Significance of Jesus' Death and Resurrection

Every Christian affirms as a central aspect of their faith that "Jesus saves." His death and resurrection are the foundational, saving events for the whole of humanity—as noted in the Acts of the Apostles, "there is no other name by which we may be saved" (Acts 4:12). However, when Christians seek to answer the question, "How does the death and resurrection of Jesus save us?," there has been little agreement as to the process by which these events are salvific. The Scriptures present us with a variety of images—healing, atonement, redemption, justification, sacrifice, ransom, and so on. How can we make sense of these many images? What do they explain about the process? For example, if we think of Jesus' death as a ransom, to whom is the ransom paid?[45] In his classical study of the doctrine of salvation, Gustaf Aulén identified three major themes: classical

---

44. See Edward Schillebeeckx, *The Eucharist* (New York: Sheed and Ward, 1968). Also George Hunsinger, *Eucharist and Ecumenism* (Cambridge: Cambridge University Press, 2008) and Joseph C. Mudd, *Eucharist as Meaning: Critical Metaphysics and Contemporary Sacramental Theology* (Collegeville: Liturgical Press, 2014).
45. The two alternatives generally proposed are God or Satan, neither of which is entirely satisfactory.

ransom theory whereby Jesus' death is a ransom or bait that induces Satan to surrender his grip on humanity (a theme of divine deception); the satisfaction model whereby Jesus' death offers God satisfaction for the sins of humanity, though in Protestant theology this becomes a model of penal substitution; and the "subjective" moral influence theory whereby Jesus' death provides us with a good example to follow for our moral guidance.[46] More recently, the explorations of cultural anthropologist René Girard have argued for the antisacrificial nature of Christianity, linking the notion of sacrifice with that of the innocent scapegoat.[47]

At the heart of these differences lies the difficulty of moving from descriptive, metaphorical, and symbolic language to explanatory, analytic language and learning to appreciate both what we gain and what we lose in such a shift. Explanatory, analytic language has an important place in theology and represents an ideal for which to strive, but it also can lack the communicative power of metaphorical language; it rarely moves the hearts of believers, and so many people unfortunately regard it as inadequate. No doubt liturgy, art, drama can communicate the truth of salvation more effectively than a theological lecture. Having sound foundations allows a theologian to move between explanatory and symbolic language in such a way that brings out more powerfully the authentic meaning of the event or text. Paul Ricœur might refer to this goal as a type of "second naiveté."[48] In chapter 5, we consider this movement under the heading of "psychic conversion," which attunes the theologian to the aesthetic dimension of theology.

---

46. Gustaf Aulén, *Christus Victor: An Historical Study of the Three Main Types of the Idea of the Atonement* (London: SPCK, 1970).

47. René Girard, *The Scapegoat* (Baltimore: Johns Hopkins University Press, 1986). For a theological appreciation of Girard's work, see Raymund Schwager, *Must There Be Scapegoats?: Violence and Redemption in the Bible*, 1st ed. (San Francisco: Harper & Row, 1987), and Robert J. Daly, *Sacrifice Unveiled: The True Meaning of Christian Sacrifice* (London: T & T Clark, 2009).

48. Paul Ricœur, *The Symbolism of Evil* (New York: Harper & Row, 1967).

Conclusion

These then in summary are the outcomes of this chapter. The project of theology needs to establish theological foundations to address a number of issues: the nature and types of theological language; the variety of approaches to undertaking theology; the interminable disputes among theologians; and the tensions between descriptive, metaphorical language and explanatory, analytic language. The position we adopt throughout this work is that the foundation of theology is the theologian herself with her fundamental orientations to meaning, truth, goodness, beauty and perhaps even genuine holiness, consolidated in religious, moral, intellectual, and psychic conversions, which shape the theologian's horizon, so that it is adequate to the theological object, God, and all things in relation to God. This is not a once and for all event, but an ongoing struggle to be authentic to the implications of such conversions and to our fundamental orientations.

And so the next four chapters spell out in detail the implications of the four conversions: religious, moral, intellectual, and psychic. From these foundations, we turn our attention to various topics normally considered within the framework of fundamental theology, topics such as God, revelation, tradition, doctrine, dogmas, and religious pluralism. In the final chapter, we address the question of theological method, as congruent with the foundations we develop in this work.

2

Religious Conversion

The guiding idea of this book contends that a theologian's personal (and communal) growth in religious, moral, intellectual, and psychic conversion marks the foundational reality of theology, and that constructing explicit theological foundations requires attention to the normative features of these conversions. This chapter focuses on religious conversion. It addresses that which strikes at the heart of who and what we are, at how we live, and toward what ends or goals our living tends. The approach to theology in this book asks that we maintain a keen awareness of the social and cultural contexts within which religious conversion takes place, but it also challenges us to identify as well the normative elements within these contexts.

Our approach uses an analysis of interiority, the inner life, to unpack the structure of religious conversion. The descriptions of religious conversion, and the other conversions we discuss later, vary in different times and places, but the basic structure of the human person's growth in self-transcendence does not change. For example, readers of Augustine may resonate quite strongly with his inner experience of restlessness and fulfillment without expecting to relive all the details of his *Confessions*. The basic structure of conversion admits verification through attending to the data of consciousness, but the structure unfolds uniquely and with different levels of intensity in concrete circumstances. If we pay attention to our inner lives, we discover the principles of creativity and benevolence that in our fidelity to those principles generate the broad lines of progress and redemption within the vicissitudes of human history.

In short, this chapter unfolds by identifying a theological foundation in religious conversion that has transcultural validity. The related category of religious experience is the key to defining this foundation; it marks the inner principle of the ongoing, holistic transformation that we call "religious conversion." However, we try to avoid the trap of proposing a universal content of religious experience. This would suggest a form of essentialism that claims to capture some essence of religion against which all actual religions could be measured. Rather, we aim to identify the basic features of religious experience by using a phenomenological approach, a method of describing the dynamics of human consciousness by focusing on the operations and structures of the inner life.

The first part of the chapter considers the question of God. Of course, this question arises differently in various communities, but the question itself has normative value for understanding the human capacity for self-transcendence. The chapter then turns to religious experience and, using a phenomenological approach, defines it structurally and heuristically (that is, as a principle of discovery). The category as defined admits verification by our attending to the dynamics of consciousness and helps us to discover or interpret the occurrence of the structure in its various intensities and expressions. Consequently, this approach engages us in concrete, personal experience and orients us toward the social and cultural realities that shape and often express our inner soundings of desire and fulfillment. The chapter also addresses the difference between sociological definitions of religion and our phenomenological approach. The last section explains how this analysis implies a critical distinction between faith and belief, and how this distinction shapes the project of theology as well as theology's engagement in secular, ecumenical, and interreligious dialogues.

On a final note, the language of this chapter often reflects the Christian commitments of its authors. Examples of central concepts in the chapter are mostly tied to voices within the Christian tradition and Scriptural references are often given. But our use of the language of the Christian tradition serves only to clarify a key methodological point, namely: although we are immersed in the historical realities of society, culture, and religion, we can verify and implement the normative, transcultural elements in our unique, contingent, historically circumscribed efforts to promote growth and flourishing in ourselves and in our world. The project of theology unfolds in the context of this personal and communal task.

The Question of God

The question of God tends to arise in our modern culture as a question of credibility. Does believing in God make sense in light of modern science and the problem of evil? Is belief in God less plausible in light of error and moral failure among Christians? Does a healthy suspicion of ideology keep theism at bay for more "mature" minds that prefer scientific truth to the supposed psychic crutch and delusion of faith?[1] There are no empirical data on God and that fact may seem to put belief in God permanently at odds with a scientific viewpoint. Modern science deals with verifiable possibilities, limiting its notion of "truth" to a "high degree of probability." If the reality of God does not admit empirical verification as a matter of principle, still it may seem even more naïve to believe in God on the basis of

1. This of course is the general thesis of Richard Dawkins, *The God Delusion* (London: Bantam, 2006).

human testimonies, especially those who wrote in more credulous times. Despite the billions of the world's believers, the authority of those who proclaim the reasonableness or necessity of belief seems dramatically undermined by their own moral failures, long histories of oppression, and endless disagreements with one another. In modern culture, the question of God arises as a question of credibility: given the uncertainty of the evidence, the question of God seems unanswerable to many people, and they contentedly dismiss it.

In a later chapter, we will discuss various approaches to the question of God and the arguments behind them, but for now it will help to consider the question itself. Of course, the question of God within a given culture reflects the symbolic and linguistic resources of the culture, and thus often becomes conflated with one of the many possible answers available in the culture. The question's strong tie to issues of credibility in contemporary culture reflects particularly modern preoccupations with empirical science and its method. But the question itself does not presuppose any elements of an answer; it does not belong to image or affect, concept or judgment. Rather, the question of God arises in the performance of human inquiry. It arises each and every time a person takes the further step beyond a question about the meaning of something to *a question about the meaning of the question.* In other words, the performance of human knowing involves an intellectual orientation, a wonder and desire to know, which can lead to the question of God.

If we reflect on our ordinary experience of knowing, we can grasp how the question of God can arise in the normal course of human living. Consider the following mundane questions: Where did I leave my car keys? Is that a stop sign? The questions that people routinely ask express their expectation that by grasping the correct answer they can then act intelligently and coordinate their actions with others. But this expectation entails the anticipation of an intelligible world. Even our most boring, everyday questions anticipate the intelligibility of the universe. Such anticipation also lies at the heart of scientific method, as physicist and natural philosopher Paul Davies notes, "Science is founded on the notion of the rationality and logicality of nature."[2] Once we recognize the success of this anticipation, we can ask if this intelligible universe has an intelligent ground. Is this meaningful world grounded in a transcendent source of all meaning or is it ultimately meaningless? If this intelligible world has no intelligent ground, then whatever intelligible order it exhibits it does so without reason, without intelligibility. Here, we arrive at the question of God. Again, to quote Davies: "If the universe as a whole is pointless, then it exists reasonlessly. . . . We are then invited to contemplate a state of affairs in which all scientific chains of reasoning are grounded in absurdity. The order of the world would have no foundation and its breathtaking rationality would have to spring, miraculously, from absurdity."[3]

We can also ask about our acts of marshaling and weighing evidence for a judgment. We marshal and weigh evidence in making judgments because the realities that we know in this world are contingent (that is, dependent on a host of conditions) rather than necessary. Does the contingent being that we grasp in making the limited judgments that we make each and every day (such as "It is a stop sign") imply the existence of a necessary being, a being whose existence does not depend on anything else? Again, science also leads to this question by its requirement that scientists verify their theories with respect to the relevant empirical data. Scientific theories reflect the contingency of creation, and contingency begs further explanation. In other words, it leads to the question of God.

Still, do our judgments of value (such as "It is good not to cause

---

2. Paul Davies, "Now is the Reason for Our Discontent," *Sydney Morning Herald*, January 1, 2003.
3. Ibid.

a car accident") participate in the transcendent reality of Supreme Goodness, or are they ultimately arbitrary assertions in a morally groundless universe? Do we simply create the good by our decisions, or are our decisions oriented to a good not of our own making? In each instance, the question of God arises as a question about the significance of our performance of knowing and choosing. Despite the many possible answers a person or group may give, the question itself lies within the horizon of our orientation to meaning, truth, and value. *These orientations frame the basic meaning of the term "God" and how we identify religious conversion.*

Religious Experience

Some people answer the question of God by referring to religious experience as "proof" or testimony to the reality of God. But the category of religious experience seems to invite several rather perplexing problems in contemporary culture. Can we, for example, speak of religious experience in the singular given the fact of religious pluralism? Should we not speak of religious *experiences*? If we maintain the validity or usefulness of the category, then how do we name that which unifies these linguistically and symbolically disparate experiences into the category "religious"? Even within a given culture, what makes certain experiences "religious" and others not? Does the category apply to cultures that do not possess or accept a concept of "religion"? Are all religious experiences true? Are any true, or none? These questions about religious experience raise many further questions about language, history, human knowing, and the human capacity for self-transcendence. How should we begin to sort out this range of issues?

Our discussion of the question of God marks a good place to start with these problems. Once we differentiate the question itself and various manifestations of the question, that is, the specific concerns or formulations with which a person or culture may treat the question, then we can identify how the question of God discloses something about the human condition. Most significantly, the question of God reveals that we are beings unrestrictedly in search of meaning, questioning beings, whose desire for meaning, truth, and goodness knows no limit.[4] Of course, the reach of human attainment knows many limits. Our questions easily outrun the answers we can discover, as every parent knows once their children begin to ask why. And even then some of our answers turn out to betray some error in thinking (ours or others') or incompleteness of the data under our consideration.[5] The undifferentiated field of our orientation to meaning, truth, and goodness also limits our attainment: though we can ask questions about anything whatsoever, we cannot ask about that which we do not yet know to ask, the "unknown unknown." Our knowing begins with some experience or data; there must first occur some phenomenon about which we can wonder and desire to understand. Consequently, we cannot ask specifically about that for which we have no data (sensible or imagined) or experience, no "something-to-be-understood."

These points may seem to bring only more problems, for though we can ask about the meaning of questioning itself and thus arrive at the question of God we cannot directly apprehend God's essence as the answer to our question. Again, there are no empirical data on God. How, then, does the question of God help us to sort out and resolve the many problems associated with the category of religious

---

4. This theme of the unrestricted scope of questioning is common to both Bernard Lonergan and Karl Rahner.
5. A good example of this flawed process is the history of scientific thinking about phlogiston and its relation to combustion. The approach was shown to be completely wrongheaded once it was realised that combustion was a form of rapid oxidation. See Encyclopaedia Britannica Online, s.v. "Phlogiston," accessed August 4, 2015, http://www.britannica.com/EBchecked/topic/456974/phlogiston.

experience? Though the question of God may lead more to a paradox than an answer—that is, the paradox of desiring to know what we cannot fully grasp—the question itself does not entail an idea of God at all.[6] The question of God offers a useful starting point for our reflections because it does not presuppose knowledge, or even a concept, of God. The question itself arises in myriad ways and at all stages of development in human history because the performance of human inquiry implies it. The question discloses the unrestricted reach of human intending as the total context for all inquiry and activity.

In turn, this disclosure leads to a question of fact: Does the human spirit's unrestricted desire for meaning ever find fulfillment? Does it ever rest in that which satisfies it? Even if our question of God orients us to the possibility of an unconditioned reality that does not directly admit empirical verification, does the anticipation expressed by the question ever meet the conscious fulfillment that would correspond with the horizon of its unrestricted anticipation? In other words, do we ever experience a fulfillment deep enough to ease all the intellectual and existential anxieties and uncertainties in our living? Do we ever encounter reality as a mystery that embraces us, that conforms us to the whole universe of being in gentle accord? Such an experience of fulfillment would allow us to define the category of religious experience with reference to the dynamic field of human consciousness rather than some specific content with the label "religious." But do such experiences occur?

The biblical and theological tradition witnesses to these kinds of

---

6. Though we have a natural desire to know God by God's essence, God's essence far surpasses the natural proportion of the human mind for understanding. Hence, we have a natural desire for that which we are incapable of attaining. The beatific vision thus becomes a theological resolution to this philosophical paradox. In the absence of revelation, we would have only the paradox. For a good discussion of this see Brian Himes, "Lonergan's Position on the Natural Desire to See God and Aquinas's Metaphysical Theology of Creation and Participation," *The Heythrop Journal* 54, no. 5 (2013): 767–83.

experiences in both first and third person accounts. St. Paul spoke of God's love poured into our hearts through the Holy Spirit given to us (Rom. 5:5), and described the Spirit's presence in us by pointing to the fruits: love, joy, peace, patience, kindness, goodness, gentleness, faithfulness, and self-control (Gal. 5:22). St. Augustine began his *Confessions* by noting the restlessness of the human spirit—"Our hearts are restless until they rest in you, Lord"—and narrated his conversion as a journey of receiving the grace needed to bring his feelings, decisions, and actions into peaceful accord with the deepest desires of his heart. Martin Luther, when asked how one might identify whether one's inner experience was from God or not, responded by saying, "A God is simply that whereon the human heart rests with trust, faith, hope and love. If the resting is right, then the God is right; if the resting is wrong, then the God, too, is illusory."[7] St. Ignatius spoke of "consolation without previous cause" in the context of elaborating a delicate, introspective technique for discerning God's desire for us in the concrete circumstances of our lives.[8] Often using powerful imagery and metaphor, the mystics describe direct experiences of union with the divine. They enter deeply into the "dark night," the "interior castle," or the "vision of light," only to return and tell of the most profound experiences of transformation and fulfillment.

When they speak of their experiences, the mystics time and again speak in poetry. St. John of the Cross, for example, wrote: "Oh, night that guided me, Oh, night more lovely than the dawn, Oh, night that joined Beloved with lover, Lover transformed in the Beloved! . . . I remained, lost in oblivion; My face I reclined on the Beloved. All ceased and I abandoned myself, Leaving my cares forgotten among

---

7. Luther's *Commentary on the Book of Daniel*, quoted in Richard Haldane, *The Pathway to Reality*, 2 volumes (London: Dutton, 1905), 2:127.
8. On consolation without a cause, see Karl Rahner, *The Dynamic Element in the Church* (New York: Herder and Herder, 1964), 131–42.

the lilies."[9] The mystics often describe the heights of mystical experience as entailing a deeply unitive silence, a wordless adoration, which moves beyond language, image, and concept. But they also describe how religious experience shapes the patterns of ordinary living. For example, the eighteenth-century mystic, Jean-Pierre de Caussade, describes how divine love transforms each moment of our lived experience.[10] "The present moment," he says, "is, as it were, a desert in which simple believers see nothing but God alone, whom they enjoy, being solely occupied with his will for them."[11] He describes his experience of the world in relation to the tradition's most profound mysteries of faith. He tells us that God calls to us beyond the veil of ordinary things much as he believes he receives the real presence of Christ in the Eucharistic elements of bread and wine. He asks: "Why should not every moment of our lives be a sort of communion with divine love, continuously producing in us the fruits of that communion when we receive the body and blood of the Son of God?"[12]

Though the heights of mystical experience may release the mystic from the world of ordinary language and everyday concerns, the appropriation of the experience invariably draws on the language of the mystic's religious tradition and culture. Notably, the return to language does not partition the experience into an isolated event in the mystic's life. Rather, these profound experiences transform ordinary engagements with the world; they place ordinary values and concerns in the light of a Supreme Goodness and Ultimate Concern;

9. St. John of the Cross, *Dark Night of the Soul*, trans. P. Silverio de Santa Teresa, ed. E. Allison Peers, *The Complete Works of Saint John of the Cross, Doctor of the Church*, 3 volumes (London: Burns Oates, 1943) 1:348.
10. Jean-Pierre de Caussade, *Abandonment to Divine Providence* (Notre Dame: Christian Classics, 2010). Since 2001, the authorship of the text has been seriously questioned. See the "Introduction" by Fr. Dennis Billy, CSsR, pp. 1-8.
11. Ibid., 124.
12. Ibid., 68.

they wipe away traces of fear, self-righteousness, and resentment; they heal the soul of hatred and despair; they fulfill the horizon of inner disposition and affect as to guide knowing and choosing into the harmony of a peaceful conscience; they return the person to language and culture with a new horizon, a principle of creativity and benevolence.[13] So Augustine famously remarked: "Love, and do what you will" (*dilige et quod vis fac*).[14]

What makes these experiences "religious"? If we identify these experiences as "religious" because of particular religious elements (such as Christian beliefs or symbols), then we logically exclude the experiences of people outside that religious tradition. In other words, if religious experiences are experiences had by Christians (or whatever the sociological definition of the privileged tradition), then non-Christians by definition do not have "religious experiences." Similar consequences unfold if we define "religious experience" in terms of a particular (conceptual) content; that is, if religious experiences are experiences of "Jesus," or "God," or "redemption," for example. Of course, "Jesus" and "redemption" are words with a unique Judeo-Christian heritage, and even if we identify a concept of God in other theistic traditions, the consequences remain the same: those whose experiences are not of "Jesus," "redemption," or "God" (however we define God) do not have "religious experiences," no matter how profound or transformative their experiences may be. In short, if we define "religious experience" according to conceptual

13. Its immediacy and transformative power notwithstanding, mystical experience is integral to the ongoing conversion of the person. Conversion is never entirely settled or complete in this life. Descriptions of mystical experience can contribute to a phenomenological definition of a heuristic limit for the process of conversion: the ongoing process is defined in approximation to the limit; see note 17 below.

14. See Augustine's Homily 7 on the First Epistle of John, §8 in *St. Augustin: Lectures or Tractates on the Gospel According to St. John*, trans. John Gibb and James Innes, *The Nicene and Post-Nicene Fathers of the Christian Church*, 14 volumes (New York: The Christian Literature Company, 1888), 7:504.

criteria (whether sociological or theological), then we logically limit the category of religious experience to people within a certain tradition, either by explicit membership or by conceptual agreement.

If we decide rather to determine the meaning of the category in relation to the dynamic field of human consciousness, if we say that "religious experiences" are experiences that fulfill the unrestricted desire for meaning, truth, and value, then our definition orients us to the data of human history without an *a priori* decision about the content or meaning of the phenomena we consider. In other words, the category prepares us to interpret religious expressions wherever they may occur. Consequently, our definition does not logically preclude anybody on the basis of historical accidents, claims to cultural normativity, or theological principles. In other words, people who simply do not encounter the Gospel in their lifetime, or who live a different religious commitment, are not by definition excluded. Likewise, our definition does not necessarily include any explicitly "religious" person in the category, either. It may happen that many Christians do not undergo religious experience, and that many people, who identify as non-Christians, or nonreligious, or even antireligious, in fact, do.[15]

The inner reality that our category anticipates does not allow us to treat religious experience as a static, uniform content that merely appears under different guises. Religious experience and its effects are dynamic principles of ongoing personal growth. The category anticipates the normative trajectory of a journey toward personal authenticity.[16] By defining the concept of religious experience

15. For example, the whole language of a "higher power" found in various applications of the Twelve Steps program speaks of "religious experience" in our terms, even though it does not require any explicit religious commitment from those who undertake them.
16. For a more extensive treatment of religious experience and conversion, see Christiaan Jacobs-Vandegeer, "Method, Meaning, and the Theologies of Religions," *Irish Theological Quarterly* 80, no. 1 (2015): 30–55.

phenomenologically (that is, in terms and relations derived from the data of consciousness), we avoid making *a priori* decisions about the content and validity of diverse religious experiences and allow for the particular variations characteristic of a process of growth.[17] The category thus functions heuristically; that is, it works as a principle of discovery in interaction with the concrete data of religious living. The category then becomes useful for interpreting the lived experience of human history and for placing the project of theology on a concrete, verifiable base.

Phenomenological and Sociological Definitions of Religion

The phenomenological approach to religion proposed here begins with our unrestricted desire for meaning, truth, and value, and with the experienced fulfillment of that desire. These two basic experiences (that is, unrestricted yearning and fulfillment) provide heuristic components for understanding the expansive volumes of data on religious living and expression. On this phenomenological anthropology, the unrestricted desire for meaning, truth, and value provides norms for our cognitional and evaluative labors in making judgments and decisions about the world. The experienced fulfillment of the inner exigencies for unrestricted intelligibility, truth, and goodness gives us the sole basis for nominating certain experiences as "religious." On this account, the category allows us potentially to speak of both atheists and devout Christians as having religious experiences in this life.[18]

17. The phenomenological approach allows us to give an implicit definition of religious experience, that is, a definition that focuses strictly on the relational element of the terms and abstracts from specific instances. For Lonergan on implicit definition, see Bernard J. F. Lonergan, *Insight: A Study of Human Understanding*, ed. Frederick E. Crowe and Robert M. Doran, *The Collected Works of Bernard Lonergan*, 25 volumes (Toronto: University of Toronto Press, 1992), 3:10–13; Lonergan, *Understanding and Being: the Halifax Lectures on Insight*, ed. Elizabeth A. Morelli, Mark D. Morelli, and Frederick E. Crowe, 2nd ed., *The Collected Works of Bernard Lonergan*, 25 volumes (Toronto: University of Toronto Press, 1990), 5:45–47.

Of course, different people describe experiences of yearning and fulfillment in many different ways. Christians and Buddhists, for example, draw on very different traditions of spiritual discipline and theological reflection. Scores of people search for words to describe the heights of their experiences of fulfillment and transcendence. Nature-lovers, poets, painters, and musicians often join their art to this precarious task of expression. The notion of religious experience proposed here has explanatory value because it refers to conscious events as related to normative elements in the structure of human inquiry. In other words, "religious experience" as "experienced fulfillment" occurs in consciousness and allows us to consider the inner core of "religion" as empirically given.[19] Because religious experience fulfills the human capacity for self-transcendence, it reveals itself over time in the sustained commitment to deeper attentiveness, intelligence, reasonability, responsibility, and love. Such habits are sown for the harvest of the Spirit (Gal. 5:22). Consequently, Christian saints and mystics often directly connect their descriptions of being in love with God to their deepened commitments to living out that redeeming love within their concrete circumstances.[20]

18. A good example of a nonbeliever having a "mystical" experience is the novelist Arthur Koestler. While in prison in Spain awaiting execution he had an experience that he described thus: "And then, for the first time, I suddenly understood the reason for this enchantment: the scribbled symbols on the wall represented one of the rare cases where a meaningful and comprehensive statement about the infinite is arrived at by precise and finite means. The infinite is a mystical mass shrouded in a haze; and yet it was possible to gain some knowledge of it without losing oneself in treacly ambiguities. The significance of this swept over me like a wave. The wave had originated in an articulate verbal insight; but this evaporated at once, leaving in its wake only a wordless essence, a fragrance of eternity, a quiver of the arrow in the blue. I must have stood there for some minutes, entranced, with a wordless awareness that 'this is perfect—perfect.'" See Arthur Koestler, *The Invisible Writing* (London: Vintage, 2005), 429. He remained nonetheless a lifelong atheist.

19. The meaning of "empirical" here includes the data of sense as well as the data of consciousness. This inclusive meaning allows us to regard conscious events and states as "something-to-be-understood" (that is, data), and thus to critically account for the interior dimensions of religious living.

20. Rowan Williams defines a mystic according to the criteria of the Paschal Mystery as applied to

Does this approach imply a common religious experience? Is mystical experience the same for everybody, no matter where or when they live? How does this approach address cross-cultural questions about religious experience and the significance of language? One approach, which could be called the perennialist perspective on these questions, contends that all mystical experiences are continuous or identical in content and comprehensible as such. And so Evelyn Underhill says:

> So we may say that the particular mental image which the mystic forms of his objective, the traditional theology he accepts, isn't essential. Since it is never adequate, the degree of its inadequacy is of secondary importance.... We cannot honestly say that there is any wide difference between the Brahman, Sufi, or Christian mystic at their best.[21]

On the perennialist perspective, the testimonies of Hindu, Christian, and Sufi mystics point to a common platform upon which the world's mystics gaze at the Ultimate.[22] Critics say that this approach marginalizes the differences in the mystics' unique expressions of their experiences, and struggles to account for its own presupposition of a common experiential content beneath language. How would we ever go about identifying that content? In the end, this approach does not recognize the constitutive role of a linguistically mediated culture in the mystics' descriptions of religious experience.

On the other hand, the approach often referred to as constructivist in this debate argues that a mystic's cultural-linguistic resources thoroughly and completely structure the mystic's experiences.[23] The

the mystic's life, that is, a Christian mystic embodies the meaning of the Paschal Mystery in the patterns of his or her life. See Rowan Williams, *Teresa of Avila* (London: Continuum, 2003), chapter 5.

21. Quoted in Avery Dulles, *Models of Revelation* (Maryknoll, NY: Orbis Books, 1992), 74.

22. For another classic example of the perennialist position, see W. T. Stace, *Mysticism and Philosophy* (London: MacMillan, 1960).

23. See, for example, Steven Katz, "Language, Epistemology, and Mysticism," in *Mysticism and Philosophical Analysis*, ed. Steven Katz (London: Oxford University, 1978), 22–74.

hope for discerning common experiential ground among diverse mystics vanishes under the weight of the priority of language over experience in human knowing. Religious expressions may exhibit similarities, but the likenesses are not due to religious experiences per se. The differences in mystical literature are then decisive; they confirm the constructivist's denial of the distinction between experience and understanding. The constructivist disallows the element of novelty in the field of human consciousness to contribute to the mystic's expressions and unique engagements with culture and tradition. For the constructivist, the mystic simply cannot speak without recapitulating the linguistic field of the tradition within which he or she encounters the world.

Our approach takes a different path. It focuses neither on an experience shorn of language nor on the concepts that inform the description of experience. It does not begin by eliminating the distinction between experience and interpretation, either by arguing for a nonlinguistic experience, or by collapsing the two. Rather, the phenomenological approach focuses on how religious experience functions in relation to the normative orientation of consciousness. It does not privilege a specific content of religious experience, but it also does not deny the possibility for mystics of different traditions to make true judgments about the commonalities in their experiences.[24] This perspective allows us to consider religious experience as integral to an ongoing process of conversion, a gradual deepening of fidelity to the inner exigencies for meaning, truth, goodness, beauty, and love.[25]

---

24. For a longer treatment of these issues, see James Price, "The Objectivity of Mystical Truth Claims," *Thomist* 49, no. 1 (1985): 81–98; and "Typologies and the Cross-Cultural Analysis of Mysticism: A Critique," in *Religion and Culture: Essays in Honor of Bernard Lonergan, SJ.*, ed. Timothy P. Fallon and Philip Boo Riley (Albany: SUNY, 1987), 81–90.

25. We will return to the issues in this debate in the chapter on the question of God. Many of the questions that are raised in this debate are not resolvable on the basis of considering religious

No doubt our religious living includes more than our inner experience alone. Our experience is integral to the patterns of our knowing and choosing in the contexts of community, culture, and society. The phenomenological approach must also account for how religious interpretations of the inner data on religion may carry the limitations and biases of a group, a culture, or even an epoch. Does a largely commonsense or metaphorical mode of religious speech run into limitations with respect to the kinds of questions it can address?[26] Does the language of the tradition mediate social inequities and power differentials (such as patriarchy and androcentrism)? Does the practice of charity inadvertently blind us to the effects of unjust economic systems in civic life, as, for example, when people generously give to the poor and yet fail to ask about the causes of poverty? The data on religious experience require that we expand our viewpoint in considering the complexities of a lived history of interpretation and human activity.

The normative structure of consciousness unfolds in a particular time and place as the history of consciousness in the world. The recipient of religious experience lives in a world of meaning and value that is created overwhelmingly by others. St. John of the Cross and Jalal ad-Din Muhammad Rumi appropriated their religious experiences in the contexts of their unique life stories, religious traditions, and cultures; they both spoke beautifully of their love for the divine, but the meanings of their poetry communicate the horizons of their respective contexts. Lived experience entails

---

experience alone. The language that a particular mystic uses to describe this experience carries with it the philosophical and theological judgments of a tradition.

26. Different religious expressions may occur in different realms and stages of meaning. Not all differences represent dialectical oppositions, though a tendency to see opposition rather than another kind of difference often results when theologians lack a differentiated understanding of the dynamics of meaning. See our chapter on intellectual conversion for a discussion of realms, stages, carriers, and functions of meaning. Note also the related discussion on differentiations of consciousness.

personal patterns of sin and grace as well as the achievements, limitations, and errors of the meanings and values that shape the person's horizon of engagement with the world. If we want to understand the lived experience of religion in history, then we must also consider the cultural and social meanings and values that interact in patterns of growth and deterioration, progress and decline, authenticity and inauthenticity.

Sociological definitions of religion can provide tremendous insight here. Depending on the perspective and methods of the sociologist, the definition of religion may vary significantly. A functionalist theory, for example, may suggest that religion expresses collective representations and acts as a force of social cohesion (Emile Durkheim);[27] another theory may describe how religion inspires the cultural imagination of a capitalist economy (Max Weber);[28] still another may explain how religion corrals complicity with economic exploitation as "the opiate of the masses" (Karl Marx). Still further, a postcolonial reading may criticize scholarly attempts to define "religion" in essentialist terms. Such essentialist attempts ignore how religious forms are embodied, interpreted, ambiguous, and embedded in social dynamics of power and discipline (Talal Asad).[29] The category of "religion" in certain instances may turn out to privilege and apply a modern, liberal worldview of society and the individual, and thus represent little more than a product of Western colonialism.

In this chapter, the emphasis lies on the inner core of religion, which we define heuristically using phenomenology, but the many complex interactions of this core with various outer expressions

27. See, for example, Emile Durkheim, *The Elementary Forms of the Religious Life*, trans. Joseph Ward Swain (New York: Free Press, 1965).

28. Max Weber, *The Protestant Ethic and the Spirit of Capitalism*, trans. Talcott Parsons (Dover Publications, 2003).

29. Talal Asad, *Genealogies of Religion: Discipline and Reasons of Power in Christianity and Islam* (Baltimore: Johns Hopkins University, 1993), 27–54.

require that we construct multiple sets of categories in order to understand religious living in its personal, cultural, and social dimensions. Not only do we anticipate descriptive understandings of religion in this project, but also an evaluation of religion's social significance becomes integral to the analysis. The phenomenological approach offers categories that enrich investigations of ethnographic data on religion and culture and aid the discernment of dynamics of power, value, and authenticity. Most importantly, the categories in this approach are heuristic in content, not culturally normative; they are oriented to the empirical data on religious living in all their diversity, ambiguity, and complexity. Such an orientation enables us to shift our viewpoint in considering volumes of data with the goal of understanding the unfolding dynamism of religious conversion for persons and communities in history.

Faith and Belief

Our notion of religious experience suggests that all people may awaken at one time or another to a sense of fulfillment for their hearts' deepest desires. They may experience the mystery of love and awe with particular acuity, and recognize inner soundings of a "call to a dreaded holiness."[30] The notion of religious experience may in principle apply to anybody from anywhere, and this point raises questions about the significance of religious belief. Is belief integral to religious experience and what is the relationship between them?

The fact that religious experience may occur widely precludes the decision to view religious conversion as simply a matter of adopting particular sets of beliefs.[31] The basic meaning of conversion here

---

30. Lonergan, *Method*, 113.
31. We understand religious conversion in relation to religious experience, which functions hermeneutically as an implicitly defined limit term. In turn, the data on religious experience is the data on a process of conversion. See notes 16 and 17 above. See also Lonergan, *Method*, 289.

requires neither creedal consensus nor membership in a group. The Greek word *metanoia* expresses the idea much better. Often translated as "repentance" in the New Testament, the word literally means a "change of mind and heart," a shift in self-understanding that entails both regret for wrongdoings and resolve for better ways of living. On this view, religious conversion refers to the shifts in our ways of knowing and choosing that reflect our ongoing growth in self-transcendence. Such shifts can and do happen in all kinds of circumstances and life stories.

The inclusivity of this category of religious experience allows us to make an important distinction between faith and belief. We use the term "faith" to denote the cognitive dimension of our religious experience. It names the difference in the horizon of our knowing that occurs as a result of our experience of being in love unrestrictedly. When a person falls in love, deeply in love, her experience of the world noticeably changes. Descriptively put, the grass simply looks greener, the sky looks a bit bluer, and the difficult person down the hall no longer seems all that bad. The experience of love discloses the potential of a transformative fulfillment in consciousness, and religious experience enriches that horizon only more profoundly. St. Francis de Sales used the analogy of human love to speak about how divine grace permeates consciousness. He noted how lovers are rapt with their beloved in each and every moment of the day, and how being in love with God only increases the depths of being consumed in unrestricted loving:

> Just as those who in love with a human and natural love almost always have their thoughts turned toward the chosen beloved, their hearts full of affection toward her, their mouth full of her praises, and in her absence, they do not lose the opportunity to express their passions by letters, and find no tree without inscribing on its bark the name of the one they love – so those who love God cannot stop thinking of him, panting for him, longing for him, and speaking of him, and would, if

it were possible, engrave on the breast of every person in the world the holy and sacred Name of Jesus.[32]

The overwhelming experience of being in love marks our point of departure for understanding religious experience. It allows us to consider faith concretely as the cognitive dimension of a profound shift in the flow of images, affects, insights, judgments, and decisions. Many people describe a different way of knowing in light of their experiences of mystery, awe, and fulfillment, and "faith" helps us to name that difference. Consider the emphasis on "realization" in Thomas Merton's description of a religious experience he had at an ordinary street corner: "In Louisville, at the corner of Fourth and Walnut, in the center of the shopping district, I was suddenly overwhelmed with the realization that I loved all those people, that they were mine and I theirs, that we could not be alien to one another even though we were total strangers."[33]

Merton recorded this experience in his personal journal on March 19, 1958. He lived as a Trappist monk at the Abbey of Gethsemani in Trappist, Kentucky, and connected this overwhelming experience of love for the passersby at the street corner to a shift in his understanding of his monastic vocation. He no longer saw his monastic life as a separate or spiritually higher life in relation to the rest of the world. He explained:

It was like waking from a dream of separateness, of spurious self-isolation in a special world, the world of renunciation and supposed holiness. The whole illusion of a separate holy existence is a dream. Not that I question the reality of my vocation, or of my monastic life: but the conception of "separation from the world" that we have in the monastery too easily presents itself as a complete illusion: the

---

32. St. Francis de Sales, *The Complete Introduction to the Devout Life*, trans. John-Julian (Brewster, MA: Paraclete Press, 2013), 103 (2.13).

33. Thomas Merton, *Conjectures of a Guilty Bystander* (Garden City, NY: Doubleday, 1966), 156.

illusion that by making vows we become a different species of being, pseudoangels, "spiritual men," men of interior life, what have you.[34]

This overwhelming experience of love shifted Merton's understanding of himself and his relation to others. This shift marks a new beginning and a change of heart, a transcending of the limitations of previous patterns of understanding: "This sense of liberation from an illusory difference was such a relief and such a joy to me that I almost laughed out loud."[35] Such a change of heart leaves sweetness and levity in the place of old burdens. Religious experience strikes to the core of who we are and to how we encounter the world in affect and intention. When we fall in love unrestrictedly, we begin to see the world with eyes of love. We become able and ready to discern God's self-disclosures in the most ordinary and unlikely of places.

If faith represents the cognitive dimension of religious experience, if it denotes the "knowledge born of religious love,"[36] still it cannot be equated with a specific categorical statement or concept. In other words, faith does not designate a belief or teaching. Rather, faith functions as a principle of evaluating, judging, understanding, and attentiveness. It marks a shift in the horizon of human knowing for the person whose growth now takes place in the state of unrestricted loving. The person of faith apprehends the transcendent value that conditions and relativizes all other values. The overwhelming goodness of the world as a whole, despite its darkness and obscurity, shines forth in the light of the lover's gaze. So a person genuinely grasps something more than what she grasps in the absence of love. She can say with Pascal: "The heart has reasons that reason does

34. Ibid., 156–57.
35. Ibid., 157.
36. Lonergan, *Method*, 115.

not know."[37] The heart grasps a value that we cannot manufacture intellectually merely by the efforts of our minds alone.

Belief, on the other hand, conforms to the structure of language and communicates knowledge of the world. The idea that belief occurs only in religious matters overlooks the necessity and function of belief in nearly every facet of human living, including science. Most of us hold a multitude of beliefs about the world, referring to them regularly in our everyday activities. I believe, for example, that when my car fails to start, it fails because of a mechanical reason. Of course, someone may challenge my belief. Someone else may say that my car fails to start because of a curse placed on it. Now I know almost as little about automotive machinations as I do about magic, but past experience informs my belief that automotive failure has a mechanical explanation. My belief, then, has a rational basis. Its rationality hinges on the empirical verifiability of a mechanic's expertise. Though I do not understand most of what takes place under the hood of my car, I believe that competent mechanics do understand and can use their knowledge to repair the problem.

Depending on our areas of expertise or ignorance, we can extend this example to any number of beliefs, ranging from the shape of the earth, to the processes of photosynthesis, to headache medicine. Belief, in this generalized understanding, represents knowledge that originates with someone else, someone other than me (that is, the person who adopts or rejects the belief). On this analysis, belief represents knowledge, but it contrasts with immanently generated knowledge. Some things I know because of a personal achievement or discovery. Most people can operate their vehicles quite well; they have a solid understanding of what happens when they do various things in their cars and can explain their movements with confidence

37. Blaise Pascal, *Pensées*, trans. W. F. Trotter (New York: E. P. Dutton, 1958), 80 (§ 277).

and relative success to a novice driver. The novice may take certain points of instruction on faith or belief before she learns the truthfulness of the instruction by experimentation and verification. Similarly, a student of geometry can attain an insight into what makes a circle a circle. Beyond merely memorizing a definition, she can learn why any particular circle represents (however imperfectly) a locus of coplanar points equidistant from a center.

We often learn to accept certain beliefs as true prior to appropriating their truthfulness through our own inquiry and experimentation. Not all immanently generated knowledge marks a discovery for all of the human family, and not all beliefs are tested and verified by all people. In fact, most of us verify only a small handful of the vast number of beliefs upon which we rely in our everyday activities and conversations. Both immanently generated knowledge and belief may tell us something true about the world. The difference between these kinds of knowledge lies in their origin.

The difference between faith and belief marks a difference in the structure of knowledge. More precisely, it marks a difference between the principle and content of knowledge. Ordinarily, our unrestricted desire to know serves as the principle of our knowing, but in religious knowing, our natural desire unfolds in the context of its total fulfillment, in the context of unrestricted loving. So faith marks a new principle of knowledge, a new horizon of knowing, and enables a person to see with the eyes of religious love.

What then does that person grasp? The object of faith may include anything whatsoever (save evil and sin). Ordinary things known in the light of faith mediate the transcendent value to which they ultimately relate. The Christian tradition's emphasis on sacramentality recognizes how finite things point beyond themselves to the reality of the divine, and "faith" names the principle by which a person apprehends that reality in ordinary living. Other people often become mediators of God's love for us, and most intensely in the context of a special loving relationship. Not all of us would love Beatrice quite like Dante, but we all might apprehend her goodness as a person. The apprehension of value in the beloved strikes much more deeply in the lover. It has transformative effects and takes on a surplus of meaning. So Dante described not only his unending love for Beatrice, but also how she made him a better person, how in loving her he experienced no less than his salvation.[38]

Moral acts and judgments are useful examples, too. A person may recognize Gandhi's fasting as a genuine value in the context of a newly liberated India. But a person may also witness Gandhi's fasting as an extraordinary act of love, an act that elicits more than a merely natural appreciation. In fact, the act may stir one to a deeper love of God and suggest such love by its intrinsic meaningfulness. So faith enables us to know in new light things that we could otherwise know naturally, but the knowledge that faith gives accounts for a significant difference in what we know.

Still, objects of faith may differ substantially. The object of faith may include a reality that exceeds the natural proportion of human knowledge. Such a reality represents a mystery in the technical, theological sense. A "mystery" here denotes a truth hidden so completely in God that we would not (and could not) know it had God not revealed it. When the object of faith includes a mystery in this precise sense, then it represents knowledge we could not naturally attain. The mysteries of the Trinity and Incarnation are objects of faith in this special sense, and the teachings on these mysteries are in a unique class called "dogma." Not all doctrines are dogmas.[39] Some teachings contain truths that we can attain naturally,

---

38. For an excellent discussion of Dante's love for Beatrice, see Charles Williams, *The Figure of Beatrice: A Study in Dante* (London: Faber and Faber, 1958), 17-30; see also Ralph McInerny, *Dante and the Blessed Virgin* (Notre Dame, IN: University of Notre Dame, 2010).

39. We will return to these issues in a later chapter on revelation.

for example, the intrinsic value of the human person or our responsibility for the common good. But no human person could ever arrive at knowledge of the Trinity in this life without divine revelation in human history.

Religious faith has a transcultural base in religious experience (heuristically defined), but religious beliefs of all kinds are tied to the history of the community within which they emerge. Hence, faith and belief are distinct, and this distinction marks a key commitment in our theological foundations. The distinction has a transcultural basis in religious experience and produces consequences for how theologians appropriate and communicate the meaning of a religion in a particular culture. The foundations of theology are presupposed in our systematic attempts at understanding the realities affirmed and described in doctrines. Scriptural references or allusions are not methodically foundational within our approach. Nor are references to revelation. Rather, Scriptural meanings (interpretation) are appropriated (dialectic) within the life of the community (history) and affirmed as revelatory (doctrines) on the basis of theologians' foundational commitments (implied or explicit) in cognitional theory, epistemology, metaphysics, and religion. We will explain these processes more fully in chapter 10.

If theologians do not admit criteria that originate apart from revelation, they almost invariably conflate faith and belief. They define faith in terms of revelation and see theology as a superior science that stands apart from (and often against) secular understandings of the world. Faith assumes an epistemic privilege in all things, and the world outside the church shrinks behind a shadowy veneer. If faith unlocks the door of salvation and always entails belief, then theologians treat the unbelieving world with suspicion. It may make sense for them to resolutely oppose the world in principle. Or perhaps they simply dismiss viewpoints that occur outside the margins of salvation. They expunge or domesticate foreign (secular) influence in theology and reframe basic categories in Scriptural or ecclesial terms, which, in their way of thinking, are nearer to revelation. Identifying faith (*fides qua*) with religious belief (*fides quae*) then collapses religious experience into doctrines. Such a move can lead to the denial of the ontological integrity of the created world. The most visible example of this (epistemic) privileging of religious authority appears in religious fundamentalism.

Several contemporary theologies also exhibit variations of this tendency toward collapsing faith into belief. Radical Orthodoxy, for example, emphasizes the overwhelming difference that revelation makes to our understanding of the world, and then critiques secular reason as a way of knowing independently of religious belief.[40] On this viewpoint, the principles of genuine knowledge are explicitly theological, so that faith would not likely wander outside the Christian community.[41] The postliberal approach to theology can appreciate different ways of understanding the world, but its reliance on Ludwig Wittgenstein elevates language over experience and concludes to incommensurability for a plurality of linguistic horizons. Doctrines set the parameters or grammar for the Christian worldview in theology. So the dynamics of faith are meaningful only according to the grammar and syntax of the Christian tradition.[42] In Avery Dulles'ss famous *Models of Revelation*, he describes propositional and dialectical models of revelation, each of which, in its own way, binds together faith and belief.[43] The propositional

40. See, for example, John Milbank, *Theology and Social Theory*. The dialectical theology of Karl Barth also exhibits this feature.
41. For example, consider Milbank's understanding of "ethics" as specifically tied to the church: "To be ethical therefore is to believe in the Resurrection, and somehow to participate in it. And outside this belief and participation there is, quite simply, no 'ethical' whatsoever" (John Milbank, *Being Reconciled: Ontology and Pardon* [New York: Routledge, 2003], 148).
42. See, for example, George A. Lindbeck, *The Nature of Doctrine: Religion and Theology in a Postliberal Age* (Philadelphia: Westminster Press, 1984).

model may recognize a natural revelation, but it defends doctrine as the unique carrier of saving truth and necessary for reconciliation with God. The dialectical view denies natural revelation and distinguishes doctrine from the saving value of hearing the Word, but maintains the exclusivity of faith's unique claim to revealed truth. Both models emphasize the identity of revelation and salvation.[44]

On the other side of the spectrum, theologians may also err in the opposite direction, identifying faith and belief on the basis of an immanentist anthropology. They may deny the disproportion and dynamism of religious experience to conclude that experiences of fulfillment are products of human achievement like any other, products that lie within the ordinary horizon of human knowing and choosing; they reduce their religious experience to the plane of immanence. If theologians do not recognize holiness as a unique dimension of our inner lives, distinct from our moral and intellectual vitality, they open a door to naturalism. The conflation of faith and belief then collapses grace into nature. It denies our (elevated) participation in the divine. Dulles's new awareness model of revelation illustrates the reductionist tendency toward this problematic viewpoint. The new awareness model rightly emphasizes the transformation of the subject and shift in awareness that enables a new way of seeing the world, but it abandons the objectivity of religious knowing and threatens to reduce revelation to whatever a person apprehends as meaningful. The different kinds of belief noted above are gathered together and relativized by the subject's religious experience.

The distinction between faith and belief on the basis of religious experience allows us to maintain the objectivity of revelation without restricting God's offer of salvation to the Christian community. It

---

43. Dulles, *Models of Revelation*. Cited in note 21.
44. They are of course related. See chapter 8 of the present work.

allows us to recognize the distinct contributions of faith and belief to our personal and collective growth. Notably, the distinction has important ramifications for ecumenical and interreligious dialogue. The foundational reality of religious experience as prior to doctrines allows the churches and religions to meet on the (heuristically defined) common ground of reciprocity with the other as loved and (potentially) loving. No doubt beliefs differ, sometimes significantly, but a theology with a foundation in the universality of religious experience contextualizes differences in religious beliefs with reference to the experienced gift that meets the inner desire for self-transcendence in each of us.

No doubt beliefs matter profoundly. Beliefs carry the wisdom of a tradition and powerfully promote the flourishing of the inner gift in unique and irreplaceable ways. Still further, beliefs may maintain the biases and blind spots of a tradition; they may diminish and even undermine cooperation with the love a person receives and experiences, however subtly. The distinction between faith and belief allows us to appreciate the complexities of their interrelations in the shifting, dynamic terms of personal and communal growth in self-transcendence. The distinction does not imply a simplistic, universalized faith that would consume all belief and undercut the significance of religious differences. Quite the contrary, the distinction enables us to recognize the importance of those differences without attaching an *a priori* judgment about their validity. It allows us to prevent rash judgments about the differences, to appreciate the historical patterns of culture and society mediated by the differences, and to hope for an encounter of persons that will allow for new experiences of community on the basis of charity, already given, to those both near and far away.

Conclusion: A Theological Example:
Religious Conversion as Foundational

In chapter 1, we argued that some theological disputes arise because of the presence or absence of various forms of conversion. We identified the debates over the historical Jesus as an example. Of course, we are not in a position to verify the presence or absence of religious conversion within the many participants in that debate. In fact, it stands outside the range of anybody's ability to decisively say that someone has undergone religious conversion. Unlike intellectual conversion, the presence or absence of which we can verify on the basis of a text, religious conversion evades the power of our judgment in many ways. Our salvation is a mystery hidden in God. Still, we can anticipate how someone with or without religious conversion might approach the text of the Gospels by recognizing the kinds of apprehension religious conversion makes possible.

The horizon of religious conversion enables theologians to recognize the New Testament as an expression of religious experience impacting upon an entire community. The documents of the New Testament are a passionate love song to the person of Jesus, through whom the members of the early church experienced a major change in their lives. Such change we describe as religious conversion. Out of the community's religious experience all kinds of questions emerged about who Jesus is and how we might understand him, and these questions go beyond foundations to questions of judgment (doctrines). Still, the early Christian community clearly identified Jesus as the one who brought about a most radical change in their lives. He was "Emmanuel," God-with-us, the focus of the fulfillment of their search for meaning, truth, and goodness. The full unpacking of christological questions took several centuries to occur, but that process unfolded as a matter of answering fundamental questions about the identity of Jesus and his relationship to God in light of the early community's experience of him.

On the other hand, reading the New Testament in the absence of religious conversion is like listening to Mozart while being tone-deaf. Rather than identifying with the impact of Jesus on the lives of the early Christians and recognizing their religious experience, the reader will find it all very puzzling and perhaps even suspicious. The language of the New Testament will sound "over the top," excessive, and will more than likely point to an agenda at work in the community. Rather than a hymn of love to Jesus, the New Testament then looks like a way of shoring up the authority of certain leaders within the early church and justifying their power over the community. Such a reading traces these power plays into the life of the church and finds them culminating in the declarations of Jesus' divinity as the ultimate consolidation of church power. The quest for the historical Jesus then becomes a search for the "real" Jesus stripped of the "accretions" of the church. A great splitting occurs between the "historical Jesus" and the "Christ of faith," and theologians may then appeal to the historical Jesus as to subvert the claims of Christian faith. No doubt this trajectory occurs in the writings of some theologians who quest for the historical Jesus.

Does this trajectory suggest the absence of religious conversion? Not necessarily. Some theologians may approach the text with a hermeneutic of suspicion out of deep love for God. Still, this trajectory of reading the text without recognizing the religious experience of the community may also represent the outcome of a theologian's refusal of that love. The task of theology in all its phases or specializations presupposes the foundational reality of the theologian's inner life. So this point applies in principle to the whole community of theologians: religious development is dialectical in this life, a constant realization of authenticity and withdrawal from inauthenticity, and this fact keeps theology going, making us hopeful of a deeper religious conversion and a fuller understanding of the mysteries of faith.

3

Moral Conversion and the Structure of the Good

In the previous chapter, we considered religious conversion in terms of an inchoate (total) fulfillment of our conscious-intentional orientation toward meaning, truth, and goodness. It is the experience of God's love flooding our hearts (Rom. 5:5), of being loved by God "before the foundation of the world" (Eph. 1:4). This involves a radical shift in our horizon so that in everything we do we act on a different level, with an expanded range of possibilities for meaning, truth and goodness. Still, as with the human experience of falling in love, this is only the first momentous step in our sustained growth in authenticity. It takes a lifetime to unpack the full implications of this transformation. One aspect of this unpacking is the issue of moral conversion, which, while often an outcome of religious conversion, is a distinct and at least partially independent reality. For example, Augustine's prayer for the gift of continence indicates both the presence of religious conversion (he prays for the gift) and the absence of elements of moral conversion (the struggle with continence).[1] The growth in authenticity enabled and sustained by the gift of God's love is a rocky path with both stumbles and setbacks on the way.

As with religious conversion, the presence or absence of moral conversion has an impact on the ways in which we approach our work as theologians. When we lack a clear foundation in moral conversion we often hold confused ideas about the nature of human freedom, about human flourishing, and the problem of sin and evil. Such confusion impacts our basic anthropology as well as our understanding of redemption. As we shall see, moral conversion also provides the basis for relating the human sciences, such as sociology and psychology, to theology in a constructive fashion. This is a particularly important outcome given the prominence of these human sciences in the wider culture. Moral conversion is thus significant in theology's mediating role between religion and culture. Of course, some might suggest that religious conversion is a sufficient basis for doing theology without other considerations. Yet, as we shall argue below, moral (and intellectual) conversion provides a normative framework for assessing the authenticity of religious conversion. Without attention to these other conversions, theology leans toward fideism.

What is Moral Conversion?

We can approach the topic of moral conversion through the narrative of someone who has undergone such a conversion. We have something like such a narrative in the story of St. Ignatius of Loyola. As a young man he was interested in martial activities, in battle and a desire for the fame that came from victory. In one battle, he was seriously injured and had to undergo an extensive period of convalescence (indeed he had a limp for the rest of his life from his

1. Augustine famously prayed, "Grant me chastity and self-control, but please, not yet." See Augustine, *The Confessions*, 198 (Book 8.17).

injuries). During this time of recovery, he could do very little, so he read. He read popular works of romance and battle that inflamed his passions, but he later found that they provided no lasting satisfaction. He also read the lives of saints. These also aroused his passions, but in a way that stayed with him and uplifted his heart. The popular works he read satisfied him in the moment, but the lives of the saints allowed him to discover his own need for genuine value. Attending to the difference in his own feelings allowed him to discern mere satisfactions from genuine values, and to then commit himself to values over satisfactions.

This short narrative illustrates key features of the process of moral conversion. We all make decisions in our lives. Our fundamental orientation to goodness drives us to ask, "Is this truly good? Is this better or worse than that?" as part of the process of coming to those decisions. However, we need to ask such questions because we know that sometimes we make decisions on the basis of something less than what is truly good. Sweet things may satisfy our hunger, but if we eat too many of them we will quickly become unhealthy. It may be satisfying to cheat on our taxes, but if everyone did it our social order would collapse. To ask whether our decisions are truly good is to recognize a distinction between the truly good, or genuine values, and the apparently good, or the merely satisfying. Moral conversion entails a commitment to the genuine good, a shift in the criteria for making our decisions. Sometimes such a commitment entails real hardship and suffering, even to the point of death. We witness something of this cost in the death of Socrates, whose commitment to the value of wisdom led to conflict with his society and his eventual execution.

Ignatius learned to distinguish between genuine value and mere satisfaction by attending to his own affective states. He later developed this into a sophisticated process of spiritual discernment, by which we can identify interior pulls and counterpulls within consciousness and their impact upon our decision making. Our affectivity responds to both satisfactions and values, but in different ways. Interior discernment assists us in learning which is which. These affective responses raise questions about the truly good course of action, the occurrence of which then requires reasoning, deliberation, and responsible decision. However, even at an affective level we can consolidate our orientation to genuine value so that our decisions are habitually guided toward the truly good. This type of habitual affective orientation is related to the notion of virtue.[2]

A Scale of Values

To suggest that some decisions intend what is truly good, as opposed to the merely satisfying, is to suggest that in some sense values are "objective" or "real," not merely the product of some individual choice. While we shall postpone a fuller discussion of terms like "objective" and "real" until the next chapter, at a first approximation, we can say that genuine values are independent of my current stage of moral development or orientation. Regardless of how I feel or think, this decision intends the truly good, or it does not. If values are objective, I have no choice about them, except to either accept them (and live accordingly) or reject them (and live according to what is merely satisfying). If we accept values as objective, freedom is not about arbitrary choice, but about freely conforming our lives to a set of values not of our own making. Freedom then has a normative structure, oriented toward the good. When we choose a mere satisfaction over a genuine value, it is not just a matter of using

---

2. In Scholasticism, this was called "connatural" knowledge, a sort of infused affective moral knowledge. For a contemporary account congruent with our approach, see Jeremy Wilkins, "Grace and Growth: Aquinas, Lonergan and the Problematic of Habitual Grace," *Theological Studies* 72, no. 4 (2011): 723–49.

freedom, but of misusing it. To recognize values as real moves us right away from the notion of freedom as arbitrary choice as found in much of our commonsense notions of freedom.

At the same time, we know that we do not *spontaneously* respond to what is truly valuable, but need to learn to appreciate some things that are genuinely of value. And so a child may not spontaneously want to eat vegetables, but over time can learn to appreciate that they are healthy to eat. Similarly, it might take a more refined sensibility to appreciate great literature, but in the absence of that sensibility it remains objectively valuable, a significant cultural achievement. Thus, we can distinguish between moral growth, as learning to appreciate genuine values as valuable and responding accordingly, and moral conversion, which involves turning from satisfactions to genuine value. Seen in this light a moral tradition is a cumulative deposit of moral wisdom that emerges from moral conversion present and operative over many generations.

We can also recognize that some values are "higher" than others. We value good health, but we might risk our physical wellbeing to defend our country from invasion. Our country might go to war, but we might view it as unjust and our conscience might then object to our participation in it, even at serious personal cost. We can fill out this observation by proposing a hierarchical and normative scale of values. It is *hierarchical* in that it suggests some values are higher than others, and *normative* in the sense that such a scale should be incorporated into any responsible decision-making process. One could argue that recognition of this scale as normative is itself an outcome of ongoing moral conversion, but for the time being we will propose it as a useful structure or model for consideration.

We begin with an account of *vital values*. We choose vital values when we make decisions in order to maintain our physical wellbeing. We exercise, eat well, keep warm in the cold, and so on. All these decisions are good because they help maintain our biological wellbeing so that we can do all the other things that we need to do. And we may not experience all these things as satisfying. Exercise on a cold morning might not feel very good, but we do it because we know it benefits us. Paradoxically, pain can be a vital value, because it tells us something is wrong that needs to be fixed, but we don't seek out pain for its own sake.

Social values on the other hand refer to the good of order that ensures the recurrence of vital values, not just for me and you, but for society as a whole. Examples of the good of order include our developing technologies, our economic system, and the political structure, which, taken together, are meant to ensure an equitable, sustainable, and just distribution of vital values for all members of the community. The good of order ensures the production and distribution of food, the maintenance of standards of living, and the socialization and education of children; we prepare the next generation to contribute to the ongoing realization of social values. Roads built today need repairs in the years ahead. Hospitals functioning now must adapt to increasing technology and changing economies in order to continue delivering current, quality healthcare. These intelligible goods of order are the products of cooperative and practical human intelligence operating over generations.

There exists a tension within social values, a tension between our spontaneous sense of communal belonging, and the drives of practical intelligence to create order in our social world. This tension is most evident when various "developments" (such as road constructions or fracking) threaten local communities. The developments may make "good economic sense," but they may damage a community by damaging local relationships, dividing communities, and so on. Both our sense of communal belonging and the demands of practical intelligence are elements of social values, and they exist in tension.

Still, it can be a creative tension, which a healthy society can use to create new forms of social order into the future.

We rightly ask critical questions when social orders break down, such that particular groups are excluded from or denied access to vital values. We can witness such breakdowns locally, within cities and nations, and most clearly on the global scale. Such breakdowns indicate that our social order fails to fully function as it should, and thus we must conceive and implement some corrective. People can be excluded from economic opportunities and political power because they are not members of certain social groups, because of their ethnicity, religious beliefs, or sexual orientation. This is a breakdown in social justice, a form of group bias, and has been a major concern of liberation theology, for example.[3] Any theology that seeks to incorporate concern for social justice must attend to the structure of social values and their relationship to vital values, the nature of distortions within the social order, and the ways in which such distortions can be healed.

A well-functioning social order provides its members with free time to think about the larger questions of life. Some of these questions will be about the social order itself: What is the best form of political life? Is our economic system just? Just because we have the technology to do something, should we do it? And so on. But there will also be larger questions: what constitutes human flourishing? Is human flourishing just a matter of having a well-oiled economic machine? What is the meaning and purpose of life? Can we understand the world around us? Such questioning and our attempts to address them in art, philosophy, theology, science, and other disciplines constitute a different form of value, namely, *cultural values*. When considering social values we mentioned the role of education

---

3. See, for example, the classic work, Gutiérrez, *A Theology of Liberation*.

in preparing children to become participants in and contributors to the social good. However, a good education does more than this. It introduces students to their cultural heritage wherein questions about the meaning and purpose of life have been debated and discussed for generations. It develops the child's critical thinking about these issues while helping them to appropriate the wisdom of the past. A well-functioning cultural order can assist with the proper operation of the social order, by raising critical questions, proposing alternative solutions, and identifying areas of breakdown. Simply put, we do not live on bread alone. We need our lives to be meaningful and purposeful.

As with the social order, it is possible to identify a tension within the order of cultural values. Political philosopher Eric Voegelin has suggested two major cultural types, what he calls cosmological and anthropological cultural types.[4] *Cosmological cultures* seek meaning in the rhythms of the cosmic order, the changing seasons, the flow of life and death, so that our earthly order is meant to mirror the cosmic order. This cosmic order is the realm of God, or the gods, and it establishes the template for what happens here below. My task as a human being is to find my place within the social order, which itself mirrors the heavenly order. Cosmological cultures promote social stability and highly value the traditions of the past. Conversely, they have difficulty coping with change, tend to be fatalistic, and suppress the role of the individual, subsuming them to the good of order. *Anthropological cultures* seek meaning, not in the rhythms of the cosmos, but in a world-transcending source of meaning and value, for example, a transcendent God or in human reason considered as a universal principle. The task of the individual is not to conform to the social order, but to shape their lives according to this world

4. Eric Voegelin, *The New Science of Politics, An Introduction* (Chicago: University of Chicago Press, 1952). Also see Doran, *Theology and the Dialectics of History.*

transcendent source of meaning and value. In doing so, they reshape the social order. Anthropological culture views the social order as malleable, a human construction subject to major transformation. Rather than fatalism, these cultures view human history as the outworking of human forces for change, as we build and rebuild our economies and our political institutions according to the demands of reason. Historically, we can witness a shift from a more cosmological to a more anthropological culture in the emergence of Greek philosophy in the ancient world. The death of Socrates captures the tensions that can arise in such a shift. Socrates's search for universal principles called into question the existence of "local" gods, to such an extent that he was accused of denying religion and corrupting the youth. For this, he was sentenced to death. So significant is this period that Karl Jaspers refers to it as an axial period, where history itself begins to pivot in a new direction.[5]

Voegelin posits a third cultural type, which he refers to as "soteriological" culture. Such a possibility occurs when divine meanings and values enter into human history in a way that maintains the fruitful tension between cosmological and anthropological types. Voegelin identifies such a possibility in the Judeo-Christian heritage. This is a larger scale cultural outcome of the dynamic of religious conversion we considered in the previous chapter. We shall consider this again later when we study the question of revelation.

As with the level of social values, we can identify distortions at the level of culture. Some of these arise from distortions in the social order itself, which then seek justification in political ideologies, systems of meaning and value, which enthrone the distortions of the social order as somehow "natural." We can see this, for example,

---

5. Karl Jaspers, *The Origin and Goal of History* (New Haven: Yale University Press, 1953).

in patriarchy, which provides ideological justification for a social order that marginalizes women by restricting possibilities for their economic and political participation. This marginalization is a particular concern for feminist theology and other forms of political theology.[6] However, there are also distortions that arise from a breakdown in the tension between cosmological and anthropological culture. As we noted above, a culture strongly oriented to cosmological meanings and values tends to be fatalistic and to lose sight of divine transcendence. This is less an issue for Western culture, but such cultures can still be found in Asia and Africa.[7] A culture strongly oriented to anthropological meanings and values, to the neglect and even denigration of cosmological meanings and values, becomes out of touch with the natural world and the inherent value of the biosphere. Such a culture views the natural world strictly according to its instrumental value, that is, its ability to satisfy human needs and wants. The end result can be massive environmental destruction. This distortion of the cultural dialectic is of importance to ecological theologies.[8]

Cultural values are themselves the products of human agents, persons who through their cultural products—writings, artworks, teachings, and so on—shape the way we think and feel about a range of issues. This observation points to the arena of *personal values*.

6. See the classic work, Rosemary Radford Ruether, *Sexism and God-talk: Toward a Feminist Theology*, 10th anniversary ed. (Boston: Beacon, 1993). There are also theologies that focus on issues of racism, for example, James H. Cone, *A Black Theology of Liberation*, 40th anniversary ed. (Maryknoll NY: Orbis Books, 2010).

7. Confucianism and the religious traditions of India (often referred to as Hinduism) are strongly cosmological in their structure as are the primal religions of Africa.

8. See, for example, the ground-breaking work of Sean McDonagh, *To Care for the Earth: A Call to a New Theology*, 1st U.S. ed. (Santa Fe: Bear & Co, 1987). More recently, see Denis Edwards, *Earth Revealing—Earth Healing: Ecology and Christian Theology* (Collegeville: Liturgical Press, 2001); Rosemary Radford Ruether, *Gaia and God: An Ecofeminist Theology of Earth Healing*, 1st ed. (San Francisco: HarperSanFrancisco, 1992); Leonardo Boff, *Ecology and Liberation: A New Paradigm* (Maryknoll, NY: Orbis Books, 1995).

As personal beings oriented to meaning, truth, and value, we are also creators of meaning, truth, and value through our fidelity or lack thereof to that orientation. Our own personal horizon is shaped by the culture in which we live, which we in turn shape through our actions and decisions. Inasmuch as we are faithful to our native orientation to meaning, truth, and value, we contribute to the good of culture; inasmuch as we fail to be faithful we contribute to cultural distortions and decline. Indeed, moral conversion itself is our own appropriation of ourselves as creators of meaning and value, so that we become both self-constituting and world-constituting beings through the exercise of our freedom. Through our decisions we not only shape the persons we are to be, opting for either a life of virtue or vice, but also constitute our world by shaping our social and cultural orders.

As with the social and cultural orders, there is a tension within the realm of personal values. On the one hand, there is our native orientation toward meaning, truth, and goodness, which drives us relentlessly toward a fuller participation in those intentional goals. On the other hand, we must enlist our groundedness in biological rhythms into our broader search for meaning. Theologically, this tension results in concupiscence, the inertial resistance of our bodiliness to the urgings of our spirit.[9] Of itself, it is morally neutral; indeed, virtue lies in maintaining the tension between these two aspects. As Aristotle taught, virtue lies in the mean, between the excesses of either aspect.[10] This mean is not however a homeostatic

9. See Karl Rahner, "The Theological Concept of *Concupiscentia*," in *Theological Investigations*, 23 vols., trans. Cornelius Ernst, vol. 1: 347-82. London: Darton, Longman and Todd, 1961. Rahner illustrates the neutrality of the concept by reference to the fact that we may blush when telling a lie. The bodily reaction of blushing betrays our intent to deceive.

10. As Aristotle states, "Virtue is a state of character concerned with choice, lying in a mean, that is, the mean relative to us, this being determined by a rational principle, and by that principle by which the person of practical wisdom would determine it," (Aristotle, *Nicomachean Ethics*, trans. W. D. Ross [Oxford: Oxford University Press, 1980], 39 (2.6).

balance since the drive for meaning, truth, and value transforms our bodiliness by conforming it increasingly to the demands of our conscious intentionality.[11]

This conscious orientation to meaning, truth, and value can be derailed in two basic ways. It can be derailed by a social and cultural context that distorts our search, by normalizing the distortions present in the social and cultural orders, adding a layer of confusion and obfuscation to our personal journey. Social and cultural sin impacts us interiorly. However, our own decisions can also derail our spiritual orientation, leading to distortions toward one or other aspects of the tension—either cutting ourselves off from our bodiliness, failing to recognize our limitations, and falling for the temptation to "be like gods" (Gen. 3:5), or losing ourselves in the rhythms and flows of our biological drives, with the larger horizon of meaning and value vanishing in the distance.

Left to our own resources the likelihood of such derailment is very high, indeed almost certain, particularly in a context of significant social and cultural distortions. Failings at the level of personal value have the meaning of sin in the theological sense of a personal act. It may have its preconditions and excuses, but there remains a question of personal responsibility for one's decisions and actions. The problem we then face is how we can remedy these distortions. Do we have the resources on our own to address them, or need we have recourse to a "higher power"? The inability to address our distortions is known as moral impotence, a phenomenon most evident in the problem of addictions. Augustine captures this experience well: "The truth is that disordered lust springs from a perverted will; when lust is pandered to, a habit is formed; when habit is not checked, it hardens into compulsion. There were like interlinking rings forming what I have described as a chain, and my harsh servitude used it to keep

11. See Wilkins, "Grace and Growth," 725–29.

me under duress."[12] While addicts freely engage their addiction, they are not free not to so engage.[13] How can they resolve this situation if their addiction captures their interiority and leaves them feeling helpless?

These questions raise in turn the question of *religious value*. We identified the important role of religious value in chapter 2 on religious conversion. The experience of religious value is an inchoate experience of fulfillment of our natural orientation to meaning, truth, and value, in a way that goes beyond what we could ever achieve through our own efforts. It is not the product of a decision on our part, but a radical shift in our horizon that affects all our future decisions. To claim that this experience goes beyond what we could ever achieve on our own is to claim that such an experience is "supernatural," that is, beyond the resources of human nature to attain. The experience "elevates" us to a new level of conscious operation. We considered this experience under the heading of religious conversion in chapter 2. However, to put this experience in the context of human moral failing is to highlight another aspect of this same experience: its ability to heal distortions within consciousness and set us anew on the path to authenticity, by grounding us in an overwhelming experience of love.[14]

---

12. Augustine, *The Confessions*, Book 8.10 (192).

13. For discussion on the issues of addiction and religious experience, see Gerald May, *Addiction and Grace* (San Francisco: Harper and Row, 1988); and May, *The Awakened Heart: Living beyond Addiction*, 1st ed. (San Francisco: HarperSanFrancisco, 1991).

14. This is simply a restatement of the observation of Aquinas: "And thus in the state of perfect nature man needs a gratuitous strength superadded to natural strength for one reason, viz. in order to do and wish supernatural good; but for two reasons, in the state of corrupt nature, viz. in order to be healed, and furthermore in order to carry out works of supernatural virtue, which are meritorious." (*ST* 1-2.109.2). For a contemporary theological anthropology informed by these concerns, see Neil Ormerod, *Creation, Grace and Redemption* (Maryknoll, NY: Orbis, 2007).

Implications of the Scale of Values—
Theology and the Social Sciences

The scale of values has a number of important implications for theology. First, we shall consider the scale in terms of a distinction introduced in chapter 2 between nature and grace (that is, the absolutely supernatural). Catholic theology since the thirteenth century makes a distinction between grace as a gift over and above what human nature can achieve, and a natural order, conceived metaphysically as a relatively autonomous realm with its own ends and powers. The scale of values helps us unpack the relatively compact notion of "human nature" by allowing us to distinguish among personal morality, cultural meanings and values, the social orders of community, technology, economy, and politics, and the level of human vitality grounded in our biological needs. This unpacking then provides us with categories for an account not only of the individual human person, as was so thoroughly provided by Thomas Aquinas and his discussion of virtues and vices,[15] but also of the human being as embedded in history, as a product of social and cultural forces and a producer of society and culture—an area often neglected or rendered invisible in more traditional metaphysical theologies. With these sets of categories we have the basic elements of a theology of history—not the history that is written, but the history that is written about.[16]

We can illustrate the utility of the scale of values by reflecting on the issue of gender. When the body-soul dualism dominates the theological understanding of human nature, theologians tend to conflate gender with biological sex (body/animality), and the questions raised in relation to sexual ethics are those of the virtues

15. In particular, Aquinas's account of the human virtues in *ST* 2-2.47-170.
16. For a full unpacking of this distinction, see Doran, *Theology and the Dialectics of History*, esp. 12-16, where he introduces his project in similar terms.

(soul/rationality) needed to regulate sexuality according to the dictates of reason (such as chastity, temperance). Most theologians are much more aware now of the complexities of sex and gender. While biology (vital values) is one aspect of gender, we also recognize that gender encompasses social roles built around a division of labor (such as "bread winner" and "home maker"), as well as the cultural meanings and values (masculinity, femininity) that attach those roles to sexual difference. Contemporary moral questions (personal values) about gender are much more complex and realistic than those framed within the traditional, dualistic understanding of human nature. At the very least, they undermine the various forms of gender essentialism found within the tradition.[17]

Further, by analyzing the movements among the levels of the scale of values, we can transpose questions of sin and grace from the horizon of a traditional focus on the individual to a broader horizon that considers the significance of community and history. We can identify a movement "from below," whereby the emergence of a higher level resolves problems on a lower level by transcending the lower level's limitations. And so problems with the recurrent supply and distribution of vital values are resolved at the social level, through technological, economic, and political innovations. Moving yet higher, we address social problems at the cultural level by calling into question existing institutions and processes and posing alternatives. And by our personal commitment to authenticity, we become agents of cultural change. Lonergan refers to this upward movement on the scale of values as a creative vector, because it depends on our commitment to our inner drive for meaning, truth, and value. Only by raising questions and seeking creative responses

17. The relationship of sex and gender is complex at each level of the scale of values. Even biological sex is not an uncontested category; that is, cultural meanings and values can aid or distort the interpretation of sex and difference.

to those questions do we move up the scale in the ongoing realization of the human good. Each level has its own proper set of "ends," but each lower level also participates in the higher ends of the scale. The unity of the human good includes these hierarchically ordered, interdependent dimensions.

The scale of values also allows us to discern a movement "from above." Such a movement begins at the religious level and transforms our personal values by reorienting us along the path of authenticity. In turn, we grow in genuineness as agents of cultural change, attempting to shift our cultures toward the intentional goals of meaning, truth, and value, and thereby shaping our social order in view of a just distribution of vital values for all members of the human family. The movement "from above" heals the distortions and breakdowns that occur at each level of the scale. In this way, we can recognize that sinful human decisions impact the cultural (such as ideologies) and social orders (such as sinful institutions, group biases), while also discerning the transforming influence of grace at these levels as well. Indeed, some social and cultural situations are the result of God's graciousness, and in turn assist in the further mediation of that graciousness in the unfolding of human history. This possibility is important in any consideration of the theology of the church (ecclesiology).[18]

The introduction of these categories also raises questions about theology's relationship to other disciplines, which seek to understand social and cultural orders (such as economics, sociology, and cultural anthropology). This is not a simple problem. We must first recognize that these disciplines include significant divisions within them. These divisions often reflect different approaches to their subject matter; for

---

18. See Neil J. Ormerod and Shane Clifton, *Globalization and the Mission of the Church*, for an example of this suggestion. Also Neil Ormerod, *Re-Visioning the Church: An Experiment in Systematic-Historical Ecclesiology* (Minneapolis: Fortress Press, 2014).

example, the divisions between neoclassical economics and political economics; between functionalist and conflictualist sociological approaches; between psychologists who focus on brain physiology and depth psychologists who interrogate our dreams. These divisions can also have an ideological character; they can reflect differing commitments to ways of conceiving the human person and society.[19] Recognizing these divisions raises questions for theologians seeking to utilize these human sciences: Which form of sociology/ psychology/economics shall I engage? If they are in fact based on truncated or distorted visions of human existence, then will this truncation or distortion undermine their usefulness for theology? For example, some psychologists working with brain physiology seek to reduce all human thought processes to brain biochemistry. Such a reductive approach entails philosophical assumptions beyond empirical, scientific method, and effectively denies what we might call the "spiritual" dimension of human living, that is, our orientation to meaning, truth, and value. Human freedom is then not self-determination, but is rather predetermined by underlying biological processes. Beyond the philosophical problems here, this reductionism is incompatible with theology. At least, it would be extremely difficult to develop a theological account of grace and sin under such circumstances, where human responsibility and the need for repentance are basically denied.

In short, theologians need to carefully consider the human sciences and their outcomes. The outcomes of the studies of the human sciences cannot simply be taken at face value. However, we can push the matter further. Can a relationship between theology and the human sciences have a positive impact on those sciences? Can

---

19. Alternatively the differences may lie in philosophical differences, reflecting empiricist, idealist, or realist assumptions. This however takes us into the area of intellectual conversion rather than moral conversion.

the human sciences be reoriented so that they are congruent with the broad perspectives taken by theologians while preserving their basic autonomy as sciences? Using what we have already discussed on the nature of human freedom and on the scale of values that result from moral conversion, we can begin to formulate a response to this suggestion.

A Reorientation of the Social Sciences through Moral Conversion

Let us begin by asking about the goal of the human sciences.[20] The human sciences attempt to understand human actions within their social and cultural contexts and in terms of their personal, social, and cultural effects. Human society and culture are the cumulative outcomes of human decisions and indecisions, insights and oversights, judgments and misjudgments, spanning millennia of human activity. Each generation's achievements and failures contextualize the attempts of successive generations to discover the meaning and purpose of life and coordinate human action accordingly. If we operate within the horizon of moral conversion, human decisions are intelligible inasmuch as they are oriented toward realizing and motivated by values, and respectful of the integrity of the hierarchical and normative scale of values. Where human decisions fail to respond to genuine value, they fall short of the meaning of responsible human existence. This falling short of full human flourishing occurs within our personal lives as moral failure, within our cultures as distorting ideologies, and within our societies as an unjust maldistribution of basic goods and of political and economic power. As Alasdair MacIntyre concisely argues: "Unintelligible actions are failed candidates for the status of

20. For a fuller account of the reorientation of the social sciences through moral conversion, see Ormerod, *Re-Visioning the Church*, chs. 2–3.

intelligible action; and to lump unintelligible actions and intelligible actions together in a single class of actions and then characterize actions in terms of what items of both sets have in common is to make the mistake of ignoring this."[21]

If the human sciences are seeking to understand our human world, then they need to recognize the basic distinction between "intelligible" and "unintelligible" actions (that is, in terms of the scale of values). We simply cannot understand unintelligible actions, for they cannot be "understood." Such a distinction can only properly arise from the perspective of moral conversion, which recognizes that some actions succeed while others fail to be properly moral. If we accept such a conclusion then the fact-value distinction that operates within many contemporary conceptions of the social sciences is simply not valid.

Social sciences that seek to model themselves strictly on the so-called "hard sciences" of physics and chemistry inevitably fail to fully understand human actions, societies, and cultures. In the natural sciences, there exists a prior assumption that the physical order is intrinsically intelligible, that it will inevitably succumb to the human drive for understanding.[22] However, when we consider the human world, this is simply not the case. As social theorist Roy Bhaskar notes, "the *phenomena* themselves may be false."[23] For example, beliefs held by social agents, for example, in the inherent superiority of one race over another, or of maleness over femaleness, are false, though they still may be embedded in social institutions and cultural ideologies. Such falsehood cannot be properly understood, except as

---

21. Alasdair MacIntyre, *After Virtue: A Study in Moral Theory*, 2nd ed. (Notre Dame, IN: University of Notre Dame, 1984), 209.
22. We shall consider the implications of this further when we look at the question on intellectual conversion in the next chapter.
23. Roy Bhaskar, "Societies," in *Critical Realism: Essential Readings*, ed. Margaret Archer, et al. (London: Routledge, 1998), 206–57 (231).

a personal, cultural, and social failure to live intelligently, reasonably, and responsibly. In terms of moral conversion, this means that the social sciences cannot be properly scientific, that is, have a goal of understanding correctly, unless they take into account the problem of moral failure and evil. In this sense, the problem of moral failure and evil is a "natural" problem, one that arises within the horizon of our natural orientation to meaning, truth, and value; however, its solution may lie beyond our natural resources to solve, because the problem itself distorts that very orientation.

Of course, many social scientists would not readily accept such a conclusion. Still, we argue that theology and the social sciences can and should learn from each other. While theologians can work with the outcomes of the social sciences, they need to recognize that the pronouncements of the social sciences do not have the same standing as the outcomes of the natural sciences. Theologians can also challenge the social sciences to be truly scientific, by recognizing the intrinsically moral orientation of those disciplines. In this way, one can begin the slow cultural task of reorienting the human sciences toward their proper goal.

A Question of Categories

Our discussion of social sciences and theology relates to our explanation of theological language and the derivation of categories in chapter 1. In this chapter, we have introduced a variety of categories: values and satisfactions; a hierarchical and normative scale of values as vital, social, cultural, personal and religious; a social dialectic (spontaneous intersubjectivity and practical intelligence); cultural types (cosmological, anthropological, and soteriological); virtues and vices; and so on. Most of these categories are relevant within a nontheological field of discourse. They are what we call "general categories," not specific to theology and most often arising from other disciplines.[24] However, just as Thomas Aquinas could spend enormous effort in discussing questions of "natural" virtues and vices within a theological context, drawing on the work of the pagan philosopher Aristotle, so too today theologians can and should draw upon the range of categories made available to them through the human sciences and other disciplines—not uncritically, but as essential tools in understanding the human context within which God is operating. To restrict ourselves to supposedly strictly "theological" terms, on the basis that they are "biblical" or more "traditional" is to limit the resources we can bring to bear in understanding God and all things in relation to God. Though religious conversion adds something new and unexpected into human living, as the scholastic axiom says, grace does not destroy nature but completes and perfects it. This relationship between our native orientation to meaning, truth, and goodness, which is the source of all general categories, and the divine gift of grace is important to recognize, for the native orientation provides a normative frame of reference against which to measure our growth in personal, cultural, and social flourishing, through our fidelity to the normative exigencies of that orientation. If theologians neglect or deny this relationship, they almost invariably end up advancing some form of fideism, the opposition of faith and reason.

Our approach opposes the idea that theology should exclude the use of the human sciences. Though different forms of social science may fail to recognize the specifically moral dimension of their studies, the disciplines in principle are important contributors to theological inquiry. By contrast, for example, John Milbank and the movement known as Radical Orthodoxy[25] express a number of more serious

---

24. Lonergan, *Method*, 285–88.
25. John Milbank, *Theology and Social Theory*. This same rejection of general categories is evident in the approach of Hans Urs von Balthasar, or at least in the approach of his followers, and notably in the work of Protestant theologian Karl Barth.

concerns with the social sciences *as they are currently constituted*. Far from seeking to reorient the human sciences through moral conversion, Milbank rejects them root and branch, arguing that ecclesiology is the only true form of the human sciences, because the Christian community is the only true form of human society.[26] His position rejects the idea that social science can contribute genuine insight into human flourishing. However, as we explained in chapter 1, theology has always drawn from sources beyond itself, particularly philosophical sources, and it need not do otherwise in relation to the human sciences.

A Theological Example

To clarify some of the theological significance of this issue we shall turn our attention to liberation theology, a theological movement that arose in the latter half of the twentieth century in Latin America, within a context of extreme poverty and political oppression. A central thrust of liberation theology was to theologize within this context, making their historical situation a theological source for reflection. As Gustavo Gutiérrez, the grandfather of liberation theology, notes: "The theology of liberation attempts to reflect on the experience and meaning of the faith based on the commitment to abolish injustice and to build a new society; this theology must be verified by the practice of that commitment, by active, effective participation in the struggle which the exploited classes have undertaken against their oppressors."[27] However, the question then

---

26. Ibid., 380: "The theory [that is, the Christian theory of society], therefore, is first and foremost an *ecclesiology*, and only an account of other human societies to the extent that the Church defines itself, in its practice, as in continuity and discontinuity with these societies. As the Church is *already*, necessarily, by virtue of its institution, a 'reading' of other human societies, it becomes possible to consider ecclesiology as also a 'sociology.'" For a fuller critique of Milbank in this regard see Ormerod, *Re-Visioning the Church*, 55–58.
27. Gutiérrez, *A Theology of Liberation*, 307.

arises as to how one might "read" one's social and economic context. What tools, what language, must one adopt in order to understand one's present context in order to undertake a truly contextual theology? Are religious categories and theological language sufficient or is something more needed?

In order to apply a suitable social analysis, liberation theology turned to Marxism as a "scientific" account of society, particularly in its context of conflict and oppression.[28] Indeed, we can hear echoes of Marx in the quote above from Gutiérrez with its invocation of "struggle," "exploited classes," and "oppressors." Working on the paradigm of "see, judge, act," Marxism provided liberation theologians with a lens through which to "see" their social reality, whereas the "judge" and "act" aspects would be undertaken in light of the Gospel. Theological activity would thus subsume the outcomes of a social scientific analysis into itself in order to become a contextual theology adequate to the concrete, political, and economic situation.

This brief account presents us with a good example of the issues we discussed above in regard to the relationship between theology and the social sciences and the types of categories used within theology. Liberation theologians knew the variety of approaches within the social sciences, for example: those more oriented to maintaining social harmony (generally referred to as functionalist) and those more focused on class conflict (generally referred to as conflictualist, of which Marxism is a prime example). They did not seek to reorient these two approaches into a more comprehensive social theory, but rather adopted the approach most suited to their circumstances, namely: the Marxist. The danger was that whatever the shortcomings of Marxist theory, simply because it is not a complete social account,

---

28. See the basic introduction Boff and Boff, *Introducing Liberation Theology* (Maryknoll NY: Orbis Books, 1987). For a more detailed account of the relationship between theology and the social sciences, see Clodovis Boff, *Theology and Praxis: Epistemological Foundations* (Maryknoll, NY: Orbis Books, 1987).

these shortcomings would then be incorporated into their reading of the social situation, and thus distort their theological outcomes.

One of these shortcomings is precisely the way in which Marxism, claiming to be a "scientific" account of social reality, suggests the adoption of the fact-value distinction. Indeed, this is often how liberation theology stated the matter, where Marxism would provide a reading of the social reality that would then be judged in terms of Gospel values. On the other hand, it could be argued, and in fact was argued by the Congregation for the Doctrine of the Faith, that Marxism already incorporates a significant value framework (or ideology), one antithetical to faith because of its inherent atheism:

> In the case of Marxism, in the particular sense given to it in this context, a preliminary critique is all the more necessary since the thought of Marx is such a global vision of reality that all data received form [sic] observation and analysis are brought together in a philosophical and ideological structure, which predetermines the significance and importance to be attached to them. The ideological principles come prior to the study of the social reality and are presupposed in it. Thus no separation of the parts of this epistemologically unique complex is possible. If one tries to take only one part, say, the analysis, one ends up having to accept the entire ideology.[29]

This is the problem liberation theology faced. If the fact-value split is problematic, and with it Marxism's claims to be scientific in a value-free sense, then the implicit values or ideological framework of Marxism will already be influencing the outcomes of its reading of the social reality. Without proper care, one could end up accepting the entire ideology into one's theology. A good example of this issue is a question in relation to the notion of "class struggle" found in Marxism and often present in some form within liberation theology. Is class struggle simply the recognition of existing conflicts that need

---

29. Congregation for the Doctrine of the Faith, "Instruction on Certain Aspects of the Theology of Liberation," 7n6.

to be resolved (a fact), or is it something to be promoted (a value) in order to change society?

On the other hand, if values are indeed inherent to the social scientific project itself, how is this to be done? Which values do we choose? Here the Congregation for the Doctrine of the Faith offers its own proposal: "A critical examination of the analytical methods borrowed from other disciplines must be carried out in a special way by theologians. It is the light of faith which provides theology with its principles. That is why the use of philosophical positions or of human sciences by the theologian has a value which might be called instrumental, but yet must undergo a critical study from a theological perspective. In other words, the ultimate and decisive criterion for truth can only be a criterion which is itself theological."[30] Here we might part company with the Congregation, if by this it suggests that theological criteria are brought in as extrinsic to the social sciences themselves, as a way of trumping all other considerations ("ultimate and decisive criteria"). According to the argument we have developed above, on the basis of moral conversion, what is needed is not theological criteria (strictly speaking, that is, revealed), but the overall scale of values, which provides a heuristic structure for identifying human flourishing. A reoriented social science must incorporate the heuristic structure of the scale of values, with its normative and hierarchical features, if it is to be truly scientific. The dialectic structures within the social and cultural levels of value leave ample room for both functionalist and conflictualist insights to emerge without requiring a choice between them.

On the other hand, the scale of values provides us with an entry point for discussing in an explanatory fashion the most significant contribution of liberation theology, namely, the preferential option for the poor. Within liberation theology itself this principle is derived

---

30. Ibid., 7n10.

from reading the social situation in light of the Gospel tradition.[31] However, it can also arise directly from our reading of the social reality through the incorporation of the scale of values into that reading. The existence of widespread poverty is indicative of a breakdown of the social order, the purpose of which is to provide a just, equitable, and sustainable distribution of vital values to the whole community—and increasingly so, on a global scale. The long term solution to this distortion of the social order lies not just in a realignment of forces within that order, but through the supervention of a cultural order that promotes social justice, solidarity, compassion, and so on. Without such a cultural shift, we change the social order at the risk of simply replacing one set of group biases with another. Of course, the cultural shift is itself the outcome of creative cultural change agents, whose moral conversion makes them incarnate sources of genuine value for the whole community. Such moral conversion is unsustainable in the long run without the help of divine grace, healing us of distortions and supporting us through hardship. Within the framework of the scale of values, the preferential option for the poor expresses the realization that the existence of large-scale poverty indicates a breakdown in human flourishing not only at the social level, but also at the cultural and personal levels. It is indicative of the power of sin operative in human history. Seen through this lens, the breakdown in the distribution of vital values is a barometer of social and cultural malaise.

Moral Conversion and the Problem of Evil

Our consideration in this chapter of human freedom and the

---

31. Since its promotion by liberation theology, the preferential option for the poor has been adopted as a principle within Catholic social teaching. See Rohan Michael Curnow, *The Preferential Option for the Poor: A Short History and A Reading Based on the Thought of Bernard Lonergan*, Marquette Studies in Theology (Milwaukee: Marquette University Press, 2012). The option for the poor is particularly prominent in the teaching and preaching of Pope Francis.

hierarchical and normative scale of values led us to note the significance of the problem of evil for theology. As a moral problem, the problem of evil arises when we make our decisions on the basis of mere satisfactions rather than genuine values. In the next chapter, we return to the problem of evil, not in moral terms, but in intellectual and ontological terms, through the lens of intellectual conversion. This added perspective greatly helps in avoiding any form of dualism that makes evil part of the ontological constitution of reality.

However, at this stage, we note the existential tension between the experience of religious conversion, of God's love flooding our hearts, and the experience of moral evil. There is a deep chasm between these two experiences, a chasm of light and darkness, of life and death. For some, the experience of evil can be so profound that they find nothing of value remains in human existence. Human existence is viewed as inherently perverted by the presence of sin, incapable of genuine transformation.[32] The alternative position, which we have foreshadowed above, is to suggest that our experience of religious conversion has as one of its objectives, precisely to bring about a genuine transformation of the human heart, to pluck out the heart of stone and replace it with a heart of flesh (Ezek. 36:26). In traditional terms, grace is both elevating and healing. In that case, while the problem of evil is, as we noted above, a "natural" problem, its solution is supernatural, something more than can be achieved through human effort alone.

The primary element of the experience of religious conversion is one of being loved, of an otherworldly source of love which affirms us as lovable. As such, it provides a stronger counter-voice to the self-accusations that trap us in patterns of self-harm and self-hatred and that drive our addictive and compulsively self-destructive actions:

32. Such a theological pessimism can be found in some of Augustine's work, but is amplified in the writings of some of the reformers during the Reformation.

"And by this we will know that we are from the truth and will reassure our hearts before him whenever our hearts condemn us; for God is greater than our hearts, and he knows everything. Beloved, if our hearts do not condemn us, we have boldness before God" (1 John 3:19–21). This experience of God's love is both gift and invitation. It is gift inasmuch as it is not something we can generate or force; it is something freely given by God in the wisdom of divine providence. Nonetheless, it is also an invitation to make that love our own through the return of love, to love God with all our mind and heart and strength, and to love our neighbor as ourselves (see Mark 12:30-31). And who is my neighbor, so much as those denied access to the most necessary of vital values—the hungry, the sick, the homeless—because of the disruption of human sinfulness in history (Luke 10:25-37; 16:19-31)? Scholastic theology speaks of these two aspects of religious experience as sanctifying grace and the virtue of charity.

The experience of being loved can produce two further elements that play a role in overcoming the problem of evil. Just as the gift of love heals our weakened willingness to do what is good, and empowers us to achieve the good, so too prevalent ideologies can distort and truncate our understanding of our present context and the possibilities within it. And so we need a source of wisdom to break the shackles of our minds and open us up to the whole truth of human existence. This wisdom, which is not solely of human origin, we can call faith. Faith is then an apprehension of transcendent value manifest in religious conversion, and it conforms or harmonizes us to historical communities that bear witness to transcendent truth.[33] Finally, in a world where sin and violence are normal rather than exceptional, we must overcome the aversion to suffering attendant

---

33. Lonergan defines faith as "knowledge born of religious love" (see Lonergan, *Method*, 115).

upon the challenge to choose the good in the face of human evil.[34]
The gift of God's love can then ground a hope that goes beyond
all human hope, a hope against hope (Rom. 4:18). As St. Paul puts
it: "Therefore, since we are justified by faith, we have peace with
God through our Lord Jesus Christ, through whom we have obtained
access to this grace in which we stand; and we boast in our hope
of sharing the glory of God. And not only that, but we also boast
in our sufferings, knowing that suffering produces endurance, and
endurance produces character, and character produces hope, and
hope does not disappoint us, because God's love has been poured into
our hearts through the Holy Spirit that has been given to us" (Rom.
5:1–5). These theological virtues, faith, hope, and love, which emerge
out of the experience of religious conversion, provide the framework
for a religious solution to the problem of evil, one which provides a
religious scaffolding to reinforce a moral conversion which turns our
willingness from mere satisfactions to genuine human values. We fill
out these observations more in chapter 8.

Conclusion

So far we have explored the ways in which religious and moral
conversions provide foundations for theology. They clarify for the
theologian the meaning of terms such as "religious experience,"
"God," and "value." We derived categories that can provide an
enriched account of human existence as religious, moral, cultural,
social, and vital. These are powerfully suggestive categories that
illuminate a number of existing theological debates, on questions
such as grace-nature and the role of the social sciences in theology.
And we did not need to rely on a far more traditional set of
metaphysical categories that arise from the study of being. While

---

34. On the significance of hope in overcoming adversity, see Dominic Doyle, *The Promise of
Christian Humanism: Thomas Aquinas on Hope* (New York: Herder & Herder, 2011).

some have proposed metaphysics as foundational for theology, for example, the claims of the encyclical *Fides et ratio*, our concern would be that without a proper grounding in intellectual conversion, the terms and relations used in metaphysics are not subject to a proper control of meaning. Just as religious and moral conversions reorient us to the intentional goals of holiness and genuine value, intellectual conversion is required for a proper reorientation to the intentional goals of being, truth, and the real. From this perspective it is then not metaphysics that is foundational, but the needed intellectual conversion in order to critically control our metaphysical terms. To this we now turn.

4

Intellectual Conversion and Meaning, Truth, and Reality

In the second century CE, Tertullian asked the question, "What indeed has Athens to do with Jerusalem?"[1] It is a question that has continued to echo through the learned books and journals, the lecture halls and classrooms of theological institutions in the ensuing centuries. What is the relationship, if any, between philosophical reason, captured by the symbol of Athens, the home of Greek philosophy, and Christian faith, captured in the symbol of Jerusalem? Whatever one might think of the question and its theoretical answers, historically there has been a strong tendency for philosophical questions and issues to arise within the context of seeking to understand the nature and content of Christian faith. In the early debates on belief in the Trinity, Christian thinkers asked questions about the relationship between the Father and the Son, and in their response borrowed the metaphysical concept of "substance" to argue that the Father and the Son are the same "substance" or consubstantial/*homoousios*. But how are we to understand the

---

1. Tertullian, *On Prescription Against Heretics*, 7 (246).

meaning of the term "substance" in this context? To grapple with that, we are inevitably drawn into philosophical debates.

It is easy to multiply examples of this kind of interaction. For example, Catholic theology speaks of the "real" presence of Jesus in the Eucharist that arises from a change of substance, or "transubstantiation." But what do we mean by the terms "real" and "substance"? Or we can ask, "Does God exist?" But what exactly do we mean by "exist" here? If we think of existence as implying occurrence within space and time, then the answer for many will be: no, God does not "exist" in that sense, but this need not lead to the conclusion that God does not exist at all. Just as our previous two chapters examined how at a foundational level the performance of theology has the need for basic religious and moral orientations or conversions, so this chapter takes up the need for a basic intellectual orientation. In particular, intellectual conversion involves a shift in our criteria for reality from the already-out-there-now real of extroverted consciousness to the basic orientations of rational consciousness. That is, with intellectual conversion, we explicitly identify our criteria for knowledge of reality with our performance of knowing "the real," not by taking a look, but by satisfying our questions for intelligibility (e.g., what is it?) and reflection (is it so?). Intellectual conversion thus reorients our prephilosophical commitments concerning questions of reality, truth, being, existence, knowing, and objectivity, in order that they more clearly and explicitly cohere with one another.

Of course, there are those, such as Tertullian perhaps, who reject the idea that philosophy and theology are inextricably linked. They might refer to St. Paul, for example, insisting on a juxtaposition: where "Greeks search for wisdom" Christians "preach Christ crucified" (1 Cor. 1:21-23). Such a tendency is evident in the work of Karl Barth, who famously urged that "faith takes reason by the throat and strangles the beast."[2] Undeniably, Christian theologians should "cling to Jesus Christ," crucified and risen, but unless they also address philosophical questions of reality, truth, and existence, they invariably operate from implicit and often naïve and unexamined notions of these terms. Addressing these kinds of questions allows us to avoid confusions and resolve difficulties that would otherwise arise. And so we must include the question of intellectual conversion within the foundations of theology.

The Example of St. Augustine

A good place to start in our consideration of intellectual conversion is the experience of St. Augustine narrated in Book 7 of his *Confessions*. Augustine begins Book 7 by drawing attention to his major intellectual difficulty in coming to faith: "I was unable to grasp the idea of substance except as something we can see with our bodily eyes."[3] This severely limited his ability to conceive of God as other than a body: "I was still forced to imagine something corporeal spread out in space, whether infused into the world or even diffused through the infinity outside it . . . *because anything to which I denied these spatial dimensions seemed to me to be nothing at all.*"[4] Augustine reinforces this point in another passage: "Hence I thought that even you, Life of my life, were a vast reality spread throughout space in every direction: I thought that you penetrated the whole mass of the earth and the immense, unbounded spaces beyond it on all sides, that earth, sky,

---

2. Karl Barth, *The Epistle to the Romans*, trans. Edwyn Clement Hoskyns (London: Oxford University Press, 1933), 143. Barth here echoes Martin Luther, "Whoever wants to be a Christian should tear the eyes out of his reason." This quote is frequently cited on various web sites as coming from Luther (such as http://jmm.aaa.net.au/articles/14223.htm, accessed 4 August 2006) but we have not yet found the original source. One secondary source is Walter Kaufmann, *The Faith of a Heretic* (Garden City, NY: Doubleday, 1963), 75, which does not give the original in Luther.

3. Augustine, *The Confessions*, 7.1.1 (158).

4. Ibid., 7.1.1 (159). Emphasis added.

and all things were full of you, and that they found their limits in you, while you yourself had no limit anywhere."[5]

Augustine realizes that formulating an intellectually credible account of God's existence matters to belief and worship. A God who is just another object "out there" spread out in space hardly seemed worthy of his worship, but he lacked an adequate understanding of God's reality. He needed to reorient his idea of what constitutes existence and reality in order to conceive of God's existence in a way that allowed for him to respond more fully to God's presence in his life.

Book 7 of *The Confessions* narrates that transition. Augustine begins with the story of a conversation with his friend Nebridius, concerning the Manichaean belief in a cosmic conflict between powers of light (God) and darkness. Nebridius raises the question, "What would they have done to you [God] if you had refused to fight?"[6]. In raising this question, he intends to show that no possible answer makes any sense; they are all equally unreasonable. However, from the point of view of the unfolding argument within the narrative, what Augustine presents is an alternative criterion for reality relative to the naïve position he previously held. Nebridius provides a reasoned argument against the Manichaeans:

> Those so-called powers of darkness, whom they [that is, the Manichaeans] always postulate as a horde deployed in opposition to you [that is, God]: [W]hat would they have done to you if you had refused to fight? If the reply is that they could have inflicted some injury on you, it would imply that you are subject to violation and therefore destructible. If on the other hand, it is denied they had power to injure you, there would have been no point in fighting . . . it follows that if they admitted that, whatever you are, you are incorruptible . . . this whole rigmarole would be shown up as untrue and rejected with loathing; but if they

5. Ibid., 7.1.2 (159).
6. Ibid., 7.2.3 (160).

alleged that you are corruptible, their position would already be false and no sooner stated than condemned.[7]

He argues that their position is rationally incoherent and thus concludes that the realities they posit are nothing but fables and myths. Rather than the criterion of fundamentally exterior consciousness leading the way, the argument of Nebridius turns our attention to an apprehension of reality based on reason. Later on in Book 7, this transition will be realized in Augustine through his reading of "certain Platonists," who mediate for him a shift from materiality as a criterion of reality to a more "spiritual" understanding of reality.[8] Rather than taking materiality as the paradigm for what is real, Platonic doctrine views materiality as more ephemeral, more insubstantial, than the spiritual reality of form perceived intellectually. Through his reading of the Platonists the shift foreshadowed in his juxtaposition of his fixation on corporeality with the reasoned argument of Nebridius begins to take possession of his own thinking.

And so Augustine still talks about light, but now an "incommutable light . . . not this common [visible] light at all, but something different, utterly different . . . Anyone who knows truth knows it, and whoever knows it knows eternity. . . . Love knows it."[9] God is then referred to as "eternal Truth" whose reality cannot be doubted: "Is truth then a nothing, simply because it is not spread out through space, either finite or infinite?" The reality of truth is now as real to Augustine as his own existence: "[N]o possibility of doubt remained in me; I could more easily have doubted that I was alive than that truth exists, truth that is seen *and* understood through things that

---

7. Ibid., (160-61).
8. There is much dispute over the exact identity of these Platonists and the extent of Augustine's knowledge of them. See Brian Dobell, *Augustine's Intellectual Conversion: The Journey from Platonism to Christianity* (Cambridge: Cambridge University Press, 2009) for some of the details.
9. Augustine, *The Confessions*, 7.10.16 (172–73).

are made."[10] Much here depends on how one reads the conjunction "and." Is Augustine positing here two truths, one seen, the other understood? Or is there one truth that is "seen and understood" through created reality? Clearly, Augustine takes his readers in the direction of the latter rather than the former. Indeed, in a complete inversion of our normal orientation to the "already-out-there-now" real, God is what is most real, while created material realities "do not in the fullest sense exist . . . they are real because they are from you, but unreal inasmuch as they are not what you are."[11]

Augustine has made a transition from a conception of reality as "out there" to a conception of reality as the term of a sound and reasonable argument. This presents him with a very different set of criteria for determining reality from his initial more naïve criteria. While the role of the senses is not to be completely neglected, still it is reason that has the upper hand. This is a liberating shift, because it not only allows Augustine to acknowledge the existence of God as not confined within space and time, but also the reality of his own inner world, the world of thought and feeling, or what we would call consciousness. The reality of this inner world becomes very important in his Trinitarian speculations, a point we shall return to in chapter 8.

A Modern Example

Augustine had to deal with and resolve a problem that many of us face, if not all of us; indeed, one could say it is part of the human condition. The human person has a biologically oriented drive to imagine the real as "out there," the object of our sensory input, seeking out food, shelter, mates, and predators. It is a realm of stimulus-response, of flight or fight. All such responses operate

10. Ibid., 7.10.16 (173).
11. Ibid., 7.11.17 (174).

without needing the activity of reasoning, which would only slow down the process of response. Indeed, once reasoning intervenes, questions arise: What, where, when, how, why, is it so? These questions supervene upon our biological drives to place us in a world of intelligence, reason, and value, of insight, judgment, and decision. Unless we are careful we can easily get confused between these two sets of criteria, one dominated by biologically-oriented extroversion, which sense and imagination structure, the other dominated by the desire for knowledge and structured by intelligent understanding and reasonable judgment.

A good modern example of this confusion often arises in scientific discussions about whether the universe can emerge "from nothing." Here we can refer to the work of Lawrence Krauss, *A Universe from Nothing*, in which he claims that science is well on the way to explaining how the universe emerges from "nothing," thus eliminating any need for positing God in the account of the universe's beginning.[12] As Krauss notes, much hangs on what we mean by "nothing." His regular barbs at philosophers and theologians refer to their alleged imprecision with regard to the meaning of "nothing." He, on the other hand, has a perfectly clear understanding of what he means by nothing. As he often repeats, mantra-like, throughout his book, nothing means "empty space." Indeed, "'nothing' is every bit as physical as 'something,' especially if it is to be defined as the 'absence of something.'"[13] The failure of philosophers and theologians to realize this fact indicates the "intellectual bankruptcy" of "much of modern theology and some modern philosophy."[14] He explains, "By *nothing* I do not mean nothing, but

---

12. Lawrence Krauss, *A Universe from Nothing: Why there is Something rather than Nothing* (New York: Free Press, 2012).
13. Ibid., xiv.
14. Ibid.

rather *nothing*—in this case, the nothingness we normally call empty space."[15]

As with Augustine, prior to his intellectual conversion, Krauss believes that for something to be real it must occur in space and time. He makes this supposition throughout his book: real things are things "in" space and time, subatomic particles, virtual particles, fields such as electromagnetic and gravitational fields, and so on. On the other hand, one may ask about the reality of space itself. Is space "real," and does it constitute "something" rather than "nothing"? If space is "something," then Krauss's argument that something comes from nothing ("empty space") is plainly erroneous. Indeed, even he admits "I assume space exists," so it is clearly not nothing.[16]

Much of Krauss's energy is expended telling us that "nothing [that is, empty space] is not nothing" at all,[17] but a seething undercurrent of virtual particles that can "pop" into real existence through their interaction with powerful fields, something Stephen Hawking proved in relation to the gravitational field around black holes in the 1970s.[18] Scientifically, this may well be correct, but it clearly does not address the question of whether something can come from nothing. Rather, it tells us how some things can come from something else, that is, from empty space, which is not really empty at all.

Krauss's conception of "nothing" exhibits a basic confusion. Nothing is not defined as the absence of existence or being, but as the emptiness of space and time. And at the same time, space "exists." The ontological status of space is confused for Krauss. On the one hand, existence (being "something") occurs within space; on the other, space exists. Because space is actually never empty, even "nothing is something." Krauss is captured in the same basic horizon that held the

15. Ibid., 59. Italics in the original.
16. Ibid., 150.
17. As the title of chapter 9 states, "nothing is something." Ibid., 142.
18. Ibid., 156.

young Augustine. To be real is to be "out there" in space and time. This naïve conception of reality however is married to a very keen scientific appreciation of the role of intelligence and reason, manifest in the sciences through the processes of hypothesis formation and empirical verification.[19] To make the shift that Augustine made, Krauss could reorient his conception of reality to align with science's commitment to intelligence and reason. Reality would then be that which is known through the proper use of intelligence and reason. This is the beginning of intellectual conversion.

Krauss is not alone in this regard. The confusion he expresses is common, indeed it is one we tenaciously cling to and can be found even in major philosophers. Augustine struggled with it. Even when we begin to suspect the inadequacy of this confused criteria for reality, we still tend to revert in practice to the position that the real is somehow "already out there now" waiting for us to open our eyes and see it. Intellectual conversion involves a rejection of this persistent myth that the real is out there and knowing is taking a look, and the adoption of new criteria for reality, being and truth, as the intentional goals of our understanding and reason. So startling is this shift, that if you do not think it startling, you have not actually shifted.

Objectivity, Knowing, and Reality

The outcome of intellectual conversion is to appropriate the alignment of the structures of our knowing with the structures of reality. Reality proportionate to our knowing will be known through experiencing, understanding, and judging. It may be that there are realities for which we have no direct experience—that is, realities that are not proportionate to our knowing (such as God)—but that we

---

19. For more details on this see Neil Ormerod, "Bernard Lonergan and the Recovery of a Metaphysical Frame," *Theological Studies* 74, no. 4 (2013): 960–82.

can yet know through their effects. This alignment of the cognitional operations of the subject and the structure of reality, however, causes concern for some who see it as making reality "subjective," thus denying proper "objectivity" to human knowing. Their concern is often associated with their (correct) aversion to idealism, which, they say (incorrectly), inevitably follows if our account of reality begins with the subject rather than the object.

On the other hand, if reality is out there now to be seen, then objectivity consists of taking a good look, seeing what is there to be seen and not seeing what is not there to be seen. But does this truly account for our experience? When we look for someone to be "objective," that is, for them to say what is really, truly the case, "objectively speaking," do we ask someone with a good pair of eyes, or do we ask a person of experience and wisdom, someone who can provide a balanced, reasonable judgment? Do we appoint people to preside in law courts who have no knowledge of the law, or do we reserve it for people who have excelled in their studies of the law, and have worked in a legal setting for some time and know the ins and outs of its processes? When we want an authoritative opinion on scientific matters, do we turn to personal blogs or ask properly trained and qualified persons who have worked and published in the field? When we start to ask such questions we begin to think of "objectivity" more as a skill or set of skills in a particular area of human knowledge. Some people are more objective than others. Objectivity and subjectivity are not opposed categories. The real question is then: "Which skills and dispositions does this subject need to acquire in order to become objective?" Though different areas of expertise require different skills, all domains of human knowledge require fidelity to the inherent drive for meaning and truth. Or as Lonergan states it: "Genuine objectivity is the fruit of authentic subjectivity."[20]

To capture something of the startling nature of the shift that occurs with intellectual conversion we can consider its dynamics in relation to the ancient Zen koan, "First there is a mountain, then there is no mountain, then there is a mountain again." Let us take each section in turn.

First there is a mountain. On the naïve view, we know the mountain by looking. We open our eyes and it's there. What more is there to say? Our sense of reality is determined by animal extroversion, by the operations of our senses. This "reality" has an indubitable, solid quality to it until philosophical questions about the reliability of sense data unsettle it.

Then there is no mountain. When one shifts to this new criterion for reality, the "reality" of the already-out-there-now real of animal extroversion suddenly seems less real, less solid. Idealism becomes an intellectual possibility. Like Plato, we might begin to distinguish between the appearance and the reality or with Kant between the phenomena and the noumena. In Plato's myth of the cave, the world of the senses is just a shadowy reflection of the real world of ideas. The mountain known by looking is no longer "really real," but just a shadow. In fact, idealist philosophers tend to get stuck at the "there is no mountain" phase, because they neglect the role of judgment in the process of knowing. Still, the act of reasonable judgment pushes us further into personal responsibility, not away from it, which can be even more unsettling.

Then there is a mountain again. Through judgment, we return to the "reality" of the mountain, a reality of intelligent grasp and reasonable affirmation. It may be a commonsense judgment, which grasps the meaning of the word "mountain" and makes a reasonable judgment about what one sees towering over the horizon. Or it

20. Lonergan, *Method*, 292.

99

may be the judgment of a geologist who understands the forces that conspire in the formation of mountains and can identify in the prevailing geology the effects of those forces and thus affirm: "This is in fact a mountain." Or it may be the judgment of a surveyor whose rulebook specifies that mountains be of a certain height, and since this formation fits the criterion: it is a mountain.

The importance of the shift is not that it eliminates things from our list of what is real. Mountains are still mountains. But it changes the criteria by which we recognize the reality. And in doing so it opens up the possibility of other things being real that are not present to our already-out-there-now animal extroversion.

A Fuller Sense of Reality

Once we make this shift we open ourselves to a much fuller sense of reality. For example, we may be able to affirm the reality of God, not on the basis of finding God "out there," but through reasoned argument. We shall return to this question in chapter 6, but the success of such a venture is predicated on this type of intellectual reorientation. In this way, intellectual conversion consolidates the religious conversion discussed in chapter 2. It allows us to affirm the existence and reality of God in a nonmythic way, not as some old man in the sky or a fairy at the bottom of the garden. Similarly, our appeal to the criteria of intelligence and reason allows us to affirm the reality of values that arose in our discussion of moral conversion. Values are not "out there" to be inspected by our senses, but they can be known through reasonable and responsible examination of human behavior and events. In this way, intellectual conversion consolidates the moral conversion previously discussed in chapter 3. Values are "real," they have an intelligible structure, a hierarchical and normative scale, and this provides the basis of an objective morality.

More fully, this shift allows us to affirm the full reality of our human world of meanings and values, realities such as: interest rates, mortgages, contracts, vows, national constitutions, penal codes, and so on. Where do interest rates "exist"? Not in banks or financial institutions. Are they real when we cannot touch them or see them? We all spend so much time worrying about them—are we worrying about nothing? Similarly, a contract is not just the piece of paper, but the meaning the paper embodies—as is a national constitution or a penal code. Once we break the stranglehold of our animal extroversion on our thinking, we can affirm the reality of our whole world of human meanings and values, of institutions, nations, finance, and law, of human relationships, and so on.

One important area that opens up for us, as Augustine also found, is the realm of consciousness itself. According to the sense of reality for animal extroversion, consciousness is a profound mystery. It cannot be touched or tasted, seen or heard, so its reality is truly suspect. It is not "out there" to be inspected and analyzed so at most it can be assigned the status of epiphenomenon, a secondary phenomenon reflecting some other underlying "really real" reality that can be measured and quantified, in this case, brain states.[21] And so our inner life of thought and feeling, of hopes and desires, are reduced to mere shadows of our brain biochemistry. We can avoid such a stance by intelligently grasping and reasonably affirming the existence of consciousness. We can easily grasp that there is a difference between being in a coma, or under anesthetic, or in a dreamless sleep, and dreaming, being awake and alert, understanding something, making a judgment or coming to a decision. In the former states (coma, etc.), "I" am not present, I feel and think nothing. In the latter states and to various degrees, I am the subject of those experiences. I am

---

21. On the question of consciousness as epiphenomenal see J. P. Moreland, "The argument from consciousness," in *The Blackwell Companion to Natural Theology*, ed. William Lane Craig and J. P. Moreland (Oxford: Blackwell, 2009), 282–343.

present as the subject of dreaming, alertness, understanding, judging or deciding. Understanding this difference and affirming its reality is what is meant by knowing the meaning of being "conscious." This stance also allows us to avoid the mistake of thinking we can inspect consciousness through some "inner look," which is impossible because we cannot "look at the looker."[22] Knowing consciousness is not a matter of looking at it, but attending to the difference between being in a coma or dreamless sleep, and being awake and alert, understanding and not understanding, of balancing evidence and coming to a judgment, and so on. In becoming more familiar with these conscious operations, we come to know ourselves more fully, as religious, moral, and intellectual subjects.

Meaning, History, and Community

Being comfortable with asserting the reality of the human world of meanings and values is essential if theology is to deal with the realities of history and community. Basic theological realities such as sin and grace, however we might understand these terms, have their effects not just on individuals, but on communities and on larger scale movements within history, for example in wars or major economic collapses. On the other hand, religious communities are produced by, and formative for, religious conversion (or its absence) over historical timeframes, whereby people reorient their lives toward ultimate meaning, truth, and value, indeed toward true holiness. Religious traditions contain responses to ultimate questions about the meaning of human living, and some may be conceived in terms of our human response to the entry of divine meaning and value into

---

22. With great subtlety Augustine refutes this type of argument in Book 10 of *De Trinitate*. As he notes, "and it is not to be supposed that in the contemplation of non-bodily things a similar device can be provided, so that the mind can know itself, as in a mirror" See Augustine, *The Trinity*, ed. John E. Rotelle, OSA, trans. Edmund Hill (Brooklyn: New City Press, 1991), 290 (10.5).

history.[23] Whether we want to talk about Scripture or sacrament, church or salvation, we cannot avoid the question of meaning: Scripture communicates God's meaning and truth to human beings; a sacrament expresses in meaningful symbols the reality of divine grace; the church is a community held together by common meanings and values, expressed in Scripture and traditional doctrines; salvation entails a radical shift in one's personal horizon, that is, in the core meanings and values that constitute one's life commitments. As part of our theological foundations, we need to think more seriously about meaning, how it is carried in human communities, how it functions in those communities, how its potentialities can shift over historical timeframes, and so on.

How is Meaning Carried?

While many theologians focus on language as a carrier of meaning (Scripture or church documents), in fact there are a variety of other ways in which meaning is carried within human communities. There is the spontaneous intersubjective meaning of a smile or a frown between friends, the intimate gestures of lovers, the fist raised to a foe, and so on. These gestures convey meaning directly and immediately without the need for words or reflection. There is artistic meaning whereby the artist seeks to convey a mood, a disposition, a concern through the medium of artistic expression. Good art evokes a response from us, moves us interiorly, through its beauty. There is symbolic meaning where particular objects take on or convey certain meanings and values, either personally, communally or even archetypally. National (communal) symbols such as a constitution or a flag can move people to action. Archetypal symbols around birth, maturation, or death can assist us in coming to grips with

23. We shall discuss this more in chapter 7 when we consider the question of revelation.

life-changing events, common to all humanity. We can group these three carriers of meaning together because, while distinct, they share a common feature of being elemental, that is, meaning and meant are not clearly distinguished so that their full meaning is difficult to convey; they often have a "surplus" or excess of meaning that is difficult to pin down, even where their transformative impact is evident.

In the religious order, these carriers of meaning are very important. Liturgy is a communal expression of meaning carried intersubjectively, artistically, and symbolically. Liturgy done well creates a new world of meaning into which the participant is invited to enter. It has the ability to transform our consciousness, shift our horizon toward greater openness to the power of religious conversion. Indeed, many of our most important religious experiences operate at this elemental level of meaning, be it liturgical, sacramental or personal encounter. If people were asked to recount experiences of grace they might likely draw on this form of meaning to express in personal testimony how their lives were transformed. Indeed, in chapter 2 we noted the predilection for poetry among mystics.

The strength of these carriers is also to some extent their weakness. Because meaning is not clearly distinguished from what is meant, the communication of meaning can become blurred and confused. These carriers may convey such a surplus of meaning that people draw contradictory meanings from them. On the other hand, sacraments and liturgy can take on a quasi-magical significance, as if the correct performance of the ritual is more important than the intended meaning being conveyed. And so language, either spoken or written, allows us to clarify and explain, to make explicit what is implicit, to exclude what is not intended and reinforce what is intended. Indeed, language is a very important carrier of meaning because it more easily enters into (and helps create) the public sharing of meaning. This is very evident in religious communities that share a common written source or scripture, such as Judaism, Christianity, Islam, Hinduism, and Buddhism. Such a written source can help provide a communal control of religious meaning that is less ambiguous than the meanings of liturgies and other more elemental religious experiences.

Still the types of written expression available to us may differ in their significance and cultural role. Some language operates in a commonsense manner, drawing on a common pool of knowledge, wisdom, and metaphors that convey meaning directly to those who share that common pool. But for someone outside that common pool, while they may easily read such language, they may miss some of the allusions and themes it originally intended. Such language does not operate with a tight control of meaning, and so "a blink is as good as a nod to a blind horse." On the other hand, technical language, as found in mathematics is able to exercise a very precise control of meaning, so that while the meaning may be difficult to grasp, its meaning is perfectly clear to someone trained in the field. As such, it takes on a transcultural aspect, so while every culture has its own common sense, all mathematicians regardless of their culture adopt the same technical language. At a religious level, everyone feels at home reading the Scriptures, but scholars produce endless commentaries to explain to us what they really mean. Far fewer feel at home with the pronouncements of church councils, because of the technical language deployed, but the meaning is often quite clear and precise.

Because theologians normally operate with linguistic carriers of meaning, it is important for them to be familiar with these different modes of expression. It would be as wrongheaded to read commonsense meaning as technical (one of the failings of all forms of fundamentalism), as it would be to read technical meaning as just refined common sense. The Scriptures are expressed within a particular commonsense world of meaning and it would be erroneous to expect a degree of precision in them that they were never meant to attain. Similarly if one reads the *Summa Theologiae* of Thomas Aquinas one becomes aware of entering into a technical form of expression that will require some training in order to be able to properly appreciate all that it implies. Some might question the value of such a technical form of expression. Why not simply stay at a more commonsense form of expression that "everyone" can understand? Indeed technical meaning is not for everyone, just as mathematics and science are not for everyone. But if the goal is to demonstrate the intellectual coherence of Christian faith then the adoption of technical forms of expression is hard to avoid. Indeed, even the early church councils, such as Nicaea and Chalcedon, found it impossible to avoid the use of technical terms, because the opponents of orthodoxy used the imprecision of commonsense Scriptural language to distort the meanings of Christian faith.[24] More than this, we would say that this move to technical meaning is a way of honouring God, who has revealed truths to us that elicit from us a deeper desire to understand.

This distinction is important not only when one is reading theology and theological documents but also when one is writing theology. Is one content to operate within a commonsense world of meaning or does one strive for precision and coherence? In a word, do we aspire to write a theology that is truly scientific or simply popular? The more commonsense approach may gain you more

---

24. Indeed, at the Council of Nicaea, a number of bishops complained about the use of the technical language of "substance" that had been introduced into the debate, preferring the clear and simple language of the Scriptures. In the end, however, they had to concede that unless the technical terms were introduced, they could not refute Arius in his denial of the full divinity of Jesus. See Jaroslav Jan Pelikan, *The Emergence of the Catholic Tradition (100–600)* (Chicago: University of Chicago Press, 1971), 202.

readers and popularity, but it will not make a lasting contribution to theological debates. One the other hand, technical meanings are difficult to attain and can represent a major cultural achievement. They need to be tested and challenged. Not everyone will understand them, but if they are successful they can shape a theological debate over decades and even centuries, as for example the technical language of "person" and "nature" did in Trinitarian and christological debate. To commit to writing in a more technical mode is a substantial intellectual and existential undertaking. Systems of thought do not grow overnight and are rarely the work of a single individual. Collaboration, communication, cooperation are all required to achieve such an undertaking. This is not so much the work of an individual, but of a school of thought, an intellectual movement, that makes a substantial contribution to the discipline of theology in the long run.

As a further way in which meaning can be carried, we can think of the meaning of a human being, the ways in which a life embodies meanings and values, how this life impacts on others around them, on the society and their culture, indeed how it may shape history itself. In this way, a life can incarnate a certain meaning, that while expressed in gestures and symbols and in word, is most fully expressed in a life well lived. We might think of Nelson Mandela and his life of commitment to racial equality in South Africa; Mohandas Gandhi and his commitment to nonviolent resistance to political oppression in India; and of course Jesus of Nazareth whose life embodied for Christians the entry of divine meaning and value into human history. It is now close to two thousand years since his death and the events that surrounded it, and still the meanings and values he embodied in his life lived in service to God and humanity continues to impact on human history. Indeed, the meaning of a life well lived may only become apparent in time, grasped tentatively at first, but unfolding in time as a person's impact becomes more and more evident.

The Realms of Meaning

In the discussion above on linguistic meaning, we spoke about different forms of discourse, some common sense, others more technical. We can speak more generally of different realms of meaning, patterns of expression that address a particular reality in a relatively consistent manner that offer their own standards for controlling the meaning of what is meant by those patterns of expression. We have noted a commonsense realm of meaning that operated out of a common stock of shared meanings within a particular community and that expresses itself through a focus on things in relation to us and our immediate concerns. It does not seek precision but draws up its shared meanings to express itself descriptively, effectively, and immediately. The difficulty is that if one comes from a different social setting and so does not share in that common stock of shared meanings, much of the discourse can remain obscure and the communication of meaning is no longer effective. The realm of theoretical meaning seeks to overcome this specificity by developing more precise meanings that are not simply descriptive but explanatory, meanings that seek to understand things not in relation to us but to identify the relations of things to one another. This level of explanation moves toward a totality, the encompassing of all the objects of the field, not just one by one, but within a single comprehensive account. Such achievements are most evident in mathematics, the different areas of scientific and technical discourse, and at times in theology, as evidenced in the adoption and adaptation of Aristotelian metaphysics into theology in the Scholastic era.

One theological illustration of this shift can be found in the different perspectives presented in relation to the Trinity in the New Testament and in the creed of the Nicene Council. The New Testament is primarily concerned with "God-for-us," that is, how God relates to us in the economy of salvation through the sending of God's Son, and through the outpouring of the Holy Spirit. The Nicene Creed is concerned with the same reality, the triune God, but from a different perspective, of "things in relation to other things" and so when we consider the creedal statement on the Son—"God from God, Light from Light, true God from true God, consubstantial with the Father"—we are dealing with the question not of the Father or Son in their relation to us, but in terms of their relation to one another. Only after this does the perspective shift—"for us and for our salvation he came down from heaven"—to a consideration of the relation of the Son to us. In many ways, this shift to an explanatory realm of meaning was the beginning of theology properly speaking. The major reason for making this shift is to protect the same truth being expressed in the more commonsense language of the Scriptures by providing a potentially transcultural language to express it.[25]

These two realms of meaning can create tensions. In the secular arena, a commonsense perspective can clash with those of science. Special relativity sounds like nonsense to our commonsense expectations, with its predictions of clocks slowing and distance stretching, but its theoretical validity has been tested time and time again. And so science can dismiss common sense as simple ignorance, while common sense can attack science as living in an ivory tower. In religious circles, the move to theoretic meaning (theology) can sound impious or irreverent, while the direct commonsense meanings of religious life can be dismissed as mere piety or even superstition by those who have moved into a theoretic frame. One way to resolve

---

25. See, for example, Neil Ormerod, "The Transcultural Significance of the Council of Chalcedon," *Australasian Catholic Record* LXX (1993): 322–32.

this tension is to seek to ground both commonsense and theoretical perspectives within the conscious operations of the human subject, learning to distinguish those insights that relate things to us from those that relate things to things, to recognize and affirm the validity of both forms of operation and to respect the criteria with which each operates in determining their basic judgments. Such a process moves into an interior realm of meaning, where one grows increasingly familiar with one's own conscious operations and their relationships to one another. Indeed, the whole approach of this current work is predicated on such a growing familiarity via a phenomenological approach to consciousness. Again, there is a theological precedent for this move to interiority. When Augustine sought to find analogies for the Trinity, he did so by exploring the inner operations of the mind and heart. And before he did this he took his readers through a variety of exercises to assist them in becoming more familiar with their own conscious operations (in Book 8 of *De Trinitate*).[26] Similarly, our discussion of religious, moral, and intellectual conversions presumes a growing familiarity with one's own interiority.

There are other realms of meaning we could explore but one that is of significance for theological discourse is the realm of scholarship.[27] With the discovery of historical consciousness and the emergence of critical history a new realm of meaning has emerged within modern culture. This realm of meaning is not concerned with the commonsense meanings of a particular group, or the theoretic and interior explanatory realms, but with the specialized task of transposing meanings from one commonsense realm in the past into a commonsense realm of the present. Such a realm of meaning has

26. See Neil Ormerod, "Augustine's *De Trinitate* and Lonergan's Realms of Meaning," *Theological Studies* 64, no. 4 (2003): 773–94 for an analysis of how Augustine's text draws on different realms of meaning.
27. Lonergan also speaks of a realm of transcendence, but we have already explored this in chapter 2 on religious conversion. See Lonergan, *Method*, 114.

developed its own specialized controls of meaning that are not so much theoretic as practical. We can see this in "quest for the historical Jesus" literature where various criteria for historical authenticity are drawn up.[28] They serve as practical guides for making historical judgments on the commonsense literary material of the Gospels. Much theological discourse, particularly in what we shall call the first phase of theology that brings the meanings and values of the past into the present, is of this scholarly nature. Such scholarly work while vital to theology is quite different from the direct engagement with the theological object found in the more normative phase of theological work.

How Does Meaning Function?

Our final consideration in relation to meaning is to consider the ways in which meaning functions. This can assist us in recognising that not all acts of meaning have the same significance or purpose. This is important in seeking to understand the ways in which statements both past and present operate theologically.

The first and most obvious function of meaning is to convey something that is true. Here, the focus is on *cognitive* meaning. This meaning may be conveyed in various realms (such as common sense, theory, interiority, scholarship), but its intention is to convey what is the case, what is true, what the facts of the matter are. And so the New Testament, the Council of Nicaea, and *De Trinitate*'s explorations of a psychological analogy for the Trinity each seek to express something true about the Trinity within a different realm of meaning—that is, commonsense, theoretical, and interior,

---

28. See, for example, John P. Meier, *A Marginal Jew: Rethinking the Historical Jesus*, 1st ed., 3 vols., vol. 1 (New York: Doubleday, 1991), 165–84, who gives five primary and five secondary criteria for determining the historicity of events and sayings of Jesus. Most authors in the area give similar lists, with slight variations they deem important.

respectively—while a scholarly realm of meaning seeks to express something true about the New Testament, the conciliar documents, and Augustine's *De Trinitate*. Church doctrines are often a very succinct way of expressing a cognitive meaning that affirms something believed as true. However, meaning functions in other ways as well: to exhort, to bind communities together, and so on.

And so we can talk about a *constitutive* function of meaning. This is a meaning that constitutes the identity of a particular group or community. What distinguishes a genuine community from just a group of people is a shared set of meanings and values, common experiences, insight, judgments, and commitments. These may be expressed in story, art, drama, the narration of historical events, in national constitutions and institutions, and so on. A nation is constituted by its legal founding documents, its historical institutions of governance and legal process, and its historical narrative of founding or origin. At times, we may refer to this as its "founding *myth*" because we have come to see that these meanings contain both truth and falsehood.[29] Constitutive meaning does not have to be cognitively true in order to function as constitutive.

This observation is particularly pertinent when it comes to religious meanings and values. There are some theologians who would deny the possibility of cognitive truth in religious matters. Claims to religious truth are then not seen as truth claims, but as identity markers that specify the accepted form of religious speech within a particular religious community. Religious doctrines are viewed as a form of grammar for acceptable speech, for determining the linguistic limits of the identity of the community. This approach to doctrine, for example, can be found in the work of George

29. In Australia, for example, part of the founding myth was that the land was a *terra nullius*, an empty land, ignoring the existence of the native indigenous population and their social and cultural life. Similarly accounts of the founding of nation states in the new lands of the Americas often neglect or overlook the impacts on indigenous peoples.

Lindbeck.[30] Lindbeck refers to this as a cultural-linguistic approach to doctrine. Different religions then have different doctrines, but this need have no more significance than different road rules applying in different countries. Religions are different in the same way that cultures and languages are different. They are basically incommensurable.[31] Of course, most religious believers and ecclesial authorities would not accept such a stance, but it is arrived at through an exclusive focus on constitutive meaning, to the exclusion of the possibility of cognitive meaning in religious matters.

Another way in which meaning functions is to inspire action, to direct our activities, to lead us to commitments. Of course, constitutive meanings often function in this way. A national flag is an important identity marker for a historical community, but raising it in the heat of battle is an effective way of motivating soldiers to engage the enemy. *Effective* meaning motivates, moves us to action, to engagement; it persuades us, commands us, directs us. We might think of the parables of Jesus—for example, the parable of the Good Samaritan and the ways in which it shapes our actions (or should shape our actions) when we encounter the poor and suffering. Similarly, Jesus' Sermon on the Mount directs us to act as Jesus would have us act, to turn the other cheek, to go the extra mile. They are not communicating cognitive meaning so much as trying to effect a change in our actions. These are existential, not cognitive truths. Again, as with those who would understand religious statements as primarily acts of constitutive meaning, there are also those who understand such statements primarily as acts of effective meaning. For example, Gregory Baum argues, "The Christian message is not information about the divine, to be intellectually assimilated. It is,

---

30. George A. Lindbeck, *The Nature of Doctrine: Religion and Theology in a Postliberal Age* (Philadelphia: Westminster Press, 1984).
31. Ibid., 63–72.

rather, salvational truth, it raises man's consciousness; it constitutes a new awareness in man through which he sees the world in a new light and *commits himself to a new kind action.*"[32] While both constitutive and effective meanings are clearly important in religious life, to strip religion of cognitive meaning runs the risk of turning religion into a mythic construct.

Finally, meaning has a communicative function. Our acts of meaning seek to communicate to others our cognitive, constitutive, and effective meanings. Through this communicative function (preaching, lecturing, writing, creating religious art, etc.) we create human community as a people of shared meanings and values, shared not just synchronically, but also diachronically through history. In this way, our human world is completely permeated by meaning. This is especially true of our religious world, of liturgies and sacraments, of moral and dogmatic teachings, of institutional structures and communal gatherings. If we are to understand our religious world we need to understand the ways in which meaning functions.

Philosophy and Theology

Our discussion of the question of intellectual conversion raises more general questions about the relationship between theology and philosophy, or more generally, faith and reason. The encyclical *Fides et ratio* speaks of faith and reason as "two wings on which the human spirit rises to the contemplation of the truth."[33] There is a long history of theology engaging in philosophical debates and discussion within a theological discourse, as is exemplified in the work of Thomas

---

32. Quoted in Avery Dulles, *Models of Revelation* (Maryknoll, NY: Orbis Books, 1992), 101. Emphasis added.

33. Pope John Paul II, *Fides et ratio*, "Introduction," accessed August 15, 2015, http:// www.vatican.va / holy_father / john_paul_ii / encyclicals / documents / hf_jp-ii_enc_14091998_fides-et-ratio_en.html.

Aquinas. However, what our discussion of intellectual conversion makes clear is that not all philosophical approaches will be of equal assistance to theological discourse. A philosophical approach that thinks of reality in terms of an already-out-there-now of extroverted consciousness—such as materialistic and empiricist accounts of knowing and reality—will not be adequate to engaging theological realities. For example, God is not "out there" in spatial, temporal, and material terms. God's existence is other than that of the material order of the universe. Also, as we have argued above, the notion of meaning, its carriers, realms, and functions are of great assistance in engaging with the meaning and purpose of religion as a whole, as historical community are constituted by shared meanings and values, that inform the community as to the basic truths of their faith, that constitute them as a community and motivate them to action. If a philosophical system is inattentive to questions of meaning it will not be of much help in understanding religious life.

What this means in practice is that theology will tend to favor some philosophical approaches over others. This is evident in the many figures of the early church who took an active interest in Neoplatonic thought because it was more conducive to theological speculation than materialistic approaches such as Stoicism. And so Augustine's "intellectual conversion" identified above was mediated to him by the writings of "certain Platonists." In the High Middle Ages, however, some theologians, notably Aquinas, turned to the writings of Aristotle, which they found provided a better approach to questions about the nature of reality. This is not to say they simply adopted Aristotle as he stood, but they adapted and deepened his approach through a profound reflection on Christian belief in creation, leading to the recognition of a real distinction between essence and existence.[34] Indeed, the history of the relationship between theology and philosophy is one of a creative dance whereby "they offer to each other a purifying critique and a stimulus to pursue the search for deeper understanding."[35] In this way, we might think of this relationship as creating what Alasdair MacIntyre calls a "tradition of rationality," a historical movement of people and ideas working around a set of common themes and assumptions, building a body of reasoning about theological and philosophical matters that grows over time.[36] It is in this light that we should read John Paul II's affirmation of the role of this Greco-Latin tradition: "The Church cannot abandon what she has gained from her inculturation in the world of Greco-Latin thought. To reject this heritage would be to deny the providential plan of God who guides the Church down the paths of time and history."[37] The mutual purification that has been undergone over centuries of reflection has been of lasting benefit to the church's self-understanding and its communication of the faith to others.

Of course, this is not to close the door to other possible contributions to the dance of faith and reason. A tradition of rationality that closes itself off from further development will become increasingly futile if it fails to engage the issues of the day. Many theologians in the twentieth century felt that such futility was the fate of the neo-Scholasticism that attempted to keep alive the thought of Thomas Aquinas.[38] It had not readily kept pace with modern philosophical developments, with the emergence of historical

34. Because Christianity holds to "creation from nothing" (*creatio ex nihilo*) all created being is contingent, the product of God's creative decision. Hence we cannot tell from a thing's essence (what it is) that it must exist (existence). Only God's existence is necessary and hence, for God, essence and existence are one.

35. *Fides et ratio*, n. 100.

36. See Alasdair MacIntyre, *Whose Justice? Which Rationality?* (Notre Dame, IN: University of Notre Dame, 1988).

37. *Fides et ratio*, n. 72.

38. The list of names includes some of the most influential theologians of the time: Karl Rahner, Bernard Lonergan, Henri de Lubac, Hans Urs von Balthasar, Edward Schillebeeckx, and Yves Congar, to name a few.

consciousness, or with developments in modern science. In more recent times, we have also had to deal with the impact of major Asian philosophical approaches and now in the West with postmodern thought. It is important for theology to continue to engage with new philosophical approaches, while seeking to maintain the genuine achievements of the past legacy of Greco-Roman thought.

A Theological Example: The Real Presence

We shall now consider a theological debate in which the question of intellectual conversion plays a significant role. This helps illustrate how intellectual conversion offers a control of meaning of metaphysical terms, and allows for their transposition to more contemporary expression while retaining the same basic truth.

In the New Testament, Jesus is recorded as saying "This is my body, this is my blood" in relation to the bread and wine present at the Last Supper. Since that time, Christians have believed that Jesus is truly present when they gather together in his name. Yet the nature of that presence has been a matter of debate and conflict among different Christian groups. As we saw in chapter 1, the World Council of Churches document, *Baptism, Eucharist and Ministry*, puts it:

> Many churches believe that by the words of Jesus and by the power of the Holy Spirit, the bread and wine of the eucharist become, in a real though mysterious manner, the body and blood of the risen Christ, that is, of the living Christ present in all his fullness. Under the signs of bread and wine, the deepest reality is the total being of Christ who comes to us in order to feed us and transform our entire being. Some other churches, while affirming a real presence of Christ at the eucharist, do not link that presence so definitely with the signs of bread and wine. The decision remains for the churches whether this difference can be accommodated within the convergence formulated in the text itself.[39]

39. *Baptism, Eucharist and Ministry*, 10.

It is well known that in the Catholic tradition, this presence of Jesus in the consecrated bread and wine is designated by the term "transubstantiation," meaning a change in the substance of the bread and wine into the body and blood of Christ.

In order to make sense of this debate a good starting point is to consider the meaning of terms such as "real" and "substance." As we have seen in the discussion above, the meanings of these terms shifts according to whether one is intellectually converted or not. If we think of reality as already-out-there-now, we are also likely to think of substance as "stuff," a material thing such as a "chemical substance." If that is the case when we hear of a real presence or a change of substance we will think of a physical change. Then, when we do not see, or taste, any such change we will deny that any change has taken place, or we might spiritualize the nature of the presence disconnecting it from the bread and wine. If, on the other hand, we think of the real as mediated to us through acts of understanding, we might think of the change in terms of a change in the intelligibility or meaning of the bread and wine. This is what the bread and wine truly mean, the presence of Jesus to his church. However, it is a presence that is mediated through the sensory data previously associated with the bread and wine. In the human world of meaning, Jesus' words of institution create a new reality; they give the bread and wine a new meaning, a meaning they truly have. Inasmuch as the church intends what Jesus intends, it recreates the meaning Jesus gave the bread and wine in that act of institution. In this sense, a change of meaning *is* a change in the substance.

This approach to the real presence and the notion of transubstantiation was initially promoted by a number of theologians under the notion of transsignification, a change of significance or meaning.[40] This form of speaking created some concerns where people thought of meaning as extrinsic to reality, rather than reality as constituted by meaning.[41] In fact, when we look at the word "substance" we see it has the same meaning—sub=under; stance=stand—as the word "under-stand." We grasp the substance when we correctly understand the new meaning present through the appearance of bread and wine. This can assist in making a connection between the two terms, transubstantiation and transsignification. In the human world of meaning and value, a change in our understanding is a change in substance. We can grasp this in the case of a nation adopting a particular emblem as its national flag. What was previously an interesting mix of color and form truly becomes the nation's flag with all such meaning that entails.[42]

As this example illustrates intellectual conversion allows for a more direct control of meaning of the metaphysical term, substance, while also facilitating a transposition to a different terminology based on an analysis of meaning. Without intellectual conversion, we suffer from a perennial confusion over the term substance, and other metaphysical terms such as being, essence, and existence. On the other hand, while metaphysical terms remain valid, in our contemporary setting they are less effective in communicating the theological issues needed to speak at the level of our times. A more fulsome transposition into categories of meaning may communicate more effectively the same truths expressed in the tradition through metaphysical language.

Intellectual Conversion and the Problem of Evil

Intellectual conversion also plays a role in relation to a grasp of the nature of the problem of evil. Again we may approach this through

---

40. For example in Edward Schillebeeckx, *The Eucharist*.
41. Hence the criticism of the term by Pope Paul VI in his encyclical on the Eucharist, *Mysterium Fidei*.
42. This example is taken from Schillebeeckx, *The Eucharist*, 113.

the writings of St. Augustine. For Augustine, everything that exists has reasons for its existence, reasons that ultimately relate its existence to God. Everything that exists is therefore good, because God wills it to be. Evil on the other hand "cannot be a substance" and "for you [God] evil has no being at all." These denials are not a solution to the problem of evil that tries to think away evil, to think it out of existence. If we were still in a world where reality is the "already-out-there-now" real that Augustine is rejecting, this would be the case. To say that evil has no substance or being would be to eliminate it from space and time. But this is not Augustine's meaning. If reality, substance, and existence correlate with reason, then unreality, lack of substance, and nonexistence are the antithesis of reason. What Augustine is stating when he says evil has no substance is that evil has no reasons. It lacks that which is constitutive of reality, that is, sufficient reason. Evil is thus a privation of the good, the good of sufficient reason to be.

Wherein lies this lack of reason? Primarily in the human will, which when it sins acts with insufficient reason. Augustine has already prepared us for this conclusion in Book 2 of the *Confessions*, in the story of the pear tree. There, Augustine scrutinizes his childhood misdemeanor with a penetrating interrogation as to his motives for his action. He begins his account with a blunt acknowledgment that his action had "*no reason* . . . there was *no motive* for my malice except malice."[43] Indeed, the whole analysis of his and others' actions revolves around the notion of motivation, or reasons for one's actions.[44] In his critical self-examination he finds "nothing": "I found nothing to love save the theft itself."[45] In the end, recalling Ps. 18:13 (LXX), he finds his own actions unintelligible: "Who understands

43. Augustine, *The Confessions*, 2.4.9 (68).
44. Ibid., 2.5.11 (69).
45. Ibid., 2.8.16 (72).

his faults?"[46] This lack of reasonable motivation or intelligibility for the act is the psychological correlate of Augustine's metaphysical analysis of evil as lacking substance. Again, as with our analysis of transubstantiation, substance correlates with intelligibility and meaning and what lacks these lacks substance.

If within the horizon of intellectual conversion, reality is intelligible and reasonable, then that which is unintelligible and unreasonable lacks the basic constituents of reality. Evil lacks such basics; what strikes us about our encounters with evil is our inability to understand it: and so we ask, How could anyone? In more common parlance what strikes us is the meaninglessness of evil, the "banality" of evil. Here, intellectual conversion works to reinforce moral conversion. Through moral conversion we shift our decision making from satisfactions to genuine values. Genuine values provide sufficient reasons for making an authentic decision. Through intellectual conversion we can hold fast to the nonbeing of evil, denying it an ontological status, except as parasitic on the good. Good and evil are then not equiprimordial as in dualist systems; being, existence, and reality are fundamentally good.

Conclusion

In considering intellectual conversion, we have focused on operations of intelligence and reason, understanding and judgment. At the same time these operations are dependent upon our sense, imagination, and affectivity, which permeate all these operations. To attend more closely to this level of consciousness is to raise a new set of questions about beauty, art, and symbolism, and their power to hold our attention while transforming our consciousness. Such attentiveness is essential in theology because so much of revelation, the entry

46. Ibid., 2.9.17 (73).

of divine meanings and values into human history, depends upon symbol and art (elemental meaning). If we are not sensitive to the nuance of such communication, particularly at the affective level, we can easily take symbolic and artistic meaning as explanatory rather than exploratory, leading to some profound theological confusions. We take this up in the next chapter on psychic conversion.

5

Psychic Conversion and the Question of Beauty

Thus far, we have considered religious, moral, and intellectual conversions and their foundational role in the life of the theologian seeking to be an authentic subject engaged in theological work. The question can arise as to whether this is an exhaustive account of the foundational theological subject. What other types of conversion might we consider? Previously we have mentioned our fundamental orientation to meaning, truth, and goodness. Goodness and values relate to moral conversion, while questions of meaning and truth relate to intellectual conversion. We have already seen how the presence and absence of these conversions may impact on the ways in which we engage certain theological questions. But what about beauty? Where does it fit into theological foundations? Is there a conversion that relates to beauty in the same way that intellectual conversion relates to meaning, truth, and reality, and that moral conversion relates to goodness and value? And what might the implications be for the ways in which we undertake theology through attention to the question of beauty? Here, Gerald O'Collins notes that among contemporary theologies we find three major different "styles," depending upon where one's focus is: "The first style of theology searches for truth, the second for the good that justice demands to alleviate human suffering, and the third for the divine beauty encountered in common worship and personal prayer."[1] Our task in providing foundations is to see how these different styles might relate to one another through a consideration of the question of conversion.

This question of beauty and its place in theology has become more pressing as Hans Urs von Balthasar and others have challenged theology to adopt a more aesthetic sensibility.[2] Balthasar was not seeking to develop a theology of beauty (an aesthetical theology), but a theology that incorporated beauty into its very foundations (a theological aesthetics). Balthasar argued that theology has lost such a sensibility and as a result has tended toward a cold and sterile rationalism. He traces this problem to the splitting of our notion of beauty from our notions of truth, and goodness, resulting in the truncated and trivialized account of beauty as we find in David Hume: "Beauty is no quality in things themselves; it exists merely in the mind which contemplates them. One person may even perceive deformity, where another is sensible of beauty; and every individual ought to acquiesce in his own sentiment, without pretending to regulate those of others."[3]

For Hume, beauty is arbitrarily imposed upon the sensory or sensual realm. And this limitation to the sensory marks a common problem, as John Dadosky argues: "As long as aesthetics is confined to sense perception, the locus of beauty remains external rather than

---

1. O'Collins, *Rethinking Fundamental Theology*, 328. As examples, we might think of neo-Scholasticism (truth), liberation and political theologies (goodness) and the theology of Hans Urs von Balthasar (beauty).
2. See Balthasar, *Seeing the Form*, 1:17-117.
3. Quoted in John D. Dadosky, *The Eclipse and Recovery of Beauty: A Lonergan Approach* (Toronto: University of Toronto Press, 2014), 101–2.

embedded within a deeper value; for example, it remains in the physicality rather than in the being of a person."[4] Rather, Balthasar speaks of the beauty of a "life-form"[5] or what we might refer to as incarnate meaning, as a central concern of aesthetics. Beauty is then a created participation in the glory of God, which radiates through the truth and goodness of a life well lived. Or as St. Irenaeus stated, "the glory of God is a human being fully alive" (*Gloria Dei est vivens homo*).[6] And being so fully alive is truly beautiful.

In this chapter, we shall consider firstly the nature of beauty and how it relates to meaning, truth, and value, and then we will turn our attention to a further form of conversion, namely, psychic conversion. Just as intellectual conversion is more than just being intelligent and reasonable, psychic conversion is more than attaining an aesthetic sensibility. We shall then explore how the presence or absence of psychic conversion may impact on our approach to theology.

Beauty

Debates about the nature of beauty generally revolve around a number of issues, such as its objectivity (whether beauty is in the eye of the beholder) and in scholastic terms whether beauty is a transcendental, that is, a property of being as being, such as unity, truth, and value.[7] Our approach shall be more phenomenological, focusing on the conscious experience of beauty, using this as a starting point for locating these larger questions. This is congruent

4. Ibid., 56.
5. See Balthasar, *Seeing the Form*, 1:24: "What is a person without a life-form, that is to say, without a form which he has chosen for his life, a form into which and through which to pour out his life, so that his life becomes the soul of the form and the form becomes the expression of his soul."
6. Irenaeus, *Against Heresies* Lib. 4.20. 5–7 (author's translation).
7. See Dadosky, *Eclipse and Recovery of Beauty*, for a solid and insightful discussion of these questions.

with the approach we have taken in relation to religious, moral, and intellectual conversions.

In fact, we have already spoken briefly about beauty in our discussions of symbolic and artistic meaning. We noted in particular the transformative power of the artistic and symbolic carriers of meaning. They "work" on us, shifting our conscious experience, opening up new possibilities within our imaginations, evoking affects long buried or never before experienced. This conveys key aspects of the aesthetic experience. These experiences both capture our attention and shift our consciousness toward new and different possibilities. Elaine Scarry states it thus: "[A]t the moment we see something beautiful, we undergo a radical decentering. . . . It is not that we cease to stand at the center of the world, for we never stood there. It is that we cease to stand even at the center of our own world. We willingly cede our ground to the thing that stands before us."[8]

We can see something of this process at work in the life of the central character of the Oscar winning film *American Beauty*.[9] The central character, Lester Burnham, is portrayed as a pathetic middle aged man whose life has lost all sense of direction and purpose. In the opening scenes of the film, in voice-over, he states, "My name is Lester Burnham. This is my neighborhood. This is my street. This . . . is my life. I'm forty-two years old. In less than a year, I'll be dead." To which he soon adds, "And in a way, I'm dead already." His relationships with his wife and daughter are emotionally detached and disengaged. He has become in every way a "pathetic" drifter, not only sapped of meaning and purpose, but of basic human vitality.

---

8. Elaine Scarry, *On Beauty and Being Just* (Princeton University Press, 2013), 112–13, quoted in Patrick T. McCormick, *God's Beauty: A Call to Justice* (Liturgical Press, 2012), 47–48.

9. Sam Mendes, *American Beauty* (USA: DreamWorks, 1999) accessed August 5, 2015, http://www.imsdb.com/scripts/American-Beauty.html. All quotes from the film as from this script. The film was awarded the Oscar in 2000 for best picture, best leading actor (Kevin Spacey in the role of Lester Burnham), best director (Sam Mendes in his directorial debut), best original screenplay (Alan Ball) and best cinematography (Conrad Hall).

All this changes through his encounter with his daughter's friend, Angela. In the film, Angela becomes a symbol of beauty, and Lester's first encounter with her dancing in a cheer squad exemplifies the basics of an aesthetic experience: it captures and holds his attention, indeed he is transfixed by her performance, and it initiates a profound change in his character, awakening his long dead desires. Initially, the focus of this transformation is in a renewed vitality. Lester begins to exercise, to work out, in a desire to make himself sexually attractive to the young woman; as he says to his jogging partners, "I want to look good naked." All of this could be viewed as exemplifying a male midlife crisis and Lester's actions appear typically foolish in his attempts to charm his young pursuit. However, at the point of success in his conquest, something different happens. The image projected by the young woman, who has at every stage of the film portrayed herself as sexually experienced, is shown to be a façade. A different dimension of beauty is revealed, a fragility and innocence, and Lester's transformation takes on a moral aspect. He declines her offer of her body. His life is changed through his aesthetic experience leading to an eventual moral conversion. Not long after this conversion occurs, Lester is murdered, and his postmortem self reflects on the nature of beauty and its impact upon him: "I guess I could be pretty pissed off about what happened to me . . . but it's hard to stay mad, when there's so much beauty in the world. Sometimes I feel like I'm seeing it all at once, and it's too much, my heart fills up like a balloon that's about to burst . . . and then I remember to relax, and stop trying to hold on to it, and then it flows through me like rain and I can't feel anything but gratitude for every single moment of my stupid little life."[10]

The initial experience of beauty is at the sensory or sensual level. For Lester, Angela is a sexually attractive young woman, an

10. Ibid.

attractiveness accentuated by her sexual bravado. However, once that bravado falls away to reveal her in her actual innocence, new meaning and value emerge, a beauty not to be violated by Lester's desires. We can see in this a transition from a truncated notion of beauty based on appearance to one where meaning, truth, and value can be experienced as beautiful.[11] This is a beauty which can fill our hearts to the point of bursting and which generates gratitude for every single moment of our lives.

This example helps illustrate some of the issues present in debates on beauty. As long as we remain at the sensory level, there is a certain "subjectivity" to beauty, in the sense that what captures and holds one person's attention will not necessarily do so for someone else. Beauty is then considered as "in the eye of the beholder." However, once we relate beauty to meaning, truth, and value, and overcome false notions of objectivity through intellectual conversion, then beauty is properly a property of objects, of their meaning, truth, and value. It is "objective" in the same way that meaning, truth, and value are objective.

We can push this further through a closer account of the relationship between image and affect within understanding, judging, and valuing. Following Aristotle and Aquinas, acts of understanding require the use of images (sensible or imagined) in order to emerge. Insight is into images.[12] These images are themselves often affect-laden, bringing forth into consciousness a rich life of feeling. The totality of these images and affects we may refer to as psyche.[13] While this conscious level of image and affect has

---

11. There is a similarity here to the ascendency of love from transient pleasures to the transcendent experience of beauty in Plato's "Speech of Diotima." See Plato, *Symposium*, trans. Alexander Nehamas and Paul Woodruff (Indianapolis: Hackett, 1989), 48–60.

12. Images here are not just visual, but auditory, olfactory, tactile or any combination of sensory contents.

13. Doran defines the psyche as follows: "[T]he polyphony or, as the case may be, the cacophony, of our sensations, memories, images, emotions, conations, associations, bodily movements, and

its own participation in beauty, as what is "pleasing to the eye," image and affect do not cease playing a role as we move from understanding to reasonable judging, evaluating, and responsible deliberation. The participation of image and affect in these higher-level conscious activities enriches our experiences of meaning, truth, and value. It brings the body into the life of the spirit, for our bodies are not incidental to our existence. This participation of bodiliness in spirit allows us to speak of beauty as the "splendor" of meaning, truth, and value. As Robert Doran puts it: "And the psyche is endowed with this finality, not merely as an instrument of higher purposes—for example, we need sensation and images if we are to understand anything—but also as a participation in the *clarity* of insight, the *assurance* of judgment, the *peace* of a good conscience, the *joy* of love. Without the psyche, none of these states would be felt. The psyche not only serves the spirit, but it participates in its very life and functioning."[14]

This participation is most evident at the highest level of the value of a human life well lived. Balthasar refers to this as a life-form, while we have followed Lonergan in speaking of incarnate meaning. Our lives are an existential drama as we negotiate the challenges of turning our lives into our own work of art.[15] This unique edition of ourselves will be our incarnate meaning left for others to contemplate, perhaps as successful, perhaps as failed, artists. As Doran notes, "If values are apprehended in feelings, aesthetic subjectivity lies at the basis of existential subjectivity, of morals and religion. . . . Ethics is radically aesthetics, and the existential subject for whom the issue is one of

spontaneous intersubjective responses, and of the symbolic integrations of these that occur in, indeed are, our dreams" (see Robert M. Doran, *Theology and the Dialectics of History*, 46).

14. Ibid., 47–48, emphasis added.

15. As Lonergan notes, for each person, "[H]is first work of art is his own living." Bernard J. F. Lonergan, *Insight*, 210.

personal character is at base the aesthetic subject, the dramatic artist."[16]

Perhaps too we can get some insight as to why the status of beauty as a "transcendental" has been disputed. There is an irreducibly psychic component to the experience of beauty and if we focus on this alone then beauty remains within the sensory realm. However, close attention to our conscious experiences tells us that this psychic dimension of consciousness is taken up into the more spiritual acts of understanding, judging, evaluating and deliberating. Beauty can then be thought of as corresponding to the psyche's constructive (rather than disruptive) participation in meaning, truth, and value. Hence, Bonaventure will speak of beauty as the splendor of the transcendentals together.[17] More significantly, if we neglect this participation of psyche in our accounts of understanding, judging, evaluation and deliberation, our accounts of these operations will tend to view them as mechanical, colorless, insipid, almost inhuman, and somewhat less than convincing. As Balthasar notes: "In a world which no longer has enough confidence in itself to affirm the beautiful, the proofs of the truth have lost their cogency. In other words, syllogisms may still dutifully clatter away like rotary presses or computers which infallibly spew out an exact number of answers by the minute. But the logic of these answers is itself a mechanism which no longer captivates anyone. The very conclusions are no longer conclusive."[18]

In this way a neglect of the role of beauty actually creates distortions in our accounts of these other operations within

16. Robert M. Doran, *Theological Foundations*, 2 vols., Marquette studies in theology (Milwaukee: Marquette University Press, 1995), 1:327–38. Quoted in Dadosky, *Eclipse and Recovery of Beauty*, 95.
17. Dadosky, *Eclipse and Recovery of Beauty*, 36.
18. Balthasar, *Seeing the Form*, 19. Balthasar's account of the reasoning process here, which is quite mechanical, should not be viewed as defining the operations of reason per se, but of what reason becomes once it is cut off from its psychic roots.

consciousness. Here, we are getting close to grasping something of the notion of psychic conversion.

What Is Psychic Conversion?

The notion of psychic conversion is found in the writings of Robert Doran, and it provides a modality of conversion distinct from those identified by Lonergan as religious, moral, and intellectual.[19] Each conversion represents a fuller appropriation of dimensions of human consciousness and their implications. Religious conversion represents an inchoate fulfillment of our innate desire for meaning, truth, and value; moral conversion involves a shift from satisfactions to values so that we begin to act more responsibly, in not going with the flow but acting as a self-aware moral agent; in intellectual conversion, we appropriate our intelligence and reason, so that we can operate more intelligently and reasonably in questions of knowing, objectivity, and reality. Psychic conversion is then about appropriating the operations of the psyche so that we can be attentive to our attentiveness and the ways in which our psyche hinders or helps in the search for meaning, truth, and value.

Just as intellectual conversion is more than being intelligent and reasonable, but involves an appropriation of the implications of intelligence and reason for our understanding of knowing, objectivity, and reality, so too psychic conversion is more than being attentive and hence sensitized to aesthetic experience. It requires *attending to our attentiveness*, paying attention to what attracts and holds our attention, to the spontaneous images and their associated affects, even at the level of our dreams, which emerge into

---

19. See Robert M. Doran, *Subject and Psyche*, 2nd ed. (Milwaukee: Marquette University Press, 1994); Doran, *Psychic Conversion and Theological Foundations: Toward a Reorientation of the Human Sciences* (Chico, CA: Scholars Press, 1981); and most fully in Doran, *Theology and the Dialectics of History*.

consciousness and provide the raw materials for our insights, judgments, evaluations, and deliberations. Such attention helps identify the blocks and biases operating within consciousness, which prevent the emergence of images needed for insights that lead to self-correction, or societal transformation. This allows for their proper therapeutic negotiation, liberating the psyche to more fully participate in our native orientation to meaning, truth, and value so that our lives become our own "work of art." In this way, psychic conversion may be an element in good psychotherapy as the psychotherapeutic subject learns to be more attentive to their attentiveness in order to heal past hurts.

And just as we can operate intelligently and reasonably without intellectual conversion, so we can also develop an aesthetic appreciation per se without psychic conversion. But we need intellectual conversion in order to give a fully coherent account of our performance of intelligent and reasonable knowing in relationship to objectivity and reality, and similarly we need psychic conversion in order to give a coherent account of the nature of beauty and its relationships to meaning, truth, and value. We can draw yet a further parallel, for just as intellectual conversion can assist in reinforcing moral conversion by allowing us to affirm the reality of value against any reductionist account, so too psychic conversion assists in the consolidation of both moral conversion and intellectual conversion: with psychic conversion, we can become more aware of the distinction within consciousness between mere satisfactions and genuine values; we can come to know more precisely our own spontaneous scale of values, the symbols that mediate these values, and the need to align them more closely with the normative scale; we can know that the process of moral deliberation is more than a calculus of pleasure and pain, or a dutiful weighing of goods to do and evils to avoid, for it is an existential drama involving the whole of who we are, affectively as well as intellectually. With regard to intellectual conversion, psychic conversion allows us to address the *persistence* of the myth that reality is "already out there now," and thus the psychic resistance to a reality known through intelligence and reason. This resistance may have its roots in a deep wounding that occurs in our encounters with the mendacity embedded in our human world of meanings and values, causing us to retreat into the really real of the out there now.[20]

We find something similar to psychic conversion in Paul Ricœur's notion of "second naïveté."[21] As with Aristotle and Aquinas, Ricœur is aware of the necessary role of images in cognitive processes. For Ricœur, "the symbol gives rise to thought."[22] Symbols are not the product of interpretation, but what make interpretation possible. And by using the term "symbol," he identifies more clearly the affective dimension of these cognitional processes. Ricœur envisages a shift from what he calls a first naïveté where symbols and myths are read "flatly," that is, in a literal fashion, as explanatory of reality. In the modern era, we have experienced this shift through a large-scale demythologization, which has exposed the inability of myths to provide complete explanations of reality, especially concerning natural states of affairs. But this demythologization need not become so programmatic that we regard all myth and symbol as "untrue," and attempt to replace them with elements more congruent to the modern world. Such a move threatens to rob symbols of their genuine power. Rather, we need a second, postcritical naïveté that reappropriates the power of symbol and myth, not as explanatory but as exploratory: "In losing its *explanatory* pretensions the myth reveals

20. As Rahner notes, original sin has a gnoseological impact on the human spirit. See Karl Rahner, "Theology as engaged in an interdisciplinary dialogue with the sciences," in *Theological Investigations*, trans. David Bourke, 13:80–93 (90–91). New York: Seabury, 1975.
21. Paul Ricœur, *The Symbolism of Evil* (New York: Harper and Row, 1967), 352.
22. Ibid., 347.

its *exploratory* significance and its contribution to understanding, which we shall later call its symbolic function—that is to say, its power of discovering and revealing the bond between man and what he considers sacred. Paradoxically as it may seem, the myth, when it is thus demythologized through contact with scientific history, is elevated to the dignity of a symbol in modern thought."[23]

Both Doran's notion of psychic conversion and Ricœur's notion of second naïveté invite a reappropriation of myth and symbol from the "inside," to recapture the power of these carriers of meaning as transformative of human consciousness. Just as Balthasar decries the loss of beauty within theology, Ricœur laments the loss of the symbolic depth within our religious myths: "For the second immediacy that we seek and the second naïveté that we await are no longer accessible to us anywhere else than in hermeneutics; we can believe only by interpreting. It is the 'modern' mode of belief in symbols, an expression of the distress of modernity and a remedy for that distress."[24]

While we shall give a fuller example of the theological significance of psychic conversion later in this chapter, a simple example can be found in the different ways of reading the material of Genesis 2–3. Within the worldview of a first naïveté we might read these opening chapters of Genesis as an historical and scientific account of the origins of human beings and the emergence of sin in the world. A demythologizing movement would dismiss this as a primitive account of human origins, to be replaced by proper scientific and historical knowledge. The account is "untrue" according to the canons of this modern rationality. However, through the lens of psychic conversion or second naïveté we can reappropriate the Genesis story as an etiological myth of human origins and of the

23. Ibid., 5, emphasis added.
24. Ibid., 352.

problem of evil. As myth, it still conveys true meaning, but the meaning is found in exploring the impact of the myth of the "first man" as "everyman" faced with the limitations of creatureliness and the temptations to "be like God," not accepting one's creaturely status. As such, the myth is revelatory of the human condition that it "truly" represents.

Theology and Mystery

Theology is properly oriented toward God, who is identified heuristically as the goal of all our human desires for meaning, truth, and goodness, experienced inchoately in the event of religious conversion, aspired to as the supreme value through moral conversion, and known to exist through intellectual conversion as the necessary cause of an intelligible and reasonable yet contingent universe.[25] Still, in the end, we may know that God exists, but the nature of that existence remains shrouded in darkness. We see now "through a glass darkly" what we hope to know more fully in the life to come (1 Cor. 13:12). In this sense God is the ultimate "known unknown," something we know (as existing) but also don't know (the divine nature). This human encounter with the "known unknown" is what we mean by mystery, and in that encounter there is a psychic component, an intimation of unplumbed depths, that accrue to our feelings, emotions, and sentiments.[26] Studies of religious experience might refer to this as an experience of the numinous or the holy, what Rudolf Otto refers to as the *mysterium tremendum et fascinans*.[27] Lonergan speaks of it as an experience of "the ulterior unknown, of the unexplored and strange, of the undefined surplus of

---

25. On the roles of intellectual and moral conversion in relation to natural theology, see Neil Ormerod, *A Public God: Natural Theology Reconsidered* (Minneapolis: Fortress Press, 2015).
26. Lonergan, *Insight*, 555.
27. Rudolf Otto, *The Idea of the Holy: An Inquiry into the Non-rational Factor in the Idea of the Divine and its Relation to the Rational*, 2nd ed. (New York: Oxford University Press, 1950).

significance and momentousness."[28] To lose this sense of mystery, or what Balthasar refers to as the "glory" of God, makes our theology a purely rational exercise which progressively distorts it into a caricature of itself, whose "very conclusions are no longer conclusive."[29]

All proper theological truths fall under the heading of mystery. The basic dogmas concerning God as Trinity, the Incarnation, and grace are all "known unknowns." We affirm them as true, held in faith, but how they are true remains unknown to us, hidden in the darkness of the divine nature.[30] To study them theologically is to be aware of an undefined surplus of significance and momentousness, which cannot be contained within our understanding. And so we will often refer to them as the *mysteries* of faith. We shall never cease in our exploration of these truths.

However, there is another type of mystery that we encounter, something that eludes our ability to understand it, that is, the *mysterium iniquitatis*, the mystery or problem of evil. This too is a "known unknown," as something we experience, but which resists our efforts to understand, because evil is fundamentally unintelligible.[31] An encounter with evil can also lead to an intimation of unplumbed depths, which accrue to our feelings, emotions, and sentiments, and to a sense of undefined significance and momentousness. Evil too can be experienced as *tremendum et fascinans*. We can see this in the comments of Marilyn McCord Adams where she notes at the very outset of her study of evil: "Evil as topic and symbol is fascinating, alluring. It sucks into itself everything

---

28. Lonergan, *Insight*, 556.
29. Balthasar, *Seeing the Form*, 19.
30. In chapter 10, we shall explore how these truths may be approached, through analogy and through the connections between them, in the functional specialty of systematics.
31. For an exploration of this in relation to questions of theodicy, see Ormerod, *A Public God*, 153–76.

that is 'out of bounds,' not only forbidden but unthinkable, 'beyond the pale.' Undefined, it is chaotic, energetic, disruptive, full of possibility. . . . By contrast, good may seem boring, banal, superficial. Even writing or reading about evil affords the opportunity to taste that delicious dread of picking and tasting fruits primordially disallowed."[32]

There are any number of examples we could draw from within popular culture, which further illustrate the fascination and power people find in evil deeds.[33] Of course, we can know the difference between these two forms of mystery through intellectual conversion, which allows us to distinguish between religious mysteries which are so full of meaning as to be beyond the reach of our understanding, and hence are the fullest of realities, and the mystery of evil which resists our understanding because its essence lies in its lack of meaning, its meaninglessness. However, at the level of our experience of mystery itself this distinction is not necessarily clearly given. A failure to be able to make this distinction means a failure to distinguish between genuine religion and the demonic—between God and Satan. It is not too difficult to find examples of religious individuals or movements that have taken such a turn to the demonic, either through an obsession with sin and evil or through taking up violence as part of their religious identity.[34]

One of the reasons psychic conversion is important for our present conception of theological foundations at the level of our present times is the assistance it provides the theologian in negotiating this confusion between the *tremendum et fascinans* of genuine religious

32. Marilyn McCord Adams, *Horrendous Evils and the Goodness of God* (Ithaca, NY: Cornell University Press, 1999), 1.
33. This is especially evident in films that often involve the most graphic depiction of evil actions. These films have a certain fascination evident in their box office success.
34. Not only in so-called "Islamic" terrorists, but also in so-called "Christian" movements, such as those founded by David Koresh and the Branch Davidians culminating in the siege at Waco Texas, or Jim Jones and the mass murder-suicide of his followers at Jonestown, Guyana.

mystery and that of the *mysterium iniquitatis*. This confusion has always been an undercurrent within all religious traditions, but now it is writ large in the public consciousness to such an extent that some would argue that the demonic is almost constitutive of religion. As the polemic atheist Christopher Hitchens argues, "religion poisons everything!"[35] We need theological foundations equal to the task of illuminating the distinction between divine mysteries and the mystery of evil, and to orient us toward the fullness of meaning, truth, and goodness that is God.

The Saving Significance of Jesus' Death and Resurrection

One of the great mysteries of Christian faith is that of the saving significance of Jesus' death and resurrection. In light of our discussion above, this is a particularly important mystery to focus on because it is here we find most directly the encounter between divine love and the problem of evil. If we are going to encounter anywhere confusion between God and Satan, this is where it will occur, in our attempts to make sense of this struggle between good and evil. Moreover, one might go so far as to say that this mystery is the *sine qua non* of Christian faith. Everything else flows from this, doctrines of the Trinity, incarnation, grace, church, and sacraments. Yet, unlike these other doctrines, there has been no defined dogma in relation to this great mystery. Rather than a formal dogma, the mystery is enacted liturgically in the Eucharist and more fully in the Easter Triduum, the celebration of the Last Supper, the Crucifixion, and Resurrection of Jesus in three distinct but inseparable liturgies. This highpoint of the church's liturgical calendar is its most powerful communication of its central mystery, not just in words but also in the symbolism

---

35. Christopher Hitchens, *God Is Not Great: How Religion Poisons Everything*, 1st ed. (New York: Twelve, 2007).

of water, light, bread, and wine, tied together with the dramatic narrative of the liberation of Israel from the bonds of oppression, its falling away into idolatry and the prophetic voice calling it back to its true identity through a sequence of Old Testament readings. This is meaning communicated elementally, through symbolic and artistic carriers of meaning, inviting us into a personal encounter with the mystery of salvation.

However, it is when we seek to move through elemental meaning to some conceptual clarification that things become more complex. Such a process will often begin with categories drawn from the New Testament which speak of Jesus' death as a ransom, a sacrifice (Eph. 5:2, Heb. 9:26), a sin offering (Rom. 3:25), bringing about a reconciliation with God; it is the result of a struggle with principalities and powers (Eph. 6:12), with death itself (1 Cor. 15:26), resulting in the restoration of what was lost by Adam, and so on. However, this language is symbolic, artistic, and exploratory, expressive of powerful human experiences, but not explanatory of the process of salvation itself. If the task of theology is to move beyond or through the exploratory to establish an explanatory account, something more is needed.

Indeed, the first difficulty we encounter arises when we take the exploratory account as if it is explanatory. To illustrate this issue we shall focus on the notion of sacrifice and its associated notion of ransom. These become blended when we speak of the death of Jesus as the sacrifice required to pay the ransom for a sinful humanity. For example, the Latin theologian, Tertullian, developed an account that draws on the New Testament notion of ransom (Mark 10:45). He argued that Jesus' death is in some sense a ransom that had to be paid for sin:

> Oh how unworthy is it of God and His will that you try to redeem with mere money a man who has been *ransomed by the Blood of Christ*! God

spared not His own Son for you, letting Him become a cursed for us; for "cursed is he who hangs on a tree"; as a sheep He was led to sacrifice, as a lamb to the shearer. . . . And all this that He might redeem us from our sins . . . *hell lost its right to us* and we were enrolled for heaven . . . man, born of the earth, destined for hell, was *purchased for heaven.* . . . *Christ ransomed man* from the angels who rule the world, from the powers and spirits of wickedness, from the darkness of this world.[36]

In this scheme, Jesus has paid a ransom, the needed price, so that the "rights" of hell or the angelic powers have been released, or "enrolled" for heaven. According to Tertullian, the devil has gained certain rights over humanity because of the sin of Adam, so that we have become "slaves to sin." God must treat the devil "fairly" and so must pay the price demanded for our release. And what could be more valuable than the life of his Son? Yet, even in the early church others could see that there were problems associated with the image of ransom. Gregory Nazianzus, one of the Cappadocian Fathers, for example, asks the question, "to whom is the ransom paid?":

If to the Evil One, fie upon the outrage! If the robber receives ransom, not only from God, but a ransom which consists of God Himself, and has such an illustrious payment for his tyranny, a payment for whose sake it would have been right for him to have left us alone altogether. But if to the Father, I ask first, how? For it was not by Him that we were being oppressed; and next, On what principle did the Blood of His Only begotten Son delight the Father, Who would not receive even Isaac, when he was being offered by his father [i.e., Abraham], but changed the sacrifice, putting a ram in the place of the human victim?[37]

Similarly when we interrogate the notion of sacrifice, we can ask, "To whom is the sacrifice made?" Does God require a bloody

---

36. Tertullian, *Disciplinary, Moral and Ascetical Works*, ed. Hermigild Dressler, trans. Rudolph Arbesmann, Emily Daly, and Edwin Quain, *The Fathers of the Church*, 127 volumes (Washington DC: Catholic University of America Press, 1977), 40:299–300 [emphasis added].

37. Gregory of Nazianzus, *Second Paschal Oration*, trans. Charles Gordon Browne and James Edwards Swallow, From Nicene and Post-Nicene Fathers, Second Series, 14 volumes (Grand Rapids: Eerdmans, 1983) 7:431 (XXII).

sacrifice, the death of his beloved Son, to pay for our sins? Is this the image of God we have, or is it bloodthirsty, even demonic, to suggest that this is what God requires? It is here where divine goodness most profoundly encounters the problem of evil, and our confusion over the identity of God is laid bare. Is there in God "only light," or is there "darkness" even within divinity (1 John 1:5–7)?

If we focus on the language of sacrifice, we may notice that it has a dual aspect.[38] The more positive aspect is to view sacrifice as a "sacrifice of praise," the handing of one's life over to God's will in obedient love and service. Christian language of sacrifice reflects this aspect (e.g. Rom. 12:1; Phil. 4:18; Heb. 13:15; 1 Pet. 2:5). However, we should not lose sight of the more negative aspect to the same symbol. This more negative aspect is the dark underbelly of sacrifice, the disobedience of killing the innocent, a sacrifice for an evil purpose, often masked by a "religious" or ideological justification: "It is better for you to have one man die for the people than to have the whole nation destroyed" (John 11:50). For both genuine obedience and disobedience have the structure of sacrifice. Genuine obedience sacrifices mere satisfaction for the sake of the genuine good, while disobedience sacrifices the good for the sake of the merely satisfying.

The most common problem that arises in these discussions is then to conflate the two aspects of sacrifice into a single discourse. This leads to multiple confusions between God and Satan, between goodness and sin, between divine providence and evil. Such confusion is evident in the discussion of the early Fathers on the ransom model: Is the ransom paid to God or to Satan? We can find it in the writings of Luther struggling to reconcile divine goodness with the fact of sin. For Luther, divine sovereignty requires that God

---

38. For a fuller discussion, see Neil Ormerod, "The Dual Language of Sacrifice," *Pacifica* 17, no. 2 (2004): 159–69.

be the author of both salvation and sin: "Since then God moves and actuates all in all, he necessarily moves and acts also in Satan and ungodly man. . . . Here you see that when God works in and through evil men, evil things are done, and yet God cannot act evilly although he does evil through evil men, because one who is himself good cannot act evilly, yet he uses evil instruments that cannot escape the sway and motion of his omnipotence."[39]

In a more systematic mode, it is, according to Raymond Schwager, to be found in the writings of Karl Barth. According to Schwager, Barth speaks of "Jesus' opponents as the 'instruments' and 'agents' of divine judgment," leading to the conclusion "that Jesus had suddenly stopped being the revealer of God and instead his opponents had been entrusted with his mission."[40] In fact, such an approach lays the blame for sin and the dark side of sacrifice at the feet of God.

What we find in these examples is a fundamental confusion between the *mysterium fidei* and the *mysterium iniquitatis*, between God and Satan, being worked out as we move from an exploratory symbolic language to a more theoretic explanatory account of salvation. Unless this move is successfully negotiated within the psyche of the individual theologian, the outcome is an almost blasphemous image of God, a pagan caricature of a God needing the human sacrifice of his Son to appease the divine anger before human beings can be forgiven their primal guilt. On the other hand, if successfully negotiated, then we can say with the author of the Johannine epistles: "This is the message we have heard from him and proclaim to you, *that God is light and in him there is no darkness at all. If we say that we have fellowship with him while we are walking*

---

39. Martin Luther, *The Bondage of the Will*, trans. Philip S. Watson and Benjamin Drewery, *Luther's Works,* 56 volumes (Philadelphia: Fortress Press), 33:175–76.

40. Raymund Schwager, *Jesus in the Drama of Salvation: Toward a Biblical Doctrine of Redemption* (New York: Crossroad, 1999), 163. We should emphasize that this is Schwager's interpretation of Barth. An account of Barth's position would go beyond the scope of this present work.

in darkness, we lie and do not do what is true; but if we walk *in the light as he himself is in the light,* we have fellowship with one another, and the blood of Jesus his Son cleanses us from all sin" (1 John 1:5–7, emphasis added).

Girardian Insights

While difficult to classify, the thought of René Girard is important to consider in our discussion of psychic conversion for two reasons. First, while Girard himself justifies his stance in terms of various sources—myths, great literature, common experiences, and so on—the foundation of his position is a claim about the mimetic nature of *desire,* that is, that our desires are imitative. Verification of such a claim is ultimately not to be found in these external sources but through attentiveness to our attentiveness, that is, through psychic conversion. Such personal verification is a difficult project since for many of us the origins of our desiring are an unknown territory. However, without such verification Girard's position must remain hypothetical. Second, Girard's account of mimetic desire and its apotheosis in the scapegoating mechanism adds a further dimension to our discussion of the language of sacrifice and the role of God in such language.

Girard's analysis of the mimetic nature of desire finds some confirmation in the common experience of parents whose children begin to fight over a toy. The fact that one child desires the toy immediately makes the toy more desirable for the other child. More generally, "we learn to desire by copying the desires of others. Our desires are rooted not in their objects nor in ourselves, but in a third party, the model or mediator." Thus the "ground of desire resides, not in any one subject, but *between* subjects."[41] Desire is

41. Robert M. Doran, "Imitating the Divine Relations: A Theological Contribution to Mimetic

thus interpersonal. In this process of mediation, Girard distinguishes external and internal mediation, where the distinction is one of the symbolic or psychological distance between the subject and the mediator. External mediation allows for some distance or objectification of the process, so that one may be "proud to be the disciple of so worthy a model," while in internal mediation one "carefully hides [one's] efforts to imitate the model." In such internal mediation the mediator then becomes a mimetic rival, with whom one is in competition. "The mediator becomes a shrewd and diabolical enemy who tries to rob the subject of his or her most prized possessions."[42] This mimetic rivalry lies at the heart of the phenomenon of scapegoating which Girard has analyzed in various works.[43] This phenomenon works through five distinct stages: "1. Mimetic desire; 2. Mimetic doubling; 3. Mimetic crisis; 4. The Single-Victim-Mechanism; 5. Theogony and the genesis of culture."[44] The crisis engendered through mimetic doubling and rivalry threatens to destroy the society and is resolved through a focusing of violence on a single victim, the scapegoat. The sacrifice of the scapegoat restores social harmony, transforming the victim into a "divine" source of social healing and reconciliation. The efforts of the society to hide from itself this originating violence give rise to culture and religion, whose purpose is to perpetuate the lie of violence at the heart of the society.

Girard views the religious history of Israel as a progressive release

---

Theory," *Method: Journal of Lonergan Studies* 23, no. 2 (2005): 149–86 (175). We follow Doran's exposition as it is concise and focuses on the relationship of Girardian thought to that of Lonergan. Doran's main source is René Girard, *Deceit, Desire, and the Novel: Self and Other in Literary Structure* (Baltimore: Johns Hopkins Press, 1965), as well as the secondary source Chris Fleming, *René Girard: Violence and Mimesis* (Malden, MA: Polity, 2004).

42. Doran, "Imitating the Divine Relations," 174.

43. Particularly René Girard, *The Scapegoat* (Baltimore: John Hopkins University, 1986).

44. Jacob H. Sherman, "Metaphysics and the Redemption of Sacrifice: On René Girard and Charles Williams," *Heythrop Journal* 51, no. 1 (2010): 45-51, provides an excellent account. This summary of the phases is on p. 46.

from this sacrificial structure of the scapegoat mechanism. With its emphasis on the poor and marginalized, and social justice as the touchstone of righteousness before God, Israel develops a more purified religious observance. The mission of Jesus is the final stage in this process of purification. Through his commitment to nonviolence Jesus exposes the scapegoat mechanism for what it is, the unjustified murder of the innocent. In this way, Jesus' mission is one of the subversion of sacrifice, of uncovering the secret violence upon which society is built. For the sacrificial community, "Jesus appears as a destructive and subversive force, as a source of contamination that threatens the community." That community must then turn its violence against Jesus, "the most perfect victim that can be imagined, the victim that, for every conceivable reason, violence has the most reason to pick on. Yet at the same time, this victim is the most innocent."[45] In so doing, the violence of the scapegoat mechanism is exposed, releasing a powerful force for social and cultural change, the implications of which are still being realized:

> What violence does not and cannot comprehend is that, in getting rid of Jesus by the usual means, it falls into the trap that could be laid only by innocence of such a kind because it is really not a trap: there is nothing hidden. Violence reveals its own game in such a way that its workings are compromised at their very source; the more it tries to conceal its ridiculous secret from now on, by forcing itself into action, the more it will succeed in revealing itself.[46]

Girard will in fact personify this violence as the Satan, the Accuser, whose "power is his ability to make false accusations so convincingly that they become unassailable truth of entire communities," whereas Jesus is the Paraclete, "the lawyer for the defence, the defender of

---

45. René Girard and James G. Williams, *The Girard Reader* (New York: Crossroad, 1996), 182.
46. Ibid., 183.

victims."[47] For Girard, the Passion of Jesus is "a violent process, a demonic expulsion."[48]

For Girard, Christianity is in fact antisacrificial. The historic mission of Christianity is to expose the scapegoat mechanism for the violence that it is and so put an end to all sacrifice. The use of sacrificial language in the Christian tradition is basically mistaken: "There is nothing in the Gospels to suggest that the death of Jesus is a sacrifice. . . . The passages that are invoked to justify a sacrificial conception of the Passion both can and should be interpreted with no reference to sacrifice in any of the accepted meanings" of the term.[49]

Our point in invoking Girard here is again to highlight the problems we face in distinguishing the two types of mystery, the *mysterium fidei* and the *mysterium iniquitatis*. Girard seeks to resolve this problem through his analysis of the mimetic nature of desiring. Without necessarily accepting every aspect of this analysis, we suggest that it at least illustrates the problem and the necessity of its resolution, for without some resolution our images of God at the psychic level, and our understanding of the ways in which our salvation is achieved, will remain subject to constant distortion.[50]

Psychic Conversion and the Problem of Evil

From the above discussion, we can conclude that psychic conversion has a role to play in how we understand the problem of evil. We have already noted in chapter 3 how moral conversion clarifies the nature of evil in terms of human decisions which opt for mere satisfactions over genuine values, so that their decisions lack what is proper to

---

47. Ibid., 201.
48. Ibid., 195.
49. Ibid., 178.
50. For an analysis and critique of the Girardian position, see Neil Ormerod, "Desire and the Origins of Culture: Lonergan and Girard in Conversation," *Heythrop Journal* 54, no. 5 (2013): 784–95.

all good decisions, that they be based on sound reasons that achieve the proper good in a particular situation. Chapter 4 consolidates this by arguing that because evil lacks the proper intelligibility of being based in good reason, evil lacks "substance." Hence, its proper ontological status is that of a privation. Evil lacks that which is proper to reality or being, it lacks intelligibility or meaning, because the person who so acts lacks proper reasons for their actions. Evil is thus parasitic on the good. This position can only be maintained consistently on the basis of both moral and intellectual conversions, which clarify the nature of the good, the true, the real, and being. How then does psychic conversion contribute to our discussion of theological foundations?

Here, we might ask ourselves about the question of how we symbolize evil, how we speak about it? We can identify three forms of symbolism of evil operating in various popular cultural forms. The first is not uncommon in political discourse, which evokes the language of evil, of terrorists being "pure evil," or of different states being an "axis of evil." Such language verges on an ontological dualism whereby good and evil have coequal ontological status, locked in a perpetual cosmic struggle, one trying to overcome the other. Evil is like a toxic substance which permeates the cosmos. It is not difficult to think of aspects of popular culture that reflect this symbolism where "evil" is portrayed as a black, ominous swirling "stuff," which can infiltrate the innocent bystander. When we image evil in these terms, we also image our way of "solving" the problem of evil—the evil substance needs to be corralled, excluded, or destroyed, often by any means necessary including overwhelming violence. This form of symbolism of evil captures the sense that evil is to be rejected, but it also tends to make evil part of the ontological constitution of reality, so the struggle against evil is never ending, built into the very structure of existence.[51] In his youth, Augustine was a member of the Manichaean sect that promoted such a dualist position. In the end, he felt it left the believer powerless in the face of evil. This offers no real solution to the problem of evil.

A second form of symbolism of evil also views it as part of the ontological constitution of existence, but not as something to be rejected but rather as something which together with the good forms part of a greater harmony of the universe. Good and evil are not viewed in terms of a dualism, but a duality, like the yin-yang, male-female, body-mind dualities, which must be kept in creative tension with one another. The union of good and evil as a duality offers us the possibility of a position "beyond good and evil" as found in the thought of Friedrich Nietzsche. An alternate form of symbolism is drawn more from the work of depth psychologist Carl Jung and his notion of the "shadow" within the psyche. Personal harmony is found in integrating one's personal shadow into the ego. Jung went so far as to posit a shadow side in God, which he identified with Satan.[52] This symbolism is effectively captured in the children's film *The Dark Crystal*. In the film, there are two groups: the evil Skeksis, who use the power of the "Dark Crystal" to continually renew themselves, and kindly good, if somewhat ineffectual, wizards called Mystics. Initially, this structure appears as a form of dualism, however, at the culmination of the film, after various adventures of the different characters, the two groups merge bringing the "dark" and "light" elements into a single type of being, healing division within the cosmos and restoring cosmic harmony.[53] If however evil

51. Walter Wink illustrates this point in his discussion of the Babylonian creation myth, the Enuma Elish. See Walter Wink, *The Powers that Be: Theology for a new Millennium* (New York: Doubleday, 1998).

52. Jung was not consistent in this regard. He also thought of the dogmatic proclamation of the Assumption of Mary as acknowledging a shadow element in God. As Doran argues, Jung confused the moral "either/or" of good and evil with proper dualities grounded in a dialectic of transcendence and limitation. See Doran, *Theology and the Dialectics of History*, 332–37.

53. A synopsis of the film and its characters can be found at http://en.wikipedia.org/wiki/The_Dark_Crystal.

is unintelligible, the proposal of a position which is beyond good and evil, or which integrates the intelligible good with the unintelligible evil within a single intelligent perspective is in fact illusory. Again, we do not find a genuine solution to the problem of evil within this form of symbolism. In the end, evil is simply accommodated.

Finally, we can attempt to capture in symbolism the notion of evil as privation. If evil is an absence of something, how do we denote the absence? Herbert McCabe attempts this in his book *God Matters*: "Now does this mean that badness is unreal? Certainly not. Things really are bad sometimes and this is because the absence of what is expected is just as real as a presence. If I have a hole in my sock, the hole is not anything at all, it is just an absence of wool or cotton or whatever, but it is a perfectly real hole in my sock."[54] As a symbol of evil as privation, this works but presents a fairly material sense of the absence, which can be misleading. Interestingly, a far more subtle imagery for privation can be found in the children's film, *The Neverending Story*.[55] The story has two narratives, one of a child Bastian, being bullied at school and finding some escape in reading a mysterious book entitled *The Neverending Story*, the other of the main character of the book, Atreyu, on a heroic quest to save his land of Fantasia from destruction. It is the nature of the destructive force in Fantasia that best expresses the nature of evil. In an early scene of the film three characters, Rockbiter, Tiny, and Nighthob, are discussing what is destroying the land:

> Rockbiter: Near my home there used to be a beautiful lake, but then it was gone.

---

54. Herbert McCabe, *God Matters* (New York: Continuum, 2005), 29.
55. Wolfgang Petersen, "The Neverending Story," (West Germany) 1984, accessed August 5, 2015, http://www.imsdb.com/scripts/Neverending-Story,-The.html. All quotes are taken from the script. The film is based on Michael Ende, *The Neverending Story*, trans. Ralph Manheim (New York: Dutton Children's Books, 1997), a German fantasy novel originally published in 1979 under the title: *Die unendliche Geschichte*.

Tiny: Did the lake dry up?

Rockbiter: No, it just wasn't there anymore. Nothing was there anymore. Not even a dried up lake.

Tiny: A hole?

Rockbiter: No, a hole would be something. Nah, it was nothing. And it got bigger and bigger. First there was no lake anymore and then finally, no rocks.

. . . .

Tiny: Nighthob, this could be serious! Rockbiter, what you have told us is also occurring where I live in the west! A strange sort of Nothing is destroying everything.

Later in the film, the heroic Atreyu confronts in deadly battle the G'mork, a vicious creature in league with the Nothing. Their dialogue further reveals the nature of the Nothing:

Atreyu: What is the nothing?!

G'mork: It's the emptiness that's left. It's like a despair, destroying this world. And I have been trying to help it.[56]

At the conclusion of the story the two worlds of Bastian and Atreyu begin to merge, and it is revealed that it is Bastian who must save the realm of Fantasia, not Atreyu. The ruler of Fantasia, Empress Moonchild, pleads with Bastian to save the land that is all but destroyed by the Nothing. All that is left is one grain of sand:

Bastian: Fantasia has totally disappeared?

Empress Moonchild: Yes.

Bastian: Then everything has been in vain.

56. Ibid.

Empress Moonchild: No, it hasn't. Fantasia can arise in you. In your dreams and wishes Bastian.

This story effectively captures in symbolic form both the nature of evil as privation and the solution to the problem of evil, which is not found in destroying the evil, because it is "nothing" that could be destroyed, nor in accommodating evil in some imagined synthesis beyond good and evil, but in a hope-filled creative act. While the notion of "dreams and wishes" may not be as effective as one might like, certainly our imaginations too must be enlisted in this creative process, which creates new meaning out of the meaninglessness of evil. This is not the powerlessness in relation to evil that Augustine experienced with Manichaean dualism, nor the accommodation of evil within a false duality of good and evil embraced in a position "beyond good and evil." Rather, it presents in symbolic narrative a positive and practical response to evil as privation.

Conclusion

From the start of this work, we have identified our theological foundations in terms of conversion. The converted subject is the proper foundation for theology, not texts or traditions or practices since all these must themselves be "read" or appropriated by the theologian. Without conversion, in its religious, moral, intellectual, and psychic dimensions, the theologian will easily be derailed, not attuned to the full dimensions of the theological object. To study religious texts without religious conversion is like asking a deaf person to evaluate the symphony. So much will be missed simply because the reader cannot resonate with the material under consideration. We illustrated this in relation to the history of historical Jesus studies. Lack of moral conversion will lead to a misunderstanding of the relationship between religious conversion and moral behavior, on questions such as grace and freedom, the nature of sin, and the moral life. We explored this in relation to the use of the social sciences within theology. Without intellectual conversion theology will inevitably lead to misunderstandings about God's existence, the nature of being and reality, and the reality of the meanings and values that constitute human history. This aspect was illustrated through a consideration of the doctrine of real presence and transubstantiation. Finally, without psychic conversion we risk confusing at an affective level the *mysterium tremendum et fascinans* of the genuinely holy with that of evil, leading to fundamental confusion over the identity of God. This was illustrated through a consideration of the theological language of sacrifice.

Given this foundation, the next stage of our project is to explore how these foundations help us to reconceive various topics, which would normally be undertaken in a program of fundamental or foundational theology. Our foundations provide a different entry point for a consideration of topics such as revelation, God, and other traditional doctrines. The chapters that follow in that sense are a preamble to faith or apologetics that might emerge from our foundations. Good foundations should anticipate the needs of good theology. This we hope to demonstrate in the following chapters 6–9.

6

God

This chapter discusses theological foundations for knowledge of God. Our approach emphasizes the conversion of the theologian and builds on previous chapters by illustrating how a theologian's fourfold conversion determines the horizon within which discourse about God becomes meaningful. The chapter begins by identifying the main lines or themes of several major conversations about knowledge of God in the history of philosophy and theology. In this way, the reader may gain a sense of how our discussion of foundations allows us to revisit classic themes or questions about God.

The method we propose in this book contains the exigency for undertaking this task, because theological foundations presuppose evaluations of the various and divergent ways of judging what the Christian tradition brings forward in its complicated history. Consequently, subsequent sections in this chapter pivot between clarifying our foundations for knowledge of God by contrasting them with alternative approaches and using them to identify genuine achievements. Generally speaking, theological foundations combine with evaluations in generating doctrines and in grounding the search for deeper understandings of doctrines and their genuine communications.[1] By the end of this chapter, the reader should have a better understanding of how different theologians use different tools in going about these tasks for theology's perhaps most central topic: God.

The Problem of Foundations for Knowing God

On November 23, 1654, Blaise Pascal experienced an overwhelming intimacy with God and recorded his experience on a small piece of paper. He wrote not to describe the experience's content or communicate it to an audience, but to remind himself of what he clearly knew in that moment. He copied the recorded words to parchment, folded the original paper within it, and then stitched the document beneath the lining of his coat. He carried it there over his heart for the rest of his life. It was reportedly discovered just after his death. Now known as the *Memorial*, the text gives birth to a now famous distinction in discourse about God. The note begins: "Fire. God of Abraham, God of Isaac, God of Jacob. Not of the philosophers and the learned. Certainty, Certainty sentiment joy peace. . . ."[2]

The history of reflection on God in the West includes numerous debates about how we arrive at genuine knowledge of God and how we express that knowledge. Our God-talk often betrays the sources to which we appeal, and many disagree on the measure of validity that we should ascribe to certain sources and the soundness of various appeals. For example, the *Memorial* of Pascal expresses a profound religious experience that contrasts two sources of knowledge about God: philosophy and scholarship, on the one hand, and revelation (personal or communal) on the other. And the sources are not equal. The text continues: "God of Jesus Christ, My God and your God. . . . He is found only in the ways taught in the Gospel. Grandeur of the

---

1. See chapter 10 where we take up more fully the notion of functional specialization.
2. John R. Cole, *Pascal: The Man and His Two Loves* (New York: NYU Press, 1995), 105–7.

human soul. Just Father, the world has not known you, but I have known you. Joy joy joy, tears of joy."[3] Neither manifesto nor public profession of faith, this text carried deeply personal value for Pascal. It expresses his feeling of overcoming his separation from God by the power of God's self-disclosure.

By contrast, the project of establishing knowledge of God by the resources of reason independent of revelation and religious experience belongs to what the Christian theological tradition calls "natural theology." Such a project focuses largely on arguments for rationally affirming the existence of God as well as the attributes that we can predicate of God. The arguments developed in this branch of theology are often deployed apologetically, that is, in reply to objections or in defense of the faith. But questions about the cogency and validity of these arguments go beyond debates with atheists and agnostics and strike to the heart of Christian theology, for they concern the ability of human reason to arrive at genuine knowledge of God unaided by special revelation or religious experience. Or in light of Pascal's *Memorial*, we can ask: Is the God of the philosophers the true God?

Such a question has arisen in several forms since the earliest days of Christianity. Doubting their compatibility, Tertullian famously remarked: "What indeed has Athens to do with Jerusalem?"[4] Conversely, St. Justin Martyr recognized in the wisdom of Athens the "seeds of the word" (*logos spermatikos*) and understood the love of wisdom (*philo-sophia*) as anticipatory, however opaquely, of knowledge of salvation in Christ, for only the true God could animate a genuine search for truth.[5]

3. Ibid.
4. Tertullian, *On Prescription Against Heretics*, §7.9 (246). For a concise, nuanced discussion of Tertullian's view of philosophy, see Geoffrey D. Dunn, *Tertullian* (New York: Routledge, 2004), 31–34.

The New Testament does not settle the matter. The first letter to the Corinthians seems to support Tertullian, if not Pascal more closely: "For it is written: 'I will destroy the wisdom of the wise, and the discernment of the discerning I will thwart.' . . . For since, in the wisdom of God, the world did not know God through wisdom, God decided, through the foolishness of our proclamation, to save those who believe" (1 Cor. 1:19, 21). And yet in the letter to the Romans, St. Paul says: "Ever since the creation of the world his eternal power and divine nature, invisible though they are, have been understood and seen through the things he has made" (Rom. 1:20).

No doubt opponents can cite the same biblical passages with very different interpretations and agendas. But the issue at stake here has more than two sides. It does not simply focus on the possibility of knowing God, however partially or incompletely, without knowledge of the gospel and faith. It also calls into question the validity of appealing to revelation and religious experience in making claims about God and everything else.

The New Atheists are quick to sound the sirens on the latter; they condemn religious faith for what they perceive as blatantly eschewing the critical factor in human knowing, namely, evidence that we can scrutinize. Since belief in God appears to substitute religious experience or revelation for empirical processes of experimentation and verification, which we ordinarily regard as normative in the quest for knowledge, the belief remains at best unjustified in the court of common knowledge; at worst, it represents, as Sam Harris says, "so uncompromising a misuse of the power of our minds that it forms a kind of perverse, cultural singularity—a vanishing point beyond which rational discourse proves impossible."[6] Of course, noting that belief in God does not

---

5. See the "First Apology" in *Saint Justin Martyr: The Fathers of the Church, A New Translation*, trans. Thomas B. Falls (New York: Christian Heritage, 1948), 83–84 (§46).

admit empirical verification in no way undermines or even challenges that belief. Like many other objects of commonly held beliefs (for example, the moral quality of an action or the reality of a mother's love), there are no empirical data on God. But this kind of challenge yet possesses a good deal of currency in our secular culture.

Concern for the rationality of religious belief has many variations (and with significantly greater complexities than what we find in popular atheism) in the history of philosophy and theology. Such concern motivates the apologist's effort to answer the charge of "fideism," the idea that religious knowledge rests strictly on faith or revelation and contradicts reason. Numerous arguments for the existence of God—or for the rationality of belief in God—seek to refute this charge. But there are also arguments that insist on faith and revelation for securing knowledge of the world, and not in the naïve manner that popular atheism caricatures. Some dismiss even the very project of natural theology.

The most famous of these critiques undoubtedly belongs to Karl Barth, the great Swiss Reformed theologian of the twentieth century. Writing in the context of world war, and resisting the jingoist theology of his day, he condemned theological accommodations of cultural and political agendas, most notably National Socialism. He famously rejected religion as "unbelief" and emphasized the absolute disjunction or contrast between God and the world, arguing that only God can bridge the gap by God's self-revealing actions in history. Natural theology, which includes apologetics, begins with a fundamental mistake.[7] He writes: "If one occupies oneself with real theology one can pass by so-called natural theology only as one would pass by an abyss into which it is inadvisable to step if one does

---

6. Sam Harris, *The End of Faith: Religion, Terror, and the Future of Reason* (New York: Norton, 2004), 25.

7. Karl Barth, *Church Dogmatics*, ed. Geoffrey William Bromiley and Thomas Forsyth Torrance, trans. G.T. Thomson, 13 volumes (Edinburgh: T.& T. Clark, 1936), vol. 2/1:93–95.

not want to fall. All one can do is to turn one's back upon it as upon the great temptation and source of error, by having nothing to do with it and by making it clear to oneself and to others from time to time why one acts that way."[8]

For Barth, we can find no ground for resolving the contradiction between God and a sinful world if we look on the human side of the disjunction. By not adverting to revelation in Jesus Christ, natural theology basically denies God by trying to know God apart from who God is. Barth called attention to the various ways that sin darkens the human mind and distorts the use of reason, recognizing that theology too could become servant of human sinfulness in justifying and perpetuating ideas that oppose the gospel. He thus questioned how God could become an object of thought for us, and railed against the effort to fit God into the structures of human thought.[9]

Barth's critique of natural theology finds unlikely company and inspiration in the prominent representative of the Enlightenment, Immanuel Kant. Kant scrutinized the possibility of philosophically discerning the truth about God for epistemological rather than dogmatic reasons. He rejected rationalist attempts to argue for the existence of God on the basis of self-evident principles or ideas about how the world works. Somewhat echoing David Hume, he argued that knowledge about the mechanisms of the world (for example, laws of motion or causality) tells us less about the world and more about the way our cognitive structures organize our perceptions. He distinguished phenomena (things for us) and noumena (things in themselves) and sought to expose as illusory any claim to knowledge

---

8. Karl Barth and Emil Brunner, *Natural Theology* (London: Geoffrey Bles, 1946), 75, quoted in Andrew Moore, "Should Christians do Natural Theology?," *Scottish Journal of Theology* 63, no. 2 (2010):127–45 (134n24).

9. See, for example, Barth, *Church Dogmatics*, 2/1:65–66.

about the noumenal realm. Kant thus challenged the fields of natural theology and metaphysics in general.[10]

On theoretical grounds, Kant's philosophy ends in agnosticism since we can never truly know anything that transcends our experience. Interestingly enough, however, Kant did not abandon or dismiss the idea of God. On the contrary, he claimed a moral certainty for his belief in God and argued for the regulative function of religion in human living.[11]

Barth and Kant illustrate for us the wide-ranging variation in philosophical and theological approaches to attaining knowledge of God. Massively influential as they are, many contemporary theologies draw on their works or reply to them in an extensive array of proposals. Most importantly, any proposal in this realm of discourse presupposes decisions about the validity of different sources for knowledge of God, about the categories best suited to the project, about the method of deriving those categories, and about the degree of validity that accrues to them in different contexts (for example, church doctrines, natural theology, Trinitarian theology, spirituality, and preaching). Such decisions are foundational for theologies and philosophies of God. Consequently, a particular proposal may elicit many kinds of criticism, but a foundational critique focuses on decisions about sources, categories, and the expectations for validity.

For example, what Kant meant by religion does not represent what the Christian tradition generally means by the term (for example, the meaning of giving God what we owe to God does not reduce to servicing morality), and theological appropriations of the Kantian view would need to address this interpretive divergence.[12] But if we wish to critique the foundations of Kant's view, then we would need

---

10. Immanuel Kant, *Critique of Pure Reason*, trans. Norman Kemp Smith, unabridged ed. (New York: St. Martin's Press, 1965), 525–30 (A631/B659–A639/B667).
11. Ibid., 650 (A828/B856).
12. For the notion of religion as giving due honor to God, see Thomas Aquinas, *ST* 2-2.81.4.

to focus on his decisions about knowing, objectivity, the real, value, and conscious-intentional fulfillment; then we could proceed to show how his view of religion rests on prior, problematic decisions. Likewise, we could disagree with Barth's reading of Romans at an exegetical level, and wholeheartedly agree with his rejection of National Socialism at the level of dialectics, but we attend to the foundations of his theological views when we address his fideism. On the method that we propose, Barth's fideism and Kant's idealism anticipate, if only negatively, a deeper intellectual conversion that would resolve the conflicts in their performances of knowing with their positions on knowing, objectivity, and reality.

The method that we propose then does not leave a theologian neutral or unprepared to adopt a position with respect to the significant dialectical differences among the great multitude of proposals in discourses about God. But our method also does not offer a magic-key or sledgehammer solution to resolving each and every debate for all reasonable and decent people, either. The temptation to reduce theology to a series of knockdown arguments that separate the wheat from the chaff in all of Christian history suffers from a misunderstanding of what is at stake in theological foundations. The foundational positions in discourse about God do not regard premises in arguments or the authority of Scripture or the definition of Church doctrine; they are positions concerning the self-understanding that theologians affirm and invariably apply in their theological work. The project of a theology of God rests on the ongoing, personal conversion that always and everywhere underpins this application.

The Horizon for Knowing God

Making conversion the foundational reality of theology changes how we think about the theology of God. Most importantly perhaps, it dispels the notion that we can prove or demonstrate the correct point of departure for our discourse about God. Such discourse invariably takes place within a horizon of meaning—a range of concerns, commitments, and previously acquired knowledge orienting inquiry and interpretation and we cannot prove or demonstrate a horizon. As the classic hymn says, "I was lost, but now I'm found. I was blind, but now I see." Shifts in horizon occur with the discovery of a former horizon's inadequacy, and this discovery signals a growth in knowledge that simply does not line up with previous ways of focusing on the world. Sometimes this discovery so shakes us at our foundations that we cannot ignore it, and if we appropriate it, we cannot fail to live differently in turn. No wonder we often express this breakthrough with gratitude and praise: *amazing grace*.

Of the different kinds of conversion, the religious represents our inchoate, total fulfillment and holistic transformation. It can signal a massive about-face in how we think and feel about others and the world, and in how we imagine possibilities for the future. Since it most often precedes moral, intellectual, and psychic conversions, and promotes their emergence, it powerfully and comprehensively shapes our personal horizon of meaning. Consequently, discourses about God depend on the presence or absence of religious conversion. Does our thinking and talking about God occur within a horizon of steady acceptance and cultivation of unrestricted loving? Or does it occur within a horizon of avoidance and basic rejection? The existential answers to these questions dramatically shape how we think and feel about our search for meaning, truth, value, and by inference, for God.

The primacy of authentic religious conversion makes it unnecessary to separate theology and philosophy of God or to enclose any of the common binary oppositions (for example, faith vs. reason, nature vs. grace, natural vs. dogmatic or systematic theology) into neighboring silos. Religious authenticity underpins, enables, and calls forth moral and intellectual authenticity at the level of the horizon, and taken together the distinct conversions represent aspects of a single thrust to self-transcendence in the person. Common distinctions in philosophies and theologies of God do not belie their deeper origin in the theologian's existential commitment and response to unrestricted love. Discourse about God from any disciplinary perspective begins with a concrete horizon and anticipates the expansion of that horizon by a deeper self-transcendence. Consequently, philosophy and theology of God must not overlook their common origin in religious conversion and their shared objective in the ongoing growth of the person.

Deriving Categories for God

Of course, speaking about God requires that we use certain categories. But how do we derive the categories and account for their validity? The existential importance of religious conversion notwithstanding, many theologians mistakenly assume that we must separate philosophy and theology (for example, Barth's fideism or theological rationalism) in constructing categories. Or we must use a single starting point and place the other discipline clearly in tow (for example, Radical Orthodoxy). The task seems to make separation or conflation unavoidable. Either we speak about God philosophically, independent of revelation, or we begin with the dogmatic data and make revelation our point of departure. Such a view can lead theologians to privilege Scriptural or liturgical language and treat philosophical reflection as contamination or utterly dependent on revelation. Or it can lead them to focus exclusively on the achievements of reason and errantly attempt to demonstrate what revelation alone gratuitously gives. Anselm, for example, moves in this direction with his attempt to prove the rational necessity of the Incarnation in his famous *Cur homo Deus?*

Distinguishing descriptive (things in relation to us) and explanatory (things in relation to one another) ways of understanding helps to illustrate a variety of mistakes that arise with these problematic assumptions. No matter how appropriately theologians may use liturgical or Scriptural language for a given context, the privileged language does not absolve theologians from the theoretical questions that a predominantly descriptive language simply cannot answer. If someone attempts to use liturgical and Scriptural language to satisfy foundational problems that require a differentiated or nuanced explanation, then he or she invariably needs to move beyond the descriptive resources of Scripture and liturgy.

Some examples illustrate the point. The Trinitarian theology of Hans Urs von Balthasar often uses descriptive categories (for example, the image of distance) to speak about the Son's relation to the Father (*ad intra*). But descriptive images in this context lend themselves to tritheism; their material nature keeps them from adequately contributing to an explanatory analogy for the triunity of God. Similarly, many contemporary theologians criticize "substance metaphysics" for excessively "static" and "rigid" categories, in favor of relational approaches.[13] But "static" and "rigid" are descriptive terms that are not really relevant to a correct explanatory understanding of the metaphysics of substance as "intelligibility per se." These theologies are morally and spiritually valuable alternatives to decadent metaphysics, but they do not resolve the root confusions surrounding the meanings of terms. A more careful distinction between descriptive and explanatory approaches can help theologians treat

13. Such complaints are often voiced in Trinitarian theology, notably among those influenced by John Zizioulas, *Being as Communion: Studies in Personhood and the Church* (Crestwood, NY: St. Vladimir's Seminary Press, 1985). See also his later work, John Zizioulas and Paul McPartlan, *Communion and Otherness: Further Studies in Personhood and the Church* (New York: T & T Clark, 2006).

specific questions and categories according to their proper mode of discourse.

To be sure, more explanatory discourse can lose (and often has lost) touch with the range of data and experience it purports to explain. If a philosophical framework's interpretations of dogmatic data seem to reflect its own implications rather than what revelation gives, the church declares, and the community of faith receives, then a theologian needs to account for the apparent discrepancy. How do philosophical categories contribute to explaining what doxology and prayer describe? Some theologians, for example, criticize Rudolf Bultmann's existentialism and Karl Rahner's transcendentalism for conforming the Christian message to certain philosophical constraints. Such constraints may pose problems, but repudiating philosophy or refashioning it dogmatically yet implies philosophical stances on knowing, objectivity, and being, and leaves theology with problems such as fideism and antirationalism. In theology, gainsaying or dismissing basic questions about human knowing, truth, reality, and value is tantamount to obscurantism (or arbitrarily brushing questions aside). The many difficulties with constructing proper foundations do not eliminate their necessity.

We cannot avoid adopting a stance on foundational issues. But how do we go about it? The suspicion of colonizing Christian discourse with philosophy may miss the point if generalized too far, because our very performance of pursuing truth, goodness, beauty, and love provides the performative basis for constructing categories that answer basic questions about knowing, objectivity, and the structures of reality and value. Interiority allows us to fix the frame of reference and generate explanatory controls of meaning. In other words, we can derive *general* theological categories, which theology shares with other disciplines, by making explicit the normative features of our knowing and choosing, and we can use these categories heuristically to guide or control our various inquiries. The validity of the categories depends on their proper reference to the performance of intentionality. So we discover the base for general theological categories in the moral, intellectual, and psychic conversions of the theologian, and establish the validity of the categories by an intentionality analysis that refers back to these dynamics of consciousness. Similarly, we can work out the *special* theological categories that belong exclusively to theology insofar as they are constituted by the dynamic reality of religious conversion in human consciousness.

What does this mean for the foundations of a theology of God? It means that the ultimate grounding of philosophies and theologies of God is not merely conceptual. Methodologically, the performance of theology displaces the primacy of concepts generally, and specifically deconstructs the standard binaries (for example, reason and faith, nature and grace, philosophy and theology) by its return to concrete experience. The normativity of authentic performance makes heuristic application to data possible in disparate contexts and thus guides inquiry and growth in knowledge. At the same time, the concrete dynamism verified in the performance removes the putative tendency to ground theology on axioms or controversial premises. Rather than *a priori* determinations, it provides theology with a disposition of openness to data.

Catholic doctrine, for example, affirms the possibility of natural knowledge of God.[14] But by making the performance of religious interiority foundational, we can interpret this possibility in a way that renders tired debates about faith and reason irrelevant. If we can affirm our capacity for natural knowledge of God, then we must also

---

14. See the dogmatic constitution, *Dei Filius*, set forth at Vatican I. For a contemporary reading of Vatican I on natural theology, see also Fergus Kerr, "Knowing God by Reason Alone: What Vatican I Never Said," *New Blackfriars* 91, no. 1033 (2010): 215–28.

affirm the primacy of religious conversion in all our endeavors. Like Barth, we can recognize our limitations, weaknesses, and absolute need for grace in our thinking about God, but then we can go on to distinguish natural knowledge of God both in principle (*de jure*) and in fact (*de facto*).[15] In principle, we can arrive at that knowledge by reflecting on our native orientation to the whole universe of being, and in the concrete we often flee from or impede that arrival because of biases and mistaken views of reality and ourselves. Concretely, we need the grace that makes us pleasing to God, heals the blocks and biases in our minds, and enables us to know what we could otherwise know naturally, if not for sin and other limiting conditions.

The foundations for a theology of God do not belong to a chronological sequence in relation to doctrinal and systematic theologies. The tasks are functionally interdependent, and yet methodologically ordered. Our theological foundations reflect upon and anticipate the horizon within which we apprehend the truth of doctrines and systematically explore their meanings. Since foundations are prior to doctrines (in terms of method, not time), they focus on commitments that precede and anticipate the affirmations of God's existence. But they also orient our thinking about God and even anticipate the affirmations concerning divine mysteries expressed in doctrines (a point to which we shall return at length in chapter eight). The foundations provide models; they help organize data and contextualize affirmations. Only in the fields of doctrines, systematics, and communications are the models declared as referring to reality or invoked anew for explanatory understanding and appropriate expression.

The next few sections of this chapter outline models for understanding God on the basis of the theologian's fourfold

15. See Bernard J. F. Lonergan, "Natural Knowledge of God," in *A Second Collection*, ed. William Ryan and Bernard Tyrrell (Philadelphia: Westminster Press, 1974), 117–33.

conversion. Models based on intellectual and moral conversion anticipate the discourse often associated with natural theology, but our method formally distinguishes foundations from this kind of theology because they handle different questions. Since natural theology and philosophy of God attempt to understand and affirm that God exists, they belong properly to the field of systematic theology. No formal, disciplinary separation occurs between reflection on God's existence and proposals for understanding the triunity of God, for example. Both trajectories of inquiry share a common origin and objective in the ongoing conversion of the theologian, and in the communication by which the church constitutes itself and grows.

The sections below stop short of developing a natural theology, a philosophy of God, or a systematic treatise on the Trinity, but they point the way to further understanding of such revealed truths. Most pointedly, they illustrate how the foundational reality of conversion places our diverse ways of thinking about God in the context of a many-sided exploration of the transcendent mystery to which we are oriented and with which we are united ever more closely. Our foundations allow us to explain how the God of the philosophers is also the God of Abraham, Isaac, and Jacob, and how we may delight in the fruitful understanding that all of our searching for God may attain.

Religious Conversion and Models of God

Religious conversion grounds the derivation of special theological categories. The data on religious conversion are concomitant with the long narrative of personal and communal transformation—for example, overcoming biases and bad habits, healing from psychic and affective wounds, and developing in authenticity and love—and with specific reference to the principle of this transformation in religious experience. In other words, if we wish to understand the dynamic reality of religious conversion, then we must attend to the ongoing process of personal and communal growth, a process that has its efficacious ground in unrestricted love. The task of deriving special theological categories for understanding and talking about God is based on religious experience, and thus our awareness of the loving source of our unrestricted loving is heightened in both worship and witness.

Of course, the derivation does not automatically follow from taking a good look at what happens inside us. Nor do we gain access to data on God by going within ourselves. Religious experience does not include or presuppose knowledge of God. It often leads to questions about God and the search for ultimate meaning in life, but does not of itself provide categorical knowledge of God and often undercuts various images and concepts with the absoluteness of fulfillment that only love can bring. Returning to the *Memorial*, let us consider Martin Buber's reflections on Pascal's text:

> These words [i.e., the beginning of *the Memorial*] represent Pascal's change of heart. He turned, not from a state of being where there is no God to one where there is a God, but from the God of the philosophers to the God of Abraham. Overwhelmed by faith, he no longer knew what to do with the God of the philosophers; that is, with the God who occupies a definite position in a definite system of thought. The God of Abraham, the God in whom Abraham had believed and whom Abraham had loved ('The entire religion of the Jews,' remarks Pascal, 'consisted only of the love of God'), is not susceptible of introduction into a system of thought precisely because he is God. He is beyond each and every one of those systems, absolutely and by virtue of his nature.[16]

The dynamism of religious experience produces the apophatic moment that Buber elucidates, that is, the negation of a particular

16. Martin Buber, *Eclipse of God: Studies in the Relation of Religion and Philosophy* (Westport CT: Greenwood Press, 1977), 67.

attempt at knowing God. No idea or image of God can contain or adequately express the meaning of what St. Paul describes as God's love flooding our hearts through the Holy Spirit given to us (Rom. 5:5). The experience outstrips efforts to ascertain knowledge of God and resists our attempts at cognitively manufacturing it. On a phenomenological basis, we can affirm with Buber that reason does not condition or produce our deepest experiences of conscious-intentional fulfillment. As Pascal says elsewhere: "The heart has reasons that reason does not know."[17] Nor does religious experience contain some known content, for it entails an overwhelming experience of mystery and elicits wordless adoration. In fact, when we make religious experience foundational in theology, the term of an orientation to transcendent mystery "provides the primary and fundamental meaning of the name, God," and this implies that religious experience contextualizes all of our discourse about God.[18] But then we must nuance Buber's strong statements on the implications of the apophatic for our knowledge of God. He writes:

> What the philosophers describe by the name of God cannot be more than an idea. But God, 'the God of Abraham,' is not an idea; all ideas are absorbed in him. If I think even of a state of being in which all ideas are absorbed, and think some philosophic thought about it as an idea—then I am no longer referring to the God of Abraham. The 'passion' peculiar to philosophers is, according to a hint dropped by Pascal, pride. They offer humanity their own system in place of God...There is no alternative. One must choose. Pascal chose. . . .[19]

Buber correctly points out that religious experience undermines and exposes mistaken attempts to reduce God to an object of thought (that is, what he calls the *Ich-Es* or "I-It" relationship). But he unnecessarily generalizes this conceptualist problem to the whole

17. Pascal, *Pensées*, §277 (78).
18. Lonergan, *Method*, 341.
19. Buber, *Eclipse of God*, 67–68.

field of philosophy of God. As an alternative, he recommends a philosophy that self-consciously surrenders at the experiential precipice of the Absolute (that is, the *Ich-Du* or "I-Thou" relationship). He suggests that philosophy should facilitate or tentatively describe an experience of God that ideas and concepts can only ever misrepresent.

No doubt some mistakenly reduce God to an "object" on conceptualist presuppositions, but we need not repeat the generalization that Buber makes. In chapter 2, we explained how the question of God arises on the horizon of all human knowing. When we define an "object" as that which we intend in our questions for intelligibility, truth, and value, then we can identify God heuristically with the total satisfaction of our unrestricted desire for meaning, truth, and goodness. But this heuristic also allows us to identify God as the source of the unrestricted loving that fulfills our desire. Note that our "object" here is not a concept. Our natural knowing cannot attain what God is, as God is in God's self (*uti in se est*), but it can attain a heuristic anticipation of what God is in relation to the order of the universe (a point to which we return below). And it can contemplatively affirm the reality of this transcendence. So when we identify God as an "object" in this precise sense, we can recognize that in fulfilling the horizon of consciousness, religious experience provides the backdrop for our admittedly partial and incomplete understanding of God in philosophy and natural theology. In its own limited way, reason discloses our openness to the same transcendent mystery that our graced hearts adore in limitless silence.

In fact, we can say something similar about our religious beliefs. Catholic doctrine recognizes that mysteries of faith are not exhaustively known or communicated in dogmatic pronouncements.[20] In acts of faith, we attain the reality of God, but our attainment does not exhaustively grasp its proper object; an obscurity pertains to faith in this life, "for now we see in a mirror, dimly" (1 Cor. 13:12). Both our religious beliefs in and about God and our natural, philosophical knowledge belong to the same inner context of ongoing personal conversion. The mystery of love and awe experienced in our heart of hearts invites our contemplative understanding and appreciation.

By self-appropriation we can avoid the conflict over the models of God that Buber says demand a dialectical and existential choice. The primacy of religious experience places the God of the philosophers in the context of an unrestricted loving that dwells in the deepest chambers of what St. Teresa of Avila describes as the interior castle. Of course, religious experience never simply entails knowledge of God or the cognitive content of revelation. Such prescinding allows us to retrieve apophatic strategies (that is, ways of knowing God by negating what God is not) that point to a "God beyond God," or an ultimate ground and mystery, without denying or diminishing the relatedness of these strategies to kataphatic ways of knowing God by affirmation, explanation, and description. In fact, by distinguishing kinds of cognitional apprehension and functions of meaning, we can explain how Buber's attempt to construct a philosophy that (indirectly) facilitates or describes religious experience pertains less to the cognitive and more to the effective, communicative, and constitutive functions of meaning.

Not all philosophy and theology aim predominantly at explanatory, cognitive meaning; to grasp this point requires an expansion of the horizon within which we appreciate the tradition. Consequently, we can distinguish complementary functions of meaning and avoid unnecessary conflicts in discourse about God.

---

20. See the Vatican I Dogmatic Constitution of the Catholic Faith, *Dei Filius*, in Norman P. Tanner, *Decrees of the Ecumenical Councils*, 2 vols. (London/Washington, DC: Sheed & Ward/ Georgetown University, 1990), 2:804–11.

Such discourse begins at the level of the horizon constituted by religious conversion, and relies for its explanatory unfolding on each of the four modalities of self-transcendence (that is, religious, moral, intellectual, psychic). Each contributes to the quest for the loving source of our unrestricted being in love.

Moral Conversion and Models of God

When we turn to models of God grounded in moral conversion, we begin with a different kind of question. No longer wondering about whom we ultimately love, now we ask: "To whom or what are we ultimately responsible?" And this question also does not necessarily presuppose religious belief, but arises spontaneously within the horizon of human knowing. The question of God arises spontaneously even for popular atheists, if not especially for them.

If Sam Harris and Richard Dawkins argue that we must predicate rational, public discourse on the amenability of truth claims to testable measures and scrutinizable evidence in space and time, in principle available to any rational participant, they implicitly affirm our moral obligation to intelligence and reasonableness in the search for truth about the world. In other words, if Harris and Dawkins say we ought to use our minds in a particular way, then they are tacitly admitting the existence and objectivity of a moral exigency within human living. Morality, at the very least then, requires that I justify my "facts" about the world with intelligence and reasonableness rather than some other criteria (for example, personal satisfaction—"the way I want the world to be"—or cultural bias—"the way we have always believed it to be"). And this obligation leads to a (factual) question about our choices and decisions.

Do I make choices and decisions responsibly (that is, in response to the exigencies for genuine values), or arbitrarily? If I make them responsibly, then how can I justify the values that I choose in relation to my concrete living? In other words, what is the origin of my values? If I do not posit them arbitrarily, but discriminate among them attentively, intelligently, rationally, and responsibly, then how do I account for the objectivity of values? Yet again: To whom or what am I ultimately responsible?

Of course, many people who are committed to a realism of facts quickly draw back into a relativism of values. If the world tells us how it is if we pay attention to it, they say, still the world shows utter indifference to how we act or to what happens in its unimaginably long history. Most often this kind of thinking explains the objectivity of values by reducing moral reasoning entirely to the linguistic usage of a particular culture and way of life. Morality and values cannot be assessed in the way that facts can by scientific reasoning; they are cultural or social constructions lacking any ontological ground. In other words, moral orientations that have no way of adjudicating values result in a world without objective morality.

Kant emphasized this point in his argument for the moral certainty of knowledge about God's existence and the immortality of the soul. Quite famously, he said of these beliefs and their significance: "Since, therefore, the moral precept is at the same time my maxim (reason prescribing that it should be so), I inevitably believe in the existence of God and in a future life, and I am certain that nothing can shake this belief, since my moral principles would thereby be themselves overthrown, and I cannot disclaim them without becoming abhorrent in my own eyes."[21] Kant rejected what he called "transcendental theology," and argued that we can scientifically know only that we cannot know whether or not God exists, but he defended the necessity of this belief as a rational postulate in support of his performance as a moral agent. He recognized that rational

21. Kant, *Critique of Pure Reason*, 650 (A828/B856).

faith in God's existence and the immortality of the soul allow us to account for the objectivity of morality and the rationality of our orientation to pursuing complete conformity with the moral law in practical living. If he were to renounce these beliefs, he says, then he could not account for his moral principles—and this would make him "abhorrent" in his own eyes. Whatever its shortcomings, his philosophy illustrates the existential imperative to account for the question of God in the context of our moral lives.

Many theologies and philosophies that proclaim the death of God (Friedrich Nietzsche) or point to a "God beyond God" (Paul Tillich), focus largely on how we assess our existential condition. They relate the question of God to themes of human freedom, creativity, and responsibility. Such applies also to the postmodern, deconstructionist strategies of deferring to divinity in the name of a justice or forgiveness that never arrives (Jacques Derrida and John Caputo).[22] The God who dies or lies within the boundary of human thought represents the false idol of a conceptualist heritage that obscures or injures our existential responsibility to become principles of creativity and value in concrete living. For example, Tillich criticized what he called "theological theism," arguing that many theologies mistakenly construct models that conceive God as a being among other beings, and this flawed concept indicates more than theoretical problems: it leads to despair. How we assess our existential condition reflects and often influences how we think about God:

> The God of theological theism is a being beside others and as such a part of the whole of reality. . . . [H]e is bound to the subject-object structure of reality, he is an object for us as subjects. At the same time we are objects for him as a subject. And this is decisive for the necessity of transcending theological theism. For God as a subject makes me into

22. See, for example, Jacques Derrida, *On Cosmopolitanism and Forgiveness*, Thinking in Action (New York: Routledge, 2001); John D. Caputo, *The Prayers and Tears of Jacques Derrida: Religion without Religion* (Bloomington: Indiana University Press, 1997).

an object which is nothing more than an object. He deprives me of my subjectivity because he is all-powerful and all-knowing. . . . God appears as the invincible tyrant, the being in contrast with whom all other beings are without freedom and subjectivity.[23]

For Tillich, theological theism imagines the God that "Nietzsche said had to be killed," since no one can tolerate a God who turns us into objects of absolute power and control, and engenders the "widespread anxiety of meaninglessness" that he recognized in his cultural milieu.[24] Tillich's "God beyond God" rehabilitates the meaningfulness of the existential decision to live (that is, "the courage to be") in a world beset by the destabilizing realities of anxiety and doubt.

Our explanations of conversion also locate the critical moments of personal authenticity at the existential level. Do I respond to the conscious-intentional exigencies within me for attentiveness, intelligence, reasonableness, responsibility, and love? Will I contribute to the world of meaning and value by steadfastly committing myself to these inner norms? The existential answers to these questions profoundly shape the horizon for meaningful engagement and creativity in the world. Unlike the theological theism that Tillich decried, our explanations of conversion focus on the existential performance of pursuing what we always already anticipate (that is, meaning, truth, value, love) in all of our efforts to know and choose—and despite impediments and difficulties of every kind. If the absurdity that leads certain existentialists to declare the death of God also leads them to esteem autonomy and choice, still we do not dismiss their doubts or disagree with their emphasis. Rather, we part ways with the idea that autonomy is compatible with being

23. Paul Tillich, *The Courage to Be*, The Terry Lecture Series (New Haven: Yale University Press, 1952), 184–85.
24. Ibid., 185.

arbitrary and has no share of objectivity, because we recognize no opposition between the exercise of choice and the exigencies of the (interiorly) normative.

The moral conversion that marks a shift from criteria of satisfaction to criteria of genuine value does not crush subjectivity. It orients a person toward acting in harmony with the heuristic order of the universe, to creating and connecting with others, but not in a way that determines the content of morality for all times and places—or that prescribes conformity to the often xenophobic and violent undercurrents within popular culture. Since we understand and affirm universal order only heuristically (for example, as in the normative scale of values), and in virtue of our natural, spontaneous orientation to wondering about genuine value, then we get no passes on the content of the good in specific instances; there is no extrinsic or conceptual calculus to which we can appeal in securing objectivity.[25] And we cannot eradicate our vulnerability to the manifold forms of individual and group bias in the interrelated contexts of culture and religion. But we can and yet do connect with others and create something new in acts of friendship, admiration, and love. Such creativity points to elements of mystery. None of the difficulties we encounter can keep us entirely from acknowledging our lived experiences of desiring genuine value in the concrete circumstances of our existential situations, and that lived experience points us to a supreme creativity and goodness that transcends the very apprehensions and actions that it makes possible.

Our regular inability to achieve the limited goals we recognize as worthwhile leads us to ask theological questions about sin, grace,

---

25. On this approach, "genuine objectivity is the fruit of authentic subjectivity" (*Method*, 292). The various forms of epistemological objectivism—philosophical arguments for establishing the Archimedean point of all knowledge—are simply mistaken. For an excellent discussion of epistemological objectivism, see Richard J. Bernstein, *Beyond Objectivism and Relativism: Science, Hermeneutics, and Praxis* (Oxford: Blackwell, 1983).

and redemption. Our reflections on religious conversion link the individual and cooperative performance of the human good with the fulfillment of conscious intentionality that we cannot cognitively manufacture or adequately conceptualize. The authentic Christian imagination purges the oppressiveness of what Tillich characterized as "theological theism," envisioning a radical transformation of human history because of an unrestricted, redemptive being-in-love that shatters conventional expectations of the status quo. On this radical affirmation of human life and history, to which Lonergan refers as the divinely originated "solution to the problem of evil,"[26] Thomas Merton writes:

> If we consider the true meaning of the first word in the Christian message of salvation, *metanoiete*, "repent," we see that it is a summons to a complete change of life both for the individual and for society. This change did not take place, once for all, two thousand years ago. The summons to change, to man's creative self-realization and development in the spirit, as a child of God whom the truth shall make free, *is a summons to permanent newness of life.*[27]

For Merton, the Christian concept of order resonates with the dynamic quality of the modern worldview because it depends on the existential force of its call to *metanoia* (repentance), and not on a static system of a conceptualist theism that fixes a place for the human person in a determinate relation to God and the rest of creation, which has little or nothing to do with the existential dynamism of the gospel. "In such a [static] context," writes Merton, "the call to repent is simply a call to assume one's proper place in the cosmic order—in a word, a rather minor adjustment which in many cases amounts to nothing more than accepting what one already has and not protesting

---

26. Lonergan, *Insight*, 710. In fact, the whole of chapter 20 of *Insight* is concerned with the solution to the problem of evil.
27. Thomas Merton, *Love and Living* (San Diego: Harcourt Trade Publishers, 2002), 140.

or asking for more."[28] Such a call tends to reinforce social ideologies that rationalize the myriad injustices and abuses of human history.

Christian theology must undergo the authentic meaning of its first word (*metanoiete*), and in this context many existentialist and postmodern approaches to God make important contributions, if finally inadequate. As Merton observes: "One of the historic paradoxes that resulted from this fixation of the Christian world view in one static concept is that the dynamic aspect of Christianity was left to be rediscovered and emphasized by thinkers who stood outside Christian institutions and were highly critical of them."[29] The models of God that we anticipate on the basis of moral conversion orient us to the historical process of becoming agents of creativity and friendship within the physical environment of a community.

Intellectual Conversion and Models of God

Both of the previous sections on models allude to the importance of theoretical or intellectual commitments in appropriating the significance of conversion for our discourse about God. If we are going to overcome the static systematization that radically opposes the dark night of our religious experience and squashes our freedom and moral agency, and if we are to authentically appropriate the meanings and implications of our religious and moral conversions, then we must avoid the host of potential problems that beset foundational positions on knowing, objectivity, and reality. In other words, our thinking about God also reflects the extent to which we succeed in matching our criteria for reality with the exigencies that we performatively experience as normative in our lived quests for knowledge. In other words, it depends on our intellectual conversion.

Such issues tremendously influence the openness and vitality of

28. Ibid., 141.
29. Ibid.

the horizon within which we grasp the meaning of doctrines about God. Recall our discussion of Augustine in chapter 4. If we cannot mean by "reality" anything other than "body," then with the young Augustine we will also fall unavoidably into error when trying to understand the mystery of God for which our hearts are restless.[30] Moving beyond anthropomorphism in the ways we think about God requires that we overcome our tendencies toward empiricism. Of course, we recognize this need as soon as we realize that commonsense ways of imagining God cannot answer all our questions about God (for example, "Where in the world is God?"). The God imagined as dwelling in the clouds can impel us to pursue these questions until we no longer imagine God as a body. And the same point applies to the development of Christian doctrine. The understanding of Christ's consubstantiality with the Father arose only after Clement of Alexandria extirpated empiricist assumptions about the reality of God.[31] He helped set the stage for Athanasius to substitute a second order rule of scriptural assertion to apprehend a host of images that could not properly communicate the intelligibility of the Son's relation to the Father.[32] Having grasped that this way of controlling meaning goes beyond every image, Athanasius stated the scriptural understanding that: whatever is said of the Father is said of the Son, except the name Father.[33]

---

30. Augustine wrote in his *Confessions*: "Hence I thought that even you, Life of my life, were a vast reality spread throughout space in every direction: I thought that you penetrated the whole mass of the earth and the immense, unbounded spaces beyond it on all sides, that earth, sky, and all things were full of you, and that they found their limits in you, while you yourself had no limit anywhere" 7.1.2 [trans. Boulding, 159].

31. Bernard J. F. Lonergan, "Lecture 2: The Functional Specialty 'Systematics'," in *Philosophical and Theological Papers: 1965-1980*, ed. Robert Croken and R. M. Doran, *Collected Works of Bernard Lonergan*, 25 volumes (Toronto: University of Toronto Press, 2004), 17:179-98 (183n11, 184n19).

32. See the discussion of different images for understanding the relations of divine persons (such as Tertullian's use of root and tree, fountain and river, sun and ray) in the development of Trinitarian doctrine in Neil Ormerod, *A Trinitarian Primer* (Collegeville: Liturgical Press, 2011).

33. Athanasius, *Against the Arians*, trans. Cardinal Newman and ed. Archibald Robertson, *Nicene*

Most obstacles to correctly understanding God are brought about by flawed assumptions about both human cognition and reality. In fact, we can rule out many false or problematic conceptions of God by transforming (as did Augustine) our foundational commitments on these issues. This is as true for the genesis and appropriation of ecclesial doctrine as it is for philosophical arguments for God's existence. Such arguments often begin with jejune definitions of *what God is*, and then in accord with that definition attempt to establish *that God is*.[34] In both cases, foundational commitments are decisive.

St. Anselm of Canterbury (1033–1109) proposed perhaps the most famous attempt at rationally affirming God's existence. He first authored what the tradition since Kant refers to as "the ontological argument."[35] He defined God as "that than which we can conceive nothing greater," and since a being that exists only in the mind pales in comparison to a being that also exists in reality, he concluded that God must exist. In short, Anselm attempted to deduce the necessity

and *Post-Nicene Fathers of the Christian Church*, Second Series, 14 volumes (New York: Christian Literature, 1892) 4:395 (Discourse 3.4). More fully: "And so, since they are one, and the Godhead itself one, the same things are said of the Son, which are said of the Father, except His being said to be Father." Also Basil of Caesarea, "whatever one may assign to the Father as the formula of his being, the very same also applies to the Son. If someone takes the commonality of the substance in this way, we accept it and claim it as our doctrine. For this is how divinity is one" (*Against Eunomius*, trans. Mark Delcogliano and Andrew Radde-Gallwitz, *The Fathers of the Church: A New Translation*, Volume 122 [Washington, DC: Catholic University of America, 2011], 120 [1.19]).

34. The notion of "what God is" in this context is heuristic and oriented to the affirmation of existence rather than conceptual knowledge, which surpasses the natural proportion of the human mind. As Aquinas said: "We cannot know what God is, but rather what he is not" (*ST* 1.3 [14]).

35. See Anselm's *Proslogion*, trans. Matthew D. Walz (South Bend: St. Augustine's Press, 2013) 23–24 (§2–3). It is worth noting that Anselm wrote this text as an exercise in faith. In fact, the text provided a great source of inspiration to Karl Barth (see Karl Barth, *Anselm, Fides Quaerens Intellectum: Anselm's Proof of the Existence of God in the Context of his Theological Scheme*, 1st English ed., Pittsburgh reprint series (Pittsburgh: Pickwick Press, 1975). Notably, some argue that Anselm's text has been misread in the tradition of the "ontological argument," that rather than rational or conceptual "proof," the text represents a work of Western apophatic or mystical theology. See, for example, J. Burton Fulmer, "Anselm and the Apophatic: 'Something Greater Than Can Be Thought'" *New Blackfriars* 89, no. 1020 (2008): 177–93; Denys Turner, *Faith, Reason, and the Existence of God* (Cambridge: Cambridge University, 2004), 142.

of God's existence on a strictly conceptual basis (that is, without any empirical ground).

Kant famously criticized the ontological argument for treating existence incorrectly in relation to Anselm's conception of God.[36] He argued that we cannot consider existence as a predicate or property of the greatest possible being, because existence does not change the concept of anything. Rather, it attaches predicates to a subject or posits their existence in the subject. So in each of the following propositions the copula (*is*) attaches a property to the subject: the house is red; the dog is small; the child is loud; the money is green. But the copula on its own does not change the meaning of the concept: the 100 dollars in my mind means the very same thing as the 100 dollars in my bank account, though my financial situation certainly detects a difference. Since existence does not add a property to a concept, it also does not add to the concept of the greatest possible being.[37] The deduction fails.

Anselm, however, offers a variation of the argument that focuses on *necessary* existence, which we can consider as a property of a subject (since not all existent things necessarily exist), but this variation also clearly fails according to our approach to the foundational issues at stake. Kant's criticism focuses on the role of judgment in a logical analysis of predicates and copula, but our critique begins with a different understanding of how we cognitively apprehend reality.[38] If we distinguish experiencing, understanding, and judging in the construction of knowledge, and affirm the correspondence of our cognitional operations with the structure of reality, then we can recognize the cogency of the proposition—for example, "a necessary being necessarily exists"—without attributing

36. Kant, *CPR*, 500–507 (A592/B620–A602/B630).
37. Ibid., 504–5 (A598/B626–A599/B627).
38. See Lonergan, *Understanding and Being*, 237–46; *Insight*, 692–99; see also Aquinas, *ST* 1.2.1 ad2m [11].

to it the epistemic status of truth or falsity that belongs only to correct judgment. Only in judgment do we apprehend the true, the medium in which the real is known (*verum est medium in quo ens cognoscitur*). Our foundational commitments allow us to place the ontological argument in proper perspective: without deference to the concrete universe of being, the attempt to deduce existence logically from a coherent conception need not correspond to reality.[39] The validity of the argument resembles a tautology rather than establishing what it claims.[40]

How then should we address our questions about the existence of God? For Lonergan, if we begin from our foundational commitments, we change the course of the reflection and its outcome. The question about God anticipates an analogical understanding of transcendent being, and our reflections on knowing, objectivity, and reality more than suggest the possibility of this knowledge for us. If we postulate our idea of transcendent being by first reflecting on the acts of understanding and judgment that we verify in ourselves, then we can begin with a limited or restricted act of understanding and analogically extrapolate to the unrestricted act of understanding that would fully satisfy the unrestricted desire to know.[41]

Concretely speaking, our notion of being drives and makes possible all of our quests for knowledge. It is manifested in our questioning and wondering, and thus reaches for being intelligently and reasonably in all of our conscious-intentional endeavors. But our unrestricted orientation to being does not attain the meaning that it

---

39. See Lonergan's distinction between analytic propositions and principles in *Insight*, 329–34, 693–94; *Understanding and Being*, 126–31.
40. Kant also recognizes the tautological nature of the argument. Though Alvin Plantinga ultimately dismisses Kant's critique as "irrelevant," the charge of tautology can still be applied to Plantinga's modal version of the ontological argument as well. See Alvin Plantinga, *God, Freedom, and Evil* (New York: Harper & Row, 1974), 85–112.
41. Lonergan, *Insight*, 662–69.

anticipates. It grounds a heuristic notion of being as "whatever is to be intelligently grasped and reasonably affirmed," but by definition this notion does not satisfy our unrestricted orientation. It moves us toward a totality of correct answers without determining any of them. Only an unrestricted act of understanding, which grasps everything about everything, could satisfy the unrestricted desire to know, and we could name the content of that unrestricted act, the idea of being. Such an idea—identical in act with unrestricted understanding—would possess the characteristics or properties traditionally attributed to God: oneness, immateriality, eternality, personality, omniscience, supreme goodness, benevolence, omnipotence, and freedom.[42]

Most significantly, the content of an unrestricted act of understanding would not posit a duality between knower and known. Our point of departure overcomes the false image of a primordial split between subjects and objects, rules out the false problem of whether God's being or knowing has priority, and excludes the reasonableness of conceiving God as a being among other beings. The unrestricted act of understanding can create other intelligibilities, and their creation presupposes that unrestricted intelligence creatively grasps the possibility of everything else in virtue of its primary grasp of itself. This allows us to explain revealed doctrines of creation and providence without denying the immutability of God or diminishing human creativity as a created participation in the divine. In short, outside the unrestricted act of understanding, there is nothing (*contra theological theism*). And yet by that uncreated luminosity all things are creatively known in their distinctiveness (*contra pantheism*) in virtue of a single, immaterial, nontemporal and nonspatial grasp of the intelligible ordering of

---

42. Ibid., 665–69, 680–92.

everything. The unrestricted act is self-explanatory, necessary, and creative; it explains the contingency of created being.[43]

Here we see that our notion of God emerges from our basic commitment to the intrinsic intelligibility of being. Unlike process philosophy's attempt to account for novelty and creativity in metaphysics by making God a primordial accident, intrinsically conditioned by space and time (and thus not intrinsically intelligible), our approach defines God in a way that excludes the unintelligible.[44] If we define our notion of being—based on our self-appropriation as knowers—as "whatever is to be intelligently grasped and reasonably affirmed," then an unrestricted act of understanding represents the heuristic completion of our unrestricted desire to know and the ultimate explanation of all our limited cognitional achievements.

The transition to affirming *that God exists* depends on the affirmation of the complete intelligibility of being. If we grant the intelligibility of being, then we can move beyond the defects of intelligibility in this concrete universe to the completion of their intelligibility in the intelligence of God. This problem of a defect arises in science whenever scientists ask specifically about the contingency of the intelligible relations (or "laws of nature") they verify within the physical universe.[45] Contingency pertains to mere matters of fact (for example, something happens to exist or occur in this way, but it could have been otherwise), but if we identify

---

43. *Insight*, 669–80.

44. Whitehead writes: "In all philosophic theory there is an ultimate which is actual in virtue of its accidents. It is only then capable of characterization through its accidental embodiments, and apart from these accidents is devoid of actuality. In the philosophy of organism [i.e., process philosophy] this ultimate is termed 'creativity'; and God is its primordial, nontemporal accident" (Alfred North Whitehead, *Process and Reality: An Essay in Cosmology*, ed. David Griffin and Donald W. Sherburne [New York: Free Press, 1978], 7). This approach implies that God also undergoes change and development, as Whitehead says: "It is as true to say that God creates the World, as that the World creates God" (Ibid., 348).

45. For a developed explanation of this point, see Ormerod, "Bernard Lonergan and the Recovery of a Metaphysical Frame," 960–82.

being with the real, and reality with complete intelligibility, then we must ask about the intelligibility of contingency: Why any particular thing or event rather than something else, or nothing at all? In fact, Lonergan says that we can reduce each of Aquinas's five ways of arguing for the existence of God to the apprehension of incomplete intelligibility for the concrete universe and the expectation of complete intelligibility for reality.[46] If we affirm the complete intelligibility of reality, then we ground the scientific method and simultaneously move beyond it and the concrete universe to the idea of being and the unrestricted act of understanding that grasps it. And that is what people call, "God."[47]

Is this argument invulnerable? No doubt many barriers arise due to mistaken views about knowing, objectivity, and reality. If people fail to identify the real with being, if they believe that reality contains some admixture of intelligibility and unintelligibility, then to that degree the argument's persuasiveness reduces to defects concerning foundational issues. How do we arrive at knowledge of the real? Once we identify the real with what we attain by intelligent understanding and reasonable affirmation we are not far from grasping the link between God's existence and the complete intelligibility of reality. The vulnerability of the link only attests to the precariousness of intellectual conversion.

Psychic Conversion and Models of God

Our various models of God are not merely ideas. Nor are they simply the creative expressions of profound religious experience and insight. The tendency to regard them in strictly cognitive or intellectual

---

46. Lonergan, *Understanding and Being*, 245; *Insight*, 695.
47. When Aquinas reached this point in his arguments, he said something similar: "and this we call God." His comment emphasizes the continuity between the argument's philosophical notion of God and what we implicitly mean or intend in ordinary speech about God.

terms betrays a truncated self-understanding and problematic conception of theology. The genesis of our models of God requires more than our unrestricted desire for meaning, truth, and value, because our desire always regards *something* sensed or imagined, something we experience. The horizon of our thinking about God depends also on the clarity of our attentiveness. It depends on our ability to receive or form the relevant images, and we often fail because we do not pay attention, we do not listen carefully, or we harbor an entrenched, psychic aversion. Our efforts to understand truly are made all the more difficult if we nonintentionally screen certain images because of disordered attachments or unresolved wounds carried deeply within us. Our models of God are informed by our embodied sensibility in relation to others and our physical environments. In short, they are not kept simply in our heads. Our models of God reflect the totality of who we are; they belong to our bodies too.

Our discussion of psychic conversion in chapter 5 emphasizes the need for theologians to attend to their attentiveness, that is, to undergo the kind of healing that liberates their psyche to more fully participate in their interior orientation to meaning, truth, and value. Of course, this kind of healing happens dramatically with religious, moral, and intellectual conversions; we truly see the world differently when we love unrestrictedly, commit ourselves to genuine value, and appropriate ourselves as knowers; but the psyche's contribution to self-transcendence has a dimension of its own and in turn promotes the other forms of conversion.

Many debates about the varieties of religious art attest to the importance of the psyche for ways of understanding and relating to God. The prohibitions against images of God in Judaism and Islam suggest that the attraction of believers' piety to artistic representations displaces their religious faith onto something less than God: an idol.

Rather than tempt idol worship, the Islamic tradition, for example, has focused its art on geometric patterns and calligraphy that symbolically engage the believer's consciousness, encouraging humility and surrender to the transcendent source of all. Christians have grappled with similar issues, most notably during the iconoclastic controversies of the eighth century and in the sixteenth century with the Reformation. The earlier debates influenced the Orthodox tradition of iconography and its tendency to idealize the beauty of Christ, inviting the believer's gaze into divinizing contemplation of the mystery of God. In each case, religious art plays a significant role in forming desire, cultivating experience, and shaping understanding.

When our theological foundations account for psychic conversion, we gain a fuller, explanatory perspective on the horizon of theology's performance (that is, as an activity of a theologian). By attending to our attentiveness, we heighten our awareness of how our embodied sensibilities constructively inform or perhaps distort our theological insights, judgments, and decisions. Again, religious art helps us to appreciate the dynamics at play here. Such rich images can deeply engage our psychic energy, eliciting different feelings and meanings for different people. Fyodor Dostoyevsky's wife reported that she could barely pull him away from Hans Holbein the Younger's famous painting, *The Body of the Dead Christ in the Tomb* (1521). The image captivated him. And in his novel, *The Idiot*, the painting has very different effects on certain characters, and the effects align with the characters' diverging beliefs and moral habits. Ippolit Terentyev, the young and terminally ill nihilist, describes the painting's jarring portrayal in the course of reading aloud his suicide letter:

> I believe that painters are usually in the habit of depicting Christ, whether on the cross or taken from the cross, as still retaining a shade of extraordinary beauty on his face; that beauty they strive to preserve

even in his moments of greatest agony. In Rogozhin's picture [that is, the Holbein image] there's no trace of beauty. It is in every detail the corpse of a man who has endured infinite agony before the crucifixion; who has been wounded, tortured, beaten by the guards and the people when He carried the cross on His back and fell beneath its weight, and after that has undergone the agony of crucifixion.[48]

For Ippolit, the image of the brutally tortured body, with its gangrenous flesh and slightly open mouth and eyes, juxtaposes more familiar iconic idealizations of Christ. It seems to bury all hope for the resurrection with unforgiving, naturalistic indifference, as he says: "The picture expresses and unconsciously suggests to one the conception of such a dark, insolent, unreasoning and eternal Power to which everything is in subjection."[49] When Myshkin, on the other hand, the novel's "Christ-like" protagonist, comments on the painting in the context of a question about God, he demurs, if almost jokingly: "Why, that picture might make some people lose their faith."[50] For Myshkin, the picture can elicit something despairing, the end of faith, but for Rogozhin, the dark and murderous character who owns the picture, it attracts him. He says that he likes looking at it, and approvingly replies to Myshkin's observation: "That's what it is doing."[51] Each character responds spontaneously, affectively to the image of Christ's dead body according to some resonance with his virtue and beliefs about God.

Of course, this does not imply that the painting communicates a single meaning. The starkness of the brutality can elicit layers of terror and reverence, especially in the context of Western theology's attention to humanity's fall and grave need for redemption. If people respond strongly to the image of the corpse, whatever they believe

48. Fyodor Dostoyevsky, *The Idiot*, trans. Constance Garnett (Hertfordshire: Wordsworth Editions, 1996), 381.
49. Ibid.
50. Ibid., 202.
51. Ibid.

about God and the world, their response illustrates the complexities of the embodied, affective dimensions of their beliefs and values. Here, we can appreciate the importance of psychic conversion: the tendency to conflate the mysteries of faith and the mystery of sin unfolds dramatically in layered, affective engagements with terror and beauty, suffering and transcendence, divinity and death. The therapeutic process of psychic conversion helps us to resolve this confusion.

The artwork of Kaethe Kollwitz offers a striking example of how notions of sacrifice intermingle love and heroism with a glorification of death.[52] Living in Germany during the early twentieth century, the Prussian military culture of her day esteemed the maternal virtue of sacrificing sons for the good of the nation state. But when her youngest son, Peter, joined the German army in 1914 and died a few months later, she went into a deep mourning that gradually led her to recognize the distortive influence of sacrificial ideology on her experience. Kollwitz created a small statue of the *Pietà*, the traditional image of Mary holding the broken body of her son, Jesus. The cultural coopting of the image beautifies the soldier son's death and the virtue of the mother who sacrifices her son for the glory of the Fatherland, but Kollwitz recast the image to subvert the misrepresentation of suffering and the glorification of sacrifice attached to it: "In Kollwitz's *Pietà*, an 'old, lonely, darkly brooding woman' gazes into the face of her lifeless son, tenderly touching his hand as his body collapses back into her own, back into her womb as if she could somehow hold him back from the destructive forces of the world. . . . Here, in Kollwitz's *Pietà*, we face the horror of death rendered in cold, heavy bronze: the beauty and love of

---

52. Our discussion of Kollwitz draws entirely from Jayme M. Hennessy, "The Beauty and Brutality of the Pietà," in *She Who Imagines: Feminist Theological Aesthetics*, ed. Laurie M. Cassidy and Maureen H. O'Connell (Collegeville, MN: Liturgical, 2012), 37–52 (37).

mother and child recast by human brutality into a crumpled figure of grief."[53] Kollwitz resisted the militaristic appropriations of the *Pietà's* religious symbolization, refusing to wed motherhood to sacrificial ideology. Her small sculpture expresses the deep loss of her son, and her "regret for having supported his decision to sacrifice his life for the Fatherland and the sense of desolation, abandonment, betrayal that marked her life as she mourned his death."[54] Her artwork unmasks the ugly reality and horror of war with strong themes of maternal loss and sorrow, and this led Kollwitz to remark of her sculpture: "[M]ine is not religious."[55]

Kollwitz therapeutically reclaimed her genuine experience as a mother, and in her art we see something of that process: confronting and resisting the displacement of beauty onto death. Her art identifies the darkness for what it is, and reminds us of the need for religious art and theology to attend carefully to its sense of beauty. The sensibilities of sacrificial righteousness threaten to blind religion to its complicity in violence at the very points that it should offer resistance. If theology should communicate a life-giving understanding of the Paschal Mystery, then theologians must attain the psychic freedom that allows them to discern the light from the darkness.

Conclusion and a Note on Context

The reflections on God presented in this chapter in no way constitute or represent a developed natural theology or philosophy of God. Rather, they underscore the determinative foundational issues that affect any attempt at those tasks and point the way toward a

---

53. Ibid., 37.
54. Ibid., 47.
55. Entry of December 1939, in Kollwitz, *The Diaries and Letters of Kaethe Kollwitz*, ed. Hans Kollwitz, trans. Richard and Clara Winston (Evanston, IL: Northwestern University Press, 1988), 126; cited in Hennessy, "Beauty and Brutality," 48.

resolution of those issues by means of a set of commitments based in the self-appropriation of the dynamics of conversion. Natural theology and philosophy of God occur in the realm of systematic theology, formally speaking, but their foundations are decided at the level of the theologian's basic horizon. Do I respond to the gift of unrestricted being-in-love within the horizon of consciousness? Do I make genuine value rather than satisfaction the criteria for my decision making? Do I match my criteria for reality with the exigencies for intelligence and reasonability that I experience in all my efforts to know and love? Am I psychically free in my attentiveness to the entire range of my experience, or do I harbor aversions and attachments that impact my ability to listen and attend clearly? The existential answers to these questions unfold over the long process of ongoing personal growth toward authenticity, and they dramatically shape our discourse about God. Not surprisingly, how we think and speak about God changes often over the course of a single lifetime.

Our discourse about God belongs to other contexts as well. Besides the personal, existential context, we can also identify a particular culture's stage of meaning (for example, in the first stage, common sense predominates; in the second, theory and common sense are distinct). Only then can we recognize the genetic relation between Augustine's predominantly descriptive, psychological analogy for understanding divine processions, and the theoretical, explanatory use of the same in Aquinas. It does not help or increase our understanding to fault Augustine for not asking or resolving questions in ways that outstrip his culture's stage of meaning. Similarly, different theologians operate in different realms of meaning, and the failure to distinguish and relate these realms with a differentiated interiority too often results in needless conflicts among various models of God.

There are also social and cultural contexts marked by historical patterns of progress, decline, and redemption, and these contexts and patterns introduce complex layers of variables that must shape our communicative meaning. In other words, when theologians communicate a theology of God to a particular community of faith they must consider the community's history and the forces that shape it. The most profoundly true word spoken about God in a patriarchal context may refer to God as "She."[56] Or in a racist context that "Jesus is black." And these ways of speaking need not imply anthropomorphic images of God or psychological projections upon Jesus.[57] The truth at the socio-cultural level of communications springs from the existential exigency of the gospel to transform the context at the deepest, broadest, and most personal levels. No matter what its cultural matrix, theology must not lose its connection to the liberating force of the gospel. The differentiations that this approach recommends for the various tasks of Christian theology require that we ceaselessly deepen the connection among its religious, moral, intellectual, and psychic dimensions.

56. See, for example, Elizabeth A. Johnson, *She Who Is: The Mystery of God in Feminist Theological Discourse* (New York: Crossroad, 1992), 54–56.

57. For example, James Cone writes: "The 'blackness of Christ,' therefore, is not simply a statement about skin color, but rather, the transcendent affirmation that God has not ever, no not ever, left the oppressed alone in struggle. He was with them in Pharaoh's Egypt, is with them in America, Africa and Latin America, and will come in the end of time to consummate fully their human freedom" (James H. Cone, *God of the Oppressed*, rev. ed. [Maryknoll, NY: Orbis Books, 1997], 126).

7

Revelation and Divine Self-Communication

Since the era of Vatican II, it has become a commonplace to speak of revelation as an act of *divine self-communication*. This terminology, derived from the work of Karl Rahner and adopted by Pope John Paul II, seeks to express the fact that God does not simply communicate various "facts" about God's life and his relationship to us; rather God communicates God's very self to us.[1] God is both the communicator and what is communicated. As Scripture puts it, we have become sharers in the divine nature (2 Pet. 1:4). God communicates something of the divine nature to us in the act of revelation. As the Vatican II's Dogmatic Constitution on Divine Revelation *Dei Verbum* states: "Through divine revelation, God chose to show forth and *communicate Himself* and the eternal decisions of His will regarding the salvation of men. That is to say, He chose to share with them those divine treasures which totally transcend the understanding of the human mind."[2] In this sense, revelation is

---

1. Karl Rahner, *Foundations of Christian Faith: An Introduction to the Idea of Christianity*, trans. William V. Dych (New York: Crossroad, 1982), 116–33. Gerald O'Collins, "The Pope's Theology," *The Tablet*, 27, June 1992.

2. *Dei Verbum*, Dogmatic Constitution on Divine Revelation, n. 6, accessed September 5,

much more than the communication of facts about God. However, in saying this, we are not suggesting that God's communication is without meaning. Indeed, it is the most *meaning-full* communication that can occur, as it is communication from the source of all meaning. Moreover, if we think of revelation as a communication of divine meaning and value into human history, then we can open up a fruitful discussion of revelation in terms of the various categories of meaning we considered in chapter 4 on intellectual conversion. We can ask how this meaning is carried, how it functions, and within which realms of meaning it operates. Because our concern is foundational, we are not looking at specific claims to revelation, to particular doctrinal positions in relation to Scripture (such as inerrancy or inspiration) or Church doctrines (normativity), but at the structures within which such claims can meaningfully be expressed. All such specific claims are themselves doctrines (judgments), which have arisen within various Christian communities. While we shall use our previous discussion on meaning (carriers, functions, etc.) to illustrate their utility for Christian theology, we still prescind from any particular beliefs within Christian faith. Our basic position is that revelation consists of the entry of divine meaning and value into human history, where such meaning and value lie beyond what human beings could grasp or achieve left to their own resources; indeed, divine meaning and value can "totally transcend the understanding of the human mind."[3]

2015 at: http:// www.vatican.va / archive / hist_councils / ii_vatican_council /documents/vat-ii_const_19651118_dei-verbum_en.html.

3. *Dei Verbum*, n. 6; Bernard J. F. Lonergan, "Theology in its New Context," in *Second Collection*, ed. William Ryan and Bernard Tyrrell (Philadelphia: Westminster, 1974), 55–68 (62): "For revelation is God's entry into man's making of man, and so theology not only has to reflect on revelation, but also it has somehow to mediate God's meaning into the whole of human affairs." The limitation on human achievement may be absolute (for example, knowledge of the Trinity) or relative because of human finitude or sinfulness (for example, the existence of God).

How is Revelation Carried?

One of the more influential books, at least in Catholic circles, on the question of revelation is Avery Dulles's work, *Models of Revelation*.[4] In that work, Dulles proposed five models of revelation to be found in the works of major theologians, to which he then added his own model as an integrative proposal. These models were as follows:

- Revelation as *doctrine* (or a propositional model), which he associates with either evangelicals who emphasize Scripture or with Catholics who emphasize Church teaching. This model emphasizes the cognitive content of revelation.

- Revelation as *history*, which he associates with Oscar Cullman.[5] and Wolfhart Pannenberg.[6] It views revelation as given in historical events such as the Exodus or the death and resurrection of Jesus.

- Revelation as *inner experience*, which he associates with mystical authors who present revelation as a direct, immediate and often ineffable experience of the divine.

- Revelation as *dialectic presence*, which he associates with Karl Barth and Hans Urs von Balthasar. This model emphasizes the paradoxical nature of our encounter with the divine (presence and absence) and its power to dismantle all of our existing expectations.

- Revelation as *new awareness*. Here revelation is not about a new object being understood, but a new awareness or change in subjectivity within the person who sees what was always there to be seen in a new light. Here, the emphasis is less on an "objective" revelation as on a "subjective" shift in consciousness.

4. Dulles, *Models of Revelation*.
5. For example, Oscar Cullmann, *Salvation in History* (New York: Harper & Row, 1967).
6. Particularly Wolfhart Pannenberg et al, *Revelation as History* (New York: Macmillan, 1968).

- Revelation as *symbolically mediated*. Drawing on the work of Paul Ricœur and others on the nature of symbols,[7] Dulles suggests that symbolic mediation of revelation captures many aspects of the other models he has considered, while still recognizing that there are some difficulties with his proposal.

Without going into the details of the various models, their strengths and weaknesses, let us rather ask the following question: If revelation is a meaningful communication by God to humanity, how is this meaning carried into human history? The purpose here is not to seek to restrict God to one and only one way or model through which meaning can be carried, but to explore all the ways in which meaning is carried in human communities, and to make connections between these different ways and how theologians have conceived of revelation occurring. God may well choose any or all of these means to communicate Godself to humanity.

Intersubjective Meaning

As we noted in chapter 3, there is the spontaneous intersubjective meaning of a smile or a frown between friends, the intimate gestures of lovers, a fist raised to a foe, and so on. These gestures convey meaning directly and immediately without the need for words or reflection. A smile, a frown, a blush—each reveals a meaning from the one smiling, frowning, or blushing, something very personal and intimate; it is a revelation of who I am to you at this moment in time. They speak of friendship, anger, and desire. Such communication is immediate, but not unambiguous. Is the smile one of friendship genuinely offered, or manipulative? Is the blush secret desire or mere

---

7. For example, Ricœur, *The Symbolism of Evil*.

embarrassment? Such further questions can be answered, though not without further engagement with the one who is communicating.

Can we conceive of God communicating in this fashion? Certainly the Scriptures are full of images suggestive of such communication, of God's friendship, anger, love, and so on, communicated to his chosen people. However, we recognize that such language is metaphorical. God does not literally raise a right hand in anger against us, or smile beneficently down upon us. Nonetheless there may be times when God communicates to us through these gestures expressed by another person. The smile of a friend may well reveal to us the depths of God's love for us; the desire of a lover may reveal God's passionate desire for us, and so on. This possibility is powerfully expressed in the biblical Song of Songs: "Let him kiss me with the kisses of his mouth! For your love is better than wine, your anointing oils are fragrant, your name is perfume poured out; therefore the maidens love you" (Song 1:2-3).

There is something very personal and intimate about such intersubjective meaning, which makes it difficult to "carry" beyond the realm of personal relationship. While we cannot rule out that God can reveal Godself to us in this way, it would remain a very personal form of communication, one that would require significant effort to bring into a more public arena in a way that conveyed a more general meaning.

Artistic Meaning

More public, yet no less personal, is artistic meaning. A work of art expresses the meaning of the artist, not directly, but through the media of color, tone, symmetry, drama, and so on. As with intersubjective meaning, the meaning so generated is elemental and participative. Artistic meaning is elemental inasmuch as it is not distinct from what is meant. To bring it to linguistic expression will require work, engagement, unpacking. Similarly, it is participative, something into which one must enter. It will not yield its meaning to a purely detached observer. Art provokes, challenges, while allowing us to enter into a new world of perspectives and meanings beyond our own. It invites us to view the world as the artist views it, at an affective, imaginative level. New insights can then emerge for us.

Hans Urs von Balthasar has stressed the aesthetic dimension of God's revelatory activity, especially in the drama of salvation.[8] We "reproduce" something of this drama during the Easter Triduum, the liturgical celebration of the Last Supper, the Crucifixion, and the Resurrection of Jesus. The washing of the feet, the celebration of the Eucharist, the solemn reading of the Passion narrative, the lighting of the Easter fire and candle, the proclamation of the resurrection in the Gospel, followed by the initiation (baptism, confirmation, and Eucharist) of the catechumens are an elemental and participative entry into the mystery of salvation.

Perhaps it is clear from these comments that we can well consider artistic carriers of meaning within any account of revelation. God can and—indeed, for Christians—has chosen to communicate Godself to us through artistic carriers of meaning, in the dramatic artistry of the salvation narrative.[9] Still, the particulars of such a judgment pertain to doctrines, not foundations. For our purposes, what we can say is that artistic carriers of meaning would allow for a public carriage of divine meaning into human history.

Symbolic Meaning

The notion of revelation as symbolically mediated has been thoroughly explored by Dulles.[10] Symbols mediate meaning and

---

8. In particular, see Balthasar, *Seeing the Form.*
9. On the dramatic structure of the redemptive narrative, see Schwager, *Jesus in the Drama of Salvation.*

value through their power to transform consciousness. Again, such meaning is elemental and participative. For our purposes, we note that symbols can be personal, communal, or archetypal. While personal symbols may carry divine meaning at a personal level, much like intersubjective meaning, communal and archetypal symbols have a more public and transmissible meaning. Communal symbols may relate to key events or persons within the history of the community, which helped shape its identity. A cross is a powerful symbol of salvation for Christians. Still, this symbol was not immediate; it took centuries before Christians used the cross as a communal symbol because it had such a horrific meaning within the context of the time. Archetypal symbols relate to more universal experiences, birth, maturation, fertility, death, the rhythms of the seasons, and so on. Sometimes our communal symbols can take on an archetypal dimension, as when we celebrate Christmas at the time of the winter solstice, or Easter at the time of the spring equinox, which is reflected in the fertility symbols of new life (for example, rabbits, harvest). Even the name of Easter is derived from a term for fertility.[11]

There is no doubt that God can communicate divine meaning and value through symbols, though the type of symbol is more likely to be communal and/or archetypal than personal, inasmuch as they relate either to the identity of the community or to shared human experiences. However, there is also no reason why we should restrict revelation to symbolically mediated meaning. Symbols are just one carrier of meaning and there is no *a priori* reason why other carriers might not form part of the divine economy of revelation.

Both artistic and symbolic meanings operate at a preconceptual level of consciousness. Such carriers can be powerfully transformative precisely because they shift our consciousness, making available new

10. Dulles, *Models of Revelation*, 131–54.
11. Oestrus and oestrogen have the same linguistic root as Easter.

images and affects, which liberate us to grasp reality in a new way. And so for Christians, the crucifixion frees us to think of God in a new way, not as one who stands over us as a judge, but as one who offers us the gift of love and forgiveness through his only Son. As one of Dulles's models would say, they create within us a "new awareness." Or we might say, they facilitate personal and hopefully a communal conversion toward God, and toward the good, the true, the meaningful and the beautiful. However, such meaning and value is not without its ambiguities. Symbols are multivalent and carry a surplus of meaning, artistic expression requires interpretation and the interpretations may conflict as to what the artist intends, or even if the artist's intention is relevant to the meaning of the work. And so the movement from art or symbol to conceptual or linguistic meaning is fraught with difficulties. Yet, if it is truly God who is revealing Godself to us with a divine purpose of entering into human history, then we certainly cannot preclude the possibility of language also being a carrier of divine meaning.

Linguistic Meaning

The notion of language being a carrier of meaning is most clearly affirmed by what Dulles refers to as the propositional model, or revelation as doctrine. Language offers meaning its greatest liberation. It can be written down and repeated in a variety of situations. It can be used to eliminate the ambiguities present in artistic and symbolic modes of communication. Once meaning is conceptualized in language, it can be debated, discussed, argued, clarified, proclaimed not just in its original context, but in ever new contexts. Written language becomes a repository of a culture, its historical memory, through which its deepest and most banal thoughts can be written down and passed on to others.

Still, linguistic meaning is not all of one type. There is

commonsense meaning expressed in everyday language, literary meaning which employs artistic and symbolic modes of expression, and more technical meaning which aims to be univocal and precise. We can make great errors in our understanding when we confuse these differing modes of expression, for example, when we read commonsense or literary modes as if they are technical modes of expression. We see this in various forms of fundamentalism where the more commonsense and literary modes of Scripture are taken as if they were expressing technical meaning, as if they were scientific or theological texts.

Christians in general have no difficulty in affirming that the Bible consists of divinely communicated meaning. They may disagree as to what this implies in matters such as inerrancy and inspiration, but all would find in the Bible a definitive expression of God's entry into human history. Modern approaches to Scripture recognize that its modes of communication are both commonsense and literary and so scholars have developed a variety of approaches (critical historical, literary criticism, etc.) to transpose the meaning of the text from thought forms common at the time of writing, to more contemporary commonsense and literary expressions which better communicate for us today the meaning the Scriptures express.

More difficult to deal with are the types of expression we find in the teachings of church councils and other authoritative pronouncements. These expressions are not the commonsense and literary expression of the Scriptures. Rather, they aim at a more technical meaning, developing a very specific terminology (such as person, nature, substance) in an attempt to express more precisely the more ambiguous meanings found in the Bible. Can we affirm that God communicates divine meaning through such channels? Certainly, such a possibility cannot be ruled out *a priori*. Assertions that "all religious language is metaphorical," that is, commonsense and/or literary, are just that, assertions, which are impossible to prove within a commonsense frame of meaning. And if indeed the purpose of such teachings is to expound what the Scripture teaches in a more univocal mode then the meanings being taught by Scripture and authoritative teachings can in fact be the same, simply in a different mode of expression. Of course, there are a whole range of questions that need to be asked about any and all such claims at authoritative teachings in a more technical mode, but all these questions call for judgments that relate to questions of doctrine rather than foundations, in this case a doctrine about the nature of doctrine itself. And so the Council of Nicaea is first and foremost a doctrine about the Trinity. However, it creates a new situation, of the church proclaiming a definitive teaching or dogma. In time, this second order process itself becomes subject to doctrinal teaching, specifically on questions concerning the magisterium. Further, most of the difficulties we face in contemporary circles about the claims to authoritative teaching arise from post-Enlightenment issues about religious authority itself rather than intrinsic issues with such a possible mode of divine self-communication.

Historical Meaning

Can we also talk about the meaning of historical events? Certainly, Cullmann and Pannenberg have spoken about revelation as history, whereby certain historical events such as the Exodus or the Resurrection of Jesus are understood as revelatory of God's meaning and purpose in human history. Indeed, a substantial aspect of the Scriptures is a reporting of events in the history of the Chosen People, while the New Testament provides us with four narratives of the events of Jesus' mission, passion, death, and resurrection.[12]

---

12. One of the limitations of the historical model is simply to draw attention to the nonhistorical works of the Bible such as the Wisdom literature and Psalms, which are not historical narratives.

Underlying these narratives are historical events that could be viewed as the primary means through which God communicates to us.

Again, such a possibility cannot be ruled out and we must accept that if God is actively involved in human history, and divine providence orders everything according to divine wisdom, then historical events can act as revelations of God's meaning and purpose. There are however two important observations that need to be made. First, just as other nonlinguistic modes are prone to more ambiguity than linguistic carriers of meaning, so too historical events may require explication. And so in the biblical tradition, the meaning of events is expressed through the words of the prophet who faithfully speaks God's word, in good times and bad, so that God's actions in history can be clearly identified. This shifts our focus from the events themselves to the question of prophetic inspiration and its role in revelation. We shall take up this question below. Of course, a further complexity is that the very act of prophetic interpretation itself becomes part of that historical event and colors the impact of the event on subsequent tradition. This interrelationship between word and deed is well expressed in *Dei Verbum*: "This plan of revelation is realized by deeds and words having an inner unity: the deeds wrought by God in the history of salvation manifest and confirm the teaching and realities signified by the words, while the words proclaim the deeds and clarify the mystery contained in them."[13]

The second observation concerns the very nature of historical events themselves. As Joseph Komonchak has spelled out in some detail, the nature of historical events and their meaning are hard to pin down.[14] The meaning of an event shifts and expands over time. What once was seen as a minor occurrence can take on major

---

13. *Dei Verbum*, n. 2.
14. See his essay, "Vatican II as an Event," in John W. O'Malley et al, *Vatican II: Did Anything Happen?*, ed. David G. Schultenover (New York: Continuum, 2007), 24–51.

significance over time. What once was thought of as central can recede into the shadows only to reemerge at a later time. And so the New Testament proclaimed Jesus as the Jewish messiah, but this receded into the background as Christianity moved into a non-Jewish world, where the notion of a Jewish messiah was not of much interest, only to become more important as Christian communities recovered a sense of God acting in history. The meaning can change in light of the future impact of the event, making it more significant than it originally appeared. Komonchak notes in one of the final footnotes to his essay: "Mao Tse-tung (or was it Chou En-lai?), when asked what he thought of the French revolution, is said to have replied: 'It's too soon to tell.'"[15] John Henry Newman has a similar sense of the expansive nature of revelation over time. And so he views Christianity not as a theory or a collection of documents, but as containing a powerful and great idea capable of inhabiting the human heart and mind for generations: "The increase and expansion of the Christian creed and ritual, and the variations which have attended the process in the case of individual writers and churches, are the necessary attendants on any philosophy or polity which takes possession of the intellect and heart, and has had any wide or extended dominion; . . . from the nature of the human mind, time is necessary for the full comprehension and perfection of great ideas; and . . . the highest and most wonderful truths . . . have required only the longer time and deeper thought for their full elucidation."[16] So too our grasp of the significance of certain historical events often require a "longer time and deeper thought for their full elucidation."

---

15. Ibid., 51n37.
16. John Henry Newman, *Conscience, Consensus, and the Development of Doctrine*, ed. James Gaffney, 1st ed. (New York: Image Books, 1992), 67.

Incarnate Meaning

Whatever else we may say about meaning, its primary locus is not in symbols and works of art, in the written word or historical events. The primary locus of meaning is in the hearts and minds of the human subject. Human beings are the generators of meaning through their experiences, their understandings and judgments of those experiences, and in their decisions that flow from those judgments. Even when we are speaking of the entry of divine meaning and value into human history, still at some point that meaning must be grasped by and carried within human consciousness if it is to be a genuine communication. If this were not the case then how could we say that the divine meaning had actually entered into *human* history? It would be like some alien signal that we could not decipher, which in the end would be a futile exercise, a miscommunication. We have already seen some instances of this issue when we raised questions of inspiration, both in relation to the Scriptural authors and prophetic utterances. Here we can see elements of Dulles's inner experience model, whereby certain individuals have a particular experience of the divine, and the new awareness model, whereby someone experiences a transformation of their consciousness. In more traditional terms, we might speak of mystical experience, grace, and infused wisdom as ways in which divine meaning and value enter into human history.

Such meaning becomes incarnate meaning, the meaning of a human life lived in history, expressing itself through intersubjective, artistic, symbolic, linguistic meaning charged with the very shaping of history itself. In more recent history, people such as Nelson Mandela or Mohandas Gandhi come to mind, as people who powerfully expressed an incarnate meaning that shaped the historical events of their lives and their nations. We can think too of the prophets and saints who have been touched by God and have carried divine meaning and value into the concrete circumstances of their lives. When we consider the life of the prophet, the prophet is one who is touched by God so as to speak God's word. Can we push this to the limit, so that one can be so touched by God as to not only speak God's word, but to be God's Word incarnate? Such a one would truly be the revelation of God in human history. We shall return to this possibility in chapter 8.

Technical Note

We have spoken fairly loosely about the entry of divine meaning and value into human history, but it is a very difficult problem to know how one might conceive of such an entry, that is, to move from a more descriptive statement to a more theoretically precise account. Any such question must first deal with the larger question of how God acts in human history, or in creation more generally. Traditionally, this has been expressed in terms like primary and secondary causation, contingent predication whereby contingent realities may be predicated of God who nonetheless remains transcendent, and the efficacy of divine providence. All of this will involve various theological options concerning our theology of God, which pertain to questions of doctrines (judgments of what is so) and systematics (how we may understand these judgments concerning divine mystery); and such questions lie outside the scope of a work on foundations, though we have touched on them in the previous chapter. However, in chapter 8 we shall consider ways in which the foundations we are developing anticipate certain doctrinal commitments, as we have noted above in relation to incarnate meaning and the possibility of a genuine incarnation of the divine.

How Does Revelation Function?

In chapter 4, we spoke of four distinct functions of meaning: cognitive, effective, constitutive, and communicative. As with the question of how revelation is carried, so too here we can ask how does revelation function? If revelation is the entry of divine meaning and value into human history, what does it achieve, how does it function, what purpose does it serve by that entry? Again, our intention is not to limit revelation to any particular function of meaning, but to identify how revelation may in fact function in different ways and how various theologians have opted to emphasize one or other function in their writings.

Revelation and Cognitive Meaning—Doctrines

The cognitive function of meaning is concerned with what is true, with what is real, with what really is the case. While this is clearly not the only function of meaning to be considered, it is one function which we use in our everyday communication when we want to speak of the weather, the football scores, what we bought at the shops, or in more technical situations as when the scientists at CERN announced the existence of the Higgs boson. It has become less fashionable to speak of religious meaning as true in a cognitive sense, but fashion is not a good guide for theology. Traditionally, it may often have felt as if revelation was solely concerned with cognitive meaning—we must hold these doctrines as true: one God, three persons, transubstantiation, justification by faith, and so on depending upon one's ecclesial affiliation—and so there has been in more recent times a downplaying of this aspect of meaning in the religious sphere so as to emphasize other aspects. But we still must take this function of meaning into account. For example, when John 1:1 says: "In the beginning was the word, and the word was with

God and the word was God," we are entitled to ask what this might mean. Does God have a word and if so in what sense? How can the word be both distinct from God ("with God") and be identified with God ("was God")? Asking such questions leads us on the trajectory that culminated in the Council of Nicaea with its formulation of the doctrine of the Trinity. Of course, we can only ask such a series of questions if we hold that the author of the text intended a cognitive meaning to the text. If the meaning is purely metaphorical, our questioning about the nature of the word that was "with God" and "was God" goes nowhere. Similarly, Paul insists on the reality of the resurrection as grounding Christian hope (1 Cor. 15). While we may struggle to articulate what the resurrection means, as does Paul, to simply deny its existence would seem to be antithetical to the Christian life.

The cognitive meaning of revelation finds its sharpest expression in *doctrines*. Doctrines are judgments about the truth of meanings communicated in divine revelation and received within the community of faith. To assert them as true will also mean asserting other possible meanings, which would negate these true meanings, as false. How such judgments are to be made raises further questions. Whether they are the judgments of individual believers, of gathered bishops at a Council or the pope in Rome are all themselves questions calling for further judgments to be made, and different ecclesial traditions will place the locus of judgment in different places. Moreover, the problem is not a new one, as we can find contestation as to the true meanings to be found in revelation in the New Testament itself. Paul rejects those who reject the resurrection (1 Cor. 15:12-19), while the author of the Johannine letters rejects those who deny that Jesus came in the flesh (1 John 4:2-3).[17] Indeed, the history

17. This seems to be the first reference to what will be called Docetism.

of Christianity is replete with contestation as to the true meanings to be found in revelation. Such contestation would be pointless if revelation were to have no distinctive cognitive meaning.[18] To push the matter further, if revelation is the entry of divine meaning into human history and does have a cognitive meaning, then the struggle over what that meaning is and implies is to be expected. Divine truth will be missed by some and resisted by others: "And this is the judgment, that the light has come into the world, and people loved darkness rather than light because their deeds were evil" (John 3:19). Such conclusions however remain abstract and provide no assistance in the consideration of particular claims and conflicts.

Further difficulties arise when we ask questions about the ongoing normativity of such judgments. Judgments occur in particular times and places, within a certain social and cultural context. Can a judgment made at the Council of Nicaea in 325 CE still have binding force for Christian believers in the twenty-first century? Edward Schillebeeckx expresses the problem thus:

[E]arlier expressions of faith, even dogmas, are on the one hand irrevocable and irreversible: they cannot be done away with, since with a particular social and cultural system of reference they have time and again expressed and sought to safeguard the mystery of Jesus Christ . . . in a way which is sometimes more and sometimes less successful for that time. But on the other hand, in their cultural and historical forms they can become irrelevant and indeed meaningless for later generations as they are simply repeated as they stand, because earlier generations expressed their deepest convictions about Christian faith within another semantic field, in another system of communication, and through a different perspective on reality.[19]

---

18. Of course, this is why some would deny cognitive meaning, as a way of eliminating such contestation in order to be more ecumenically open. But in doing so they would also eliminate the concerns of the New Testament as well.
19. Edward Schillebeeckx, *Church: The Human Story of God*, trans. John Bowden (New York: Crossroad, 1990), 43.

In response, we might distinguish between the context of the meaning and the content of the judgment. A meaning expressed in the past will reflect the thought forms of a previous era and a different culture. And so Nicaea expresses the relationship between the Father and the Son in terms of "consubstantiality." While the meaning may be expressed in unfamiliar terms, the issue of the content of the judgment remains the same. Is the Son divine or a creature? In terms of the content of the judgment, Nicaea asserts that the Son is divine, fully divine, "God from God, light from light, true God from true God." It is the truth of this judgment that can claim to have a normative significance beyond the particularities of place and time, of social and cultural context.

Finally, in relation to the cognitive meaning of revelation, the assertion that revelation has a cognitive meaning goes against the grain of all postmodern claims to the relativity or particularity of truth. Judgments of truth pertain to what is in fact the case, not just for me or for my particular group, but to what is truly the case. In this sense doctrines have a metaphysical content—there *is* a threefold distinction in God; we may use the term 'person' to designate this distinction, but regardless of the terminology such a distinction exists, according to Christian doctrine on the Trinity. If there were no such threefold distinction our doctrine of the Trinity would be false and we would be asserting false things about God. In addition, our worship would be idolatrous.

Of all the functions of meaning, the cognitive function is the one we have most difficulty with in our contemporary setting. It is possible to identify three reasons why this is the case:

1. *The suspicion of tradition engendered by the Enlightenment.* Kant encouraged his readers to "Dare to think" unencumbered by the stale, tired doctrines of the past. In light of the emerging

sciences of the day, religious doctrine provided by comparison a dubious road to truth, replying simply on past "authorities" to argue for its truthfulness. This shift was not just a "faith vs. reason" issue, but also a total recasting of what was meant by reasoning itself. It promoted a form of reasoning in which appeal to authority had no place, with only empirical evidence providing a sound basis for judgment. At stake here are primarily questions of religious and moral conversion and the *value of believing a (religious) tradition.*

2. *The Kantian distinction between the phenomena and the noumena.* Kant's distinction created an unbridgeable epistemological gap between the cognitional activity of the subject and the reality of the object. Cognitional activity becomes projective upon reality, not illuminative of reality. The noumena, the "thing in itself" is unattainable to human knowing. In modern theological circles, this position is usually spoken of in terms of the tension between experience and interpretation, with interpretation viewed as basically a projective activity upon our more basic and fundamental experience.[20] At stake here is a question of intellectual conversion and the *relationship between knowing and reality.*

3. *The emergence of historical consciousness.* One of the great cultural discoveries of the last few centuries has been the discovery of critical history with a concomitant emergence of historical consciousness.[21] This has forced Christianity to review all its beliefs and doctrines in the light of historical reason. This emergence has impacted not only on our understanding of

20. For a good example of this approach, see Edward Schillebeeckx, *Christ: The Christian Experience in the Modern World,* trans. John Bowden (London: SCM Press, 1980), 33–56.
21. See, for example, Bernard J. F. Lonergan, "The Transition from a Classicist World-View to Historical Mindedness," in *A Second Collection,* ed. William F. Ryan and Bernard Tyrrell (Toronto: University of Toronto Press, 1996), 1–9.

Scripture but particularly on our appreciation of doctrine and its ability to bind current belief. The general thrust of this emergence is in fact a Christian commitment to history, as reflected in the incarnation itself, but *it can easily be derailed by the absence of religious, moral, and intellectual conversion.*

Taken together these factors have created a "perfect storm" to marginalize if not outright reject the place of cognitive meaning in relation to revelation.

Revelation and Effective Meaning—Mission

These difficulties with cognitive meaning led some theologians to emphasize other functions of meaning with respect to revelation. One such function is that of effective meaning or what others might call "existential truth." This is "truth," lived truth which directs us to action, to effecting a new reality in the world, through our decisions in line with the (new) values to which we are committed. This is an important reminder that revelation has a purpose, not to convey true but disengaged facts about God, but to transform us so that we may transform the world and ourselves. It is "saving knowledge" rather than "intellectual knowledge." This is made explicit in *Dei Verbum*, which notes that "through divine revelation, God chose to show forth and communicate Himself and the eternal decisions of His will *regarding the salvation of men*" and that the "Gospel . . . is the source of all *saving truth and moral* teaching."[22] Theologian Gregory Baum states it thus: "The Christian message is not information about the divine, to be intellectually assimilated. It is, rather, salvational truth; it raises man's consciousness; it constitutes a new awareness in man through which he sees the world in a new light and commits

---

22. *Dei Verbum*, n. 7.

himself to a new kind of action."[23] This perspective is very important in assisting us to read the Scriptures, for example. What the Bible presents in the opening chapters of Genesis is not scientific information about the origins of the world, which is then to be placed into a debate with the findings of science. Rather, Genesis presents us with saving knowledge about our relationship to God and the rest of creation. Through this saving knowledge, we can more clearly align ourselves with God's saving purpose. As Galileo noted, the Bible teaches us how to go to heaven, not how the heavens go.[24] Similarly, in the New Testament, Jesus reveals to us the mysteries of God's kingdom, not so that we can contemplate them peacefully, but so that we may begin to live as kingdom people, to take up his mission in the world, whatever the personal cost of discipleship may be. And so we can see from this that effective meaning relates to the theological notion of *mission*.

While it should be clear that revelation has an effective function, we can also ask about the relationship between the cognitive and effective functions of meaning. Does the cognitive function need to be fulfilled in order that the effective function operates? Clearly, this is not the case, in that even a clever lie, frequently and forcefully told, can move us to act.[25] Indeed, many human actions would seem to be motivated by untruths—acts of sexism, racism, or homophobia. All forms of fanaticism are either based on untruths or are disproportionate to the truth they may in fact hold. If, however, God is the source of all truth and goodness, both cognitive and

23. Gregory Baum, Foreword to Andrew Greeley, *The New Agenda* (Garden City, NY: Doubleday, 1973), 16.
24. See, for example, the Galileo Project site: http://galileo.rice.edu/sci/theories/copernican_system.html.
25. A lie does not fulfill the cognitive function of meaning. A truth claim is made with a lie, but because the speaker knows that the conditions for claiming truth are unfulfilled in the claim, the cognitive function of meaning is not fulfilled. Lying is different from being wrong in terms of the cognitive function of meaning.

existential truth, then a "saving" truth revealed by God must have some true cognitive content. And so when we read the Book of Genesis, while we may not take as literally true the account of creation there presented, there is a cognitive truth to be asserted, that God truly is the creator of "all things visible and invisible."

At its heart, here is a debate about the relationship between truth and love. Does truth open or close us to love; does love open or close us to the truth? If God is the source of all truth and goodness, then the two cannot be separated, and each opens us up to the other. This was the theme of the encyclical by Benedict XVI, *Caritas in Veritate* ("love in truth") where he notes: "The demands of love do not contradict those of reason. Human knowledge is insufficient and the conclusions of science cannot indicate by themselves the path toward integral human development. There is always a need to push further ahead: this is what is required by charity in truth. Going beyond, however, never means prescinding from the conclusions of reason, nor contradicting its results. Intelligence and love are not in separate compartments: *love is rich in intelligence and intelligence is full of love.*"[26] This is an important reminder that we cannot separate out the two functions without mutual damage. While the recognition of the effective function of revelation is an important advance, it cannot be made at the expense of the cognitive function of revelation.

Revelation and Constitutive Meaning—Tradition

Another type of proposal that has emerged in the writings of George Lindbeck is one that focuses on the constitutive meaning of revelation. Rather than having a cognitive meaning with metaphysical import, Lindbeck views doctrine, for example, as a

---

26. Encyclical, *Caritas in Veritate*, On Integral Human Development in Charity and Truth, n. 30 [emphasis in the original], accessed September 5, 2015 at: http://w2.vatican.va/content/benedict-xvi/en/encyclicals/documents/hf_ben-xvi_enc_20090629_caritas-in-veritate.html.

form of cultural-linguistic expression that is constitutive of a form of religious life.[27] Throughout his work, he compares and contrasts a cognitional, propositional understanding of religion and doctrines (basically, the cognitive function of meaning), and an experiential-expressivist model (with a focus on the effective function of meaning) with his own preferred account, which is a cultural-linguistic understanding of religion and doctrine.[28] The cultural-linguistic approach steps back from the metaphysical claims of the cognitive approach. Rather than doctrines being truth claims with some metaphysical reference to God, they become linguistic and grammatical rules with only an intrasystemic significance. Different religions have different doctrines, but this need have no more significance than different road rules applying in different countries. Religions are different in the same way that cultures and languages are different. They do not share fundamental principles or foundations; they are basically incommensurable.[29]

While this approach may be attractive to someone wanting to eliminate any possibility of cognitive disagreement between differing religious traditions, it is not at all clear that those traditions would like to see their claims regarding revelation or ultimate meaning to be stripped of any metaphysical significance whatsoever. Critics of the cultural-linguistic approach would claim that the end result is cultural and religious relativism and religious indifference. More seriously, it seems to limit or preclude the possibility of God actually communicating Godself to human beings through some form of cognitive meaning. This preclusion is more a result of the impact of Enlightenment prejudice against revealed religion than any deep insight into God's operation in the world. Its endpoint is Deism, a

---

27. See his seminal work, Lindbeck, *The Nature of Doctrine*.
28. We should note that Lindbeck does not adopt this terminology, but it basically correlates with his categories.
29. Lindbeck, *The Nature of Doctrine*, 63–72.

God who creates the world but ceases to interact meaningfully with it.

On the other hand, one cannot ignore the fact that revelation does exercise a constitutive function in that it grounds, indeed creates, the identity of a religious community. The Christian community was constituted as a community through its shared experiences, understandings, judgments, and decisions relating to the person of Jesus (faith in Jesus as savior). These experiences were those of the first disciples of Jesus, who not only shared his ministry and mission but experienced him as the Risen Lord. These experiences were prolonged liturgically and communally through the sharing of the Lord's Supper and the preaching of the apostles. The shared understandings and judgments that arose from these experiences were articulated through shared communications (epistles) and writings (gospels), leading to a shared form of ethical and religious life together. To be a member of the community is to share in all these things. The shared judgments in particular set the boundaries of the community. To come to a different judgment of the meanings that constitute the community is no longer to be a member of that community, unless and until the judgments of the community as a whole change. In this sense, Lindbeck is correct in that the shared judgments of the community are like a grammar or set of rules that define the "linguistic" boundaries of that community.

It should also be clear that the constitutive function of meaning is the primary function that operated for many in the Christian community, and is perhaps what initially creates the community. What was first and foremost for the early disciples of Jesus was their faith in him. That constituted their identity, as followers of "the way" (Acts 9:2). They were the "Jesus team" or as they were called, Christ-ians (Acts 11:26). The cognitive judgments (doctrines) and effective significance (mission) would only be unpacked in due course, often over centuries. For example, Christians were baptized into the threefold name (Matt. 28:19) long before they were able to articulate exactly what that might imply, with some clarity at the Councils of Nicaea (325 CE) and Constantinople (381 CE).

Moreover, this constitutive function of meaning makes revelation effective in human history. Because revelation constitutes a human community, that community is charged with a responsibility to carry revealed meaning forward into history, to become the community which takes as its special responsibility to care for the wellbeing of that meaning as it faces the challenges of misunderstanding and misrepresentation, of counter-judgments and denials, that inevitably arise as the community moves forward, encountering other forms of meaning, other systems of thought and ways of life that may or may not be compatible with their own. If these communities are in fact the carriers of the entry of divine meaning and value into human history, then this responsibility is nothing less than a sacred task. To fail in this task would be to render divine revelation ineffective in its historical purpose.

From this we can see that the constitutive function of meaning gives us something like the theological notion of *tradition*. Already in the New Testament Paul can talk about handing on what he himself was given:

> For I handed on to you as of first importance what I in turn had received: that Christ died for our sins in accordance with the Scriptures, and that he was buried, and that he was raised on the third day in accordance with the Scriptures, and that he appeared to Cephas, then to the twelve. Then he appeared to more than five hundred brothers and sisters at one time, most of whom are still alive, though some have died. Then he appeared to James, then to all the apostles. Last of all, as to someone untimely born, he appeared also to me. (1 Cor. 15:3-6)

Indeed, he goes on: "If there is no resurrection of the dead, then

Christ has not been raised; and if Christ has not been raised, then our proclamation has been in vain and your faith has been in vain" (1 Cor. 15:13–14). However, what is clear from this is that constitutive meaning is also open to contestation. This contestation arises because there is a genuine distinction between the meanings and values that empirically constitute the community at any given point in time, and the meanings and values that constitute its normative identity.[30] The early Christian community was constitutively Jewish, if we were only to consider the matter empirically. Whether this was to be normative for the community was a matter of contestation as we see in the clash between Paul and Peter in the New Testament. Such clashes will often involve questions of cognitive meaning (What is the truth about Jesus?) and effective meaning (What is our mission that arises out of Jesus?), which then can create a possible shift in the empirical constitutive meaning of the community (Gentiles did not need to become Jewish to become Christian). Here, we might recall a comment by Kathryn Tanner: "Whether or not culture is a common focus of *agreement*, culture binds people together as a common focus for *engagement*."[31] The constitutive meaning (tradition) of the community is a common focus for engagement, hence contestation, which binds the community together because they have a common commitment to the value of the tradition itself.

As with effective meaning, we can ask about the relationship between constitutive meaning and cognitive meaning. Must constitutive meaning be grounded in cognitive meaning? Clearly, the answer given to this question by Lindbeck is no, because for him the cognitive claims of revelation are absorbed entirely by the constitutive function of meaning—that is, their cognitive meaning

30. This is commonly referred to as a distinction between tradition and Tradition. The first is empirically given; the second is normative.
31. Kathryn Tanner, *Theories of Culture: A New Agenda for Theology* (Minneapolis: Fortress Press, 1997), 57.

has no metaphysical reference. Indeed, I could be a member of the Jesus team without making metaphysical claims about him, such as claims to divinity. However, I could just as easily be a member of the Buddha team or the Confucius team or even a member of multiple teams. Do we need to take the next step and make cognitive claims about Jesus' divinity? Or are such claims simply misplaced enthusiasms on our part? Clearly, we must here deal with the historical fact that such judgments have been made in the past and have acted constitutively for the Christian community ever since. The cognitive significance of the claim has been explored in our Christologies and Trinitarian theologies for centuries and found to possess an amazing intellectual coherence. We should be slow to dismiss these cognitive claims. Again, we would note that most of our difficulties with cognitive claims to revelation arise from factors identified above. In particular, Lindbeck's position, for example, relies heavily on Kantian presuppositions about the relationship between *noumena* and *phenomena*, which exclude the possibility of metaphysical truth, a position incompatible with intellectual conversion.

Revelation and Communicative Meaning—Kerygma

While above we have spoken of constitutive meanings as creative of human communities, we should not overlook the role of communication in the process. Without communicative meaning, any meaning would remain within the originator of meaning, grasped within a single mind and heart, but not shared with another person or community. In communicative meaning, one seeks to communicate to another person by adopting intersubjective, artistic, symbolic, linguistic, and (perhaps most of all) incarnate meaning to "speak" in a way that the other can best hear. For communicative meaning to be heard the speaker must be sensitive to the context of the listener, personally, socially, and culturally. Communicative meaning is always contextual. However, this is not to say that the meaning intended is bound by the immediate or proximate context. The meaning intended may well transcend the present context, but the form of communication needs to communicate to people here and now.

Communicative meaning will relate to the other functions of meaning as well, indeed is necessary for that meaning to be communicated successfully. A good speaker will know that actions (*effective* meaning) speak louder than words and that a good listener will expect personal authenticity, as incarnate meaning, to be the ultimate guarantor of the truthfulness (*cognitive* meaning) of what is communicated. A good speaker not only speaks to an audience but creates an audience (*constitutive* meaning) who wants to listen and to carry forward what is being communicated. For this reason, we can link the communicative function of meaning in relation to revelation to the theological notion of the *kerygma*.[32] This term relates to the actual proclamation or preaching of the revealed message.

Communicative and constitutive meaning together are fundamental to theological notions, such as tradition, infallibility, and the *sensus fidei*, because it is through these two functions of meaning in relation to revelation that the meaning of revelation is carried forward in human communities over historical timeframes.[33]

32. The notion of kerygmatic theology can be found in the writings of C. H. Dodd, and particularly C. H. Dodd, *The Apostolic Preaching and Its Developments* (New York: Harper & Brothers, 1936).

33. It is worth noting that the concept of the *sensus fidei* first came to prominence in John Henry Newman, *On Consulting the Faithful in Matters of Doctrine* (London: G. Chapman, 1961). This book originally appeared in 1859, but was out of print until 1961, though a German translation was available during that period. The concept was taken up at Vatican II and has become a standard theological concern since that time. See Ormond Rush, *The Eyes of Faith: The Sense of the Faithful and the Church's Reception of Revelation* (Washington, DC: Catholic University of America, 2009).

Constitutive meaning binds the community together as shared or common meaning. Communicative meaning ensures that the message is passed on to its new members, both those brought into the community and those raised within it. Through the communication of shared experiences, meanings, judgments, and decisions, members are formed into the identity of the community, and to the extent that each member carries the meaning within them, they develop a sense of what is authentic to that identity and what is inauthentic. Again, if we are speaking of a divine revelation, the ways in which meaning is carried within the community take on theological significance and are part of the process of revelation. Every generation is charged with the sacred responsibility of both receiving and passing on the meaning of revelation: first, to receiving from those who have gone before who bear witness to the originating revelatory events; and then, to pass on that meaning to a new generation. Teaching and learning go hand in hand, for what is not learned cannot be taught. Both teaching and learning are part of the overall process of revelation and so have theological significance within an overarching safeguard of divine providence. Newman captures beautifully the complexity of the process of both receiving and passing on the tradition through multiple carriers of meaning thus:

> [T]he body of the faithful is one of the witnesses to the fact of the tradition of revealed doctrine, and . . . their *consensus* through Christendom is the voice of the Infallible Church.
>
> I think I am right in saying that the tradition of the Apostles, committed to the whole church in its various constituents and functions *per modum unius*, manifests itself variously at various times: sometimes by the mouth of the episcopacy, sometimes by the doctors [that is, theologians], sometimes by the people, sometimes by liturgies, rites, ceremonies, and customs, by events, disputes, movements, and all other phenomena which are comprised under the name of history. It follows that none of these great channels of tradition may be treated with disrespect; granting at the same time fully, that the gift of discerning,

discriminating, defining, promulgating, and enforcing any portion of that tradition resides solely in the *Ecclesia docens* [teaching Church].[34]

Does the Meaning of Revelation Develop?

Usually, this question would be explored under the heading of the development of doctrine. However, stating it in these terms allows for a more nuanced account of the issue. If we focus on one particular function of meaning, such as the cognitive function, then we risk a genuine distortion of the issues involved. For example, it is often stated that Vatican II introduced no new doctrines, as if that were the only issue at stake. While this may be true, it ignores the fact that there were significant changes in effective, constitutive, and communicative meanings within the life of the church. The fact that cognitive meanings did not change is only one part of the picture. However, even if we remain within the scope of cognitive meanings, we know that every doctrine has a history; we know something of its context, the conflicts that led to its promulgation, and the history of its reception within the church. How are we best to understand claims to a definitive revelatory event in the light of such clear historical evidence of doctrinal development? One of the greatest writers on this topic of doctrinal development, John Henry Newman, compared revelation to a big idea, the implications of which must then be unpacked over generations. He went on to posit five distinct trajectories for such unpacking, giving a clear indication that doctrinal development was not a "one-size fits all" account but requires attention to the historical particularities of each such claimed development. He also recognized that not all change is progress and so he developed seven criteria for determining the authenticity of any historical development.[35] All of these observations are simply to

34. Newman, *Consulting the Faithful*, 63.

remind us that any account of the question of development will be complex.

If we consider the foundational events of Christianity, we must first take into account the background of Jewish history, literature, and spirituality within which it finds its meaning. These act as remote preparation for the meaning of Christian revelation, so that this new meaning may find a context, a home, so that it is not just a bolt from the blue, without the needed preparation for its reception. The revelation itself is a historical event with *symbolic, artistic,* and *literary* components, but most of all the claimed incarnate meaning of Jesus Christ himself is central to the revelation that grounds Christianity. In particular, the doctrinal claims that Christianity will make about Jesus would imply that his is the definitive entry of divine meaning and value into human history, because he is in some sense divine meaning and value himself. While we might well acknowledge the ontological priority of this *incarnate meaning* as the basic source of Christian revelation, in terms of what we first encounter the priority lies with the *intersubjective, artistic,* and *symbolic* meanings Jesus communicated (*communicative* meaning) through his relationships with his disciples and the teachings he gave, and the *historical events* (*historical* meaning) that he was part of. These meanings were *elemental,* in that they were not given conceptually, and were meanings which those to whom meaning was communicated needed to participate in to "get the point." Clearly, all that happened to the first followers of Jesus had enormous significance for them, but their articulation of this (*linguistic* meaning) in letters (epistles) and narratives (Gospels) could only begin to express all that the revelatory events contained. These articulations included *cognitive, effective, constitutive,* and *communicative* components.

35. For a summary of these five trajectories and seven criteria, see Ormerod, "Vatican II—Continuity or Discontinuity?," esp. 614–20.

Development can occur then in all these different functions of meaning. There can be developments in cognitive meaning as the full significance of the original revelatory events, given as elemental meaning, are unpacked conceptually, allowing for more and clearer judgments to be made as to what is implied by that revelation. Those original events remain foundational and may be judged to constitute the content of revelation, while the unpacking that occurs must always stand in some direct relationship to that foundation. Nonetheless, the range of implications may grow over time as insights grow on insights and an ever-deeper appreciation of the significance of that original revelation occurs. There can be shifts in effective meaning as well. The nature and extent of the mission that emerges from revelation will also grow over time. For example, over a period of centuries the implications of the incarnation for human dignity can lead us to conclude that this dignity is incompatible with the institution of slavery. This was not immediately obvious, but that awareness did grow over time. As such the scope of the mission grew. We can see a similar thing happening now in relation to the environmental issue. Christians are now beginning to realize that the scope of Christian mission extends to protection of the natural environment. Similarly there are shifts in communicative meaning as the intended audience changes with different cultures and languages, levels of education, technological achievements, and so on. What once communicated effectively begins to look dated, perhaps a quaint throwback to the past. It not only no longer communicates effectively, but also is in danger of miscommunicating, of communicating the wrong message, for example, that to believe the message one must live in the past.

However, perhaps the most difficult question to work through is that of shifts in revelation's constitutive meaning for the community. Here, as we noted above there is a tension between the present empirical constitutive meanings of the community and the normative constitutive meanings. Empirically, the early Christian community was constituted as a largely Jewish community, still attending the synagogue and the Temple and observing the Jewish law. Paul argued that the significance of the revelatory events around Jesus could not be contained within Judaism as it was then constituted. The place of the law, and circumcision in particular, became a point of contention within the community. Was the Jewish law constitutive of Christian identity or not? There were no clear answers, no sayings of Jesus they could refer to, no authority to appeal to, which would settle the question. The example sets something of a pattern for the history of the church. Disagreements arise over questions of cognitive and effective meanings that are constitutive of the community's identity. New meanings may be proposed, but are they really implied by the original revelatory events? And how are these disputes to be settled? In the end, an answer to this question is an ecclesial doctrine, that is, one which reflects on the church's own performance in settling such disputes.

Why do such disagreements occur? This is the question Newman raised in relation to the different trajectories of doctrinal development. We shall identify two major trajectories without seeking to be exhaustive. The first is the deepening of cultural resources that occurs over time. In particular, a culture may begin to develop a greater control of meaning evident in the growth of technical language, such as philosophy or science. This greater control of meaning allows for more precise questions to be asked, which then necessitates the need for more precise answers. This development of a more technical control of meaning allows for new judgments (doctrines) to occur which would in some cases be unintelligible to an earlier stage of cultural development (and to anyone unfamiliar with the technical language involved). We can see something of this happening in the new doctrines that emerge in the late Middle Ages around the sacraments, all formulated in a more precise metaphysical language made possible by the impact of Aristotelian philosophy on the theology of the day. While these may be genuine developments in cognitive meaning, their effective and constitutive meaning may be lost without good communication. There is also the shift that occurs when one attempts to transpose the meaning of revelation into a completely new setting with a whole different set of cultural assumptions and historical background. The first example of this was the transposition into the Greco-Roman world as the church moved beyond being a Jewish sect and became a transcultural movement. The same story unfolds whenever the Christian message is preached in a new cultural setting. How do we know that the transpositions we attempt faithfully communicate the significance of the original revelation?

To answer this question Newman developed seven criteria for evaluating the genuineness of doctrinal developments:[36]

1. *Preservation of type*: a criterion based on an organic metaphor of bodily growth, in which "the basic proportions and relationships existing between the whole and the parts" is preserved.

2. *Continuity of principles*: as when new insights and judgments arise out of a fixed set of principles; "The different doctrines represent principles existing at a deeper level, even when these are often not recognized until a later stage."

3. *Power of assimilation*: an ability to adapt to and embrace new perspectives leading to new developments: "a living idea shows

---

36. We draw here both from Newman and the work of the International Theological Commission, "The Interpretation of Dogma," *Irish Theological Quarterly* 56, no. 4 (1990): 251–77. It is significant that the ITC, in seeking to address the question of doctrinal development, could do no better than refer to work done by Newman over a century before. It is a testament to the quality of his contribution.

its edge by its ability to get at reality, attract other ideas to itself, stimulate reflection and develop itself further without loss of its internal unity."

4. *Logical sequence*: though not a great devotee of logic in itself, Newman acknowledges it too may play a role in accounting for the development of doctrine.[37]

5. *Anticipation of its future*: "[T]rends which come to realization and succeed only later may make themselves noticeable early on, even if as isolated phenomena where the outline is still dim." These trends are likely to be genuine.

6. *Conservative action upon its past*: where developments go against the grain of earlier positions they are not likely to be genuine but corruptions; on the other hand "true development conserves and safeguards the developments and formulations that went before."

7. *Chronic vigor*: ongoing vigor and duration are themselves signs of genuine development, whereas corruptions either burn out quickly or lose life in the longer term. "Whatever is vital and durable . . . is a sign of authentic development."

While these criteria are a useful heuristic for the genuineness of development, there is always the question of who applies them. In the end, one cannot escape the subjectivity of the one drawing the conclusions from the criteria. In other words, we cannot escape from the question of religious, moral, intellectual, and psychic conversions, and their presence or absence in the one who seeks to apply any criteria whatsoever. Only where conversion in all its dimensions is present can we have confidence not only in any proposed

---

37. The ITC overstates the case when it says that there "must be logical coherence between the conclusions and the initial data." Newman's position is closer to "there must not be logical incoherence between conclusions and the initial data." More precisely he states: "The question indeed may be asked whether a development can be other in any case than a logical operation; but, if by this is meant a conscious reasoning from premises to conclusion, of course the answer must be in the negative" (Newman, *Conscience, Consensus, and the Development of Doctrine*, 188).

development, but also in those who would pass judgment on those proposed developments.

Conclusion

Revelation is one of the more significant categories we need to consider in our account of theological foundations. How we understand revelation, how it can possibly operate in human history, the nature of its impact and transmission—all require close attention to the categories of meaning we developed in chapter 4. Nonetheless, our discussion remains at a fairly general level and could be applicable in any religious context, not just Christian. We have prescinded from particular claims about the content of revelation, revelation's completion and closure, its relationship to the Scriptures, the question of the canon itself, and so on. All such questions require particular doctrinal judgments leading to a systematic exposition. They thus belong to a different phase of the theological project.

On the other hand, as can be grasped from the discussion above, there is a certain sense in which our use of the categories of meaning to explicate the notion of revelation anticipates many classical theological themes in relation to that topic. Indeed, sound foundations anticipate the sorts of doctrinal commitments and theological expositions that are the stock and trade of Christian theology. We shall explore this further in the next chapter where we consider the ways in which our foundations anticipate doctrinal commitments in relation to the Trinity, the Incarnation, and the Church.

8

Heuristic Anticipation of Doctrines

Trinity, Christology, and Ecclesiology

The task of foundations is not to preempt doctrines, but at the same time, sound foundations provide heuristic anticipations of doctrines, especially as these foundations emerge out of dialectical conflicts of interpretations of the history of doctrinal development. Without actually coming to the point of making a judgment, one can argue for the congruence of foundational categories with key doctrines such as Trinity, Incarnation, and Church. Many of the questions about the reasonableness of central doctrines are taken up in traditional fundamental theology, but in the form of apologetics and emphasizing credibility. Here, the goal is more modest, to show how foundations can be utilized to anticipate certain doctrinal stances. For example, using the category of incarnate meaning in relation to revelation allows us to ask whether there can be a definitive entry of divine incarnate meaning in human history, and what this might imply historically (that is, for the nature of the church).

Throughout this work, we have attempted to prescind from particular doctrines, except where they may help us illustrate the significance of foundational questions in theology. Within the conception of foundations in which this work operates, we seek to provide the needed foundations for the work of doctrinal and systematic theology, and in this chapter we will discuss how these foundational categories provide an anticipatory framework for doctrines and systematics. We can find a similar process at work in Karl Rahner's book, *Foundations of Christian Faith*, whereby his transcendental method provides anticipatory structures for doctrines in Christology and ecclesiology.[1] As Rahner puts it, "A keyhole forms an *a priori* law governing what key fits in, but it thereby discloses something about the key itself."[2] Thus, foundations form the keyhole into which the doctrines properly fit. The more complete our foundations, the better the fit will be. Or, in other words, if grace always completes and perfects nature, then we can anticipate heuristically something about the supernatural by understanding the world and ourselves (that is, nature). We can also note that books in fundamental theology often present an apologetics, seeking to defend particular church doctrines, by noting their "reasonableness" or perhaps more accurately provide a *praeambula fidei*, as a form of a heuristic anticipation of various doctrines.[3]

And so in this work too we shall seek to demonstrate the ways in which the foundations we have been developing anticipate certain Christian doctrines. The three areas we shall explore are doctrines in relation to the Trinity, Incarnation, and Church. One could extend this list to other areas, such as grace and sacraments, but it is not our purpose to cover all aspects here, merely to indicate how this anticipatory process might work. Further, these three doctrinal areas

1. Karl Rahner, *Foundations of Christian Faith*.
2. Ibid., 19.
3. O'Collins distinguishes the role of fundamental theology and apologetics, though historically they often merged. See Gerald O'Collins, *Rethinking Fundamental Theology*. Certainly, we do not put this material forward as a rationalist apologetic or defense of Christian beliefs. It clearly builds on religious conversion. But it seeks to indicate how the various conversions incline us toward certain doctrinal positions.

relate most directly to the previous chapter where we discussed the notion of revelation.

Divine Self-Communication and the Doctrine of the Trinity

Karl Barth recognized that there is a strong connection between the way in which we understand revelation and the doctrine of the Trinity. For Barth, the two doctrines of Trinity and Revelation form a connected pair: revelation itself has a Trinitarian structure, and in turn the Trinity is communicated in the very process of revelation. God (as Revealer) spoke God's Word (as Revelation) and God's Word is not less than God. God's Word is God. And in order that we hear the Word of God as God's Word and not reduce it to a merely human word, God's Spirit (as Revealedness) enables us to hear God's Word as truly God's Word: "God's Word is God Himself in His revelation. For God reveals Himself as the Lord and that according to Scripture signifies for the concept of revelation that God Himself is unimpaired unity yet also in unimpaired difference is Revealer, Revelation and Revealedness."[4] In a similar way, Karl Rahner draws an intimate connection between the idea of divine self-communication and belief in the Trinity. Essentially, Rahner's argument is that only a Trinitarian God can be a self-communicating God: "The differentiation of the self-communication of God in history (of truth) and spirit (of love) must belong to God 'in himself,' or otherwise this difference, which undoubtedly exists, would do away with God's self-communication. For these modalities and their differentiation either are in God himself . . . or they exist only in us, they belong only to the realm of creatures as effects of the divine creative activity."[5]

Both Rahner and Barth recognized a connection between

4. Karl Barth, *Church Dogmatics*, 1/1:339.
5. Karl Rahner, *The Trinity*, trans. Joseph Donceel (New York: Herder and Herder, 1970), 99–100.

Trinitarian doctrine and the belief that God enters the world of human affairs in a profoundly personal way. We shall now pursue this line of argument, using the categories we have been developing in the foregoing chapters. In the previous chapter we drew attention to technical issues around the phrase, "the communication of divine meaning and value," which formed the basis of our understanding of revelation. It is now time to explore what this might mean and what it might imply about God.

Of course, if God is the source of all meaning, truth, and value, then God could communicate all sorts of meanings and values to human beings, things such as scientific and mathematical truths, or about economics and sociology. Undoubtedly, these would be interesting and useful, but in general they are things that left to our own resources, we could, given time, work out for ourselves. And while there may be advantages in knowing "ahead of time," that is, before we can establish it ourselves (that string theory is a good theory to unify gravity with quantum mechanics) there is also something good and noble about working it out for ourselves.[6]

When it comes to moral truths, truths about the meaning and purpose of human living, the matter is more difficult. Here, despite centuries of moral theorizing, there is no consensus about what constitutes human flourishing, to such an extent that many would say there is no single answer, and that everyone needs to find their own path toward flourishing; this stance is commonly expressed in Western liberal societies. On the other hand, some religious persons argue that God establishes a normative mode of human flourishing, which is congruent with human reason (properly informed), even if we generally fail to grasp it because of our human sinfulness.[7] Still,

---

6. For a popular account of string theory, see Brian Greene, *The Elegant Universe: Superstrings, Hidden Dimensions, and the Quest for the Ultimate Theory* (London: Jonathan Cape, 1999). At present, the predictions of string theory cannot be empirically tested.

we could work out most of this existential truth, if not all, given the right disposition (moral conversion), and so this truth remains in principle within our grasp. Neither of these forms of communication (scientific and moral truths) constitutes divine meaning and value per se; their source may be divine, but their contents remain naturally knowable. Strictly speaking, in relation to the communication of these truths, God does not communicate Godself to us and we do not become partakers of the divine life. Such communications remain in the natural realm of the creature-Creator relationship.

The theological issue at stake here is what is referred to as the *grace-nature distinction*. Traditionally, grace is spoken of as healing and elevating. Our concern here is not with the healing aspect of grace, important though that is in a theology of sin and grace, but the notion of grace as elevating.[8] What might it mean to speak of grace as elevating? In the terms above, we may start by focusing on the creature-Creator relationship. This relationship defines our existence.[9] One way for our existence to be elevated beyond what we currently are would be for God to change this relationship with us, by adding something new which builds upon what is already given to us in our humanity. We could conceive, for example, that God could choose to communicate to us through the mediation of a higher order of creature, for example an angel, who could communicate meanings and values to us which transcend human understanding, but which for that creature are simply part of its own natural knowledge. We might think of this as relatively supernatural, in that it is supernatural for us, but not necessarily for the creature

---

7. Traditionally, original sin entails a weakening of the will and darkening of the mind. For a contemporary account, see Neil Ormerod, *Creation, Grace and Redemption*.

8. For a fuller account of grace and sin, see ibid. For a technical account of grace as elevating, see Christiaan Jacobs-Vandegeer, "Sanctifying Grace in a 'Methodical Theology'," *Theological Studies* 68, no. 1 (2007): 52–76.

9. Though as we have noted in chapter 5, such relationships do not define God's existence.

involved. Again, it would be a case of God being the communicator, but not being the content of the communication. Given the widespread belief in angels as mediators of divine communication (in fact in the Old Testament an angel is nothing but a communicator of a divine message; in the New Testament, see Heb. 2:2), this possibility should not be dismissed, even if it is not what we mean by divine *self*-communication.

The question then remains: Is it possible for God to enter into a new type of relation with us that is not simply relatively supernatural for us, though natural for some other type of creature, but one which is absolutely supernatural—that is, which transcends all possibility of merely creaturely existence, while maintaining our creaturely status? One way, and perhaps the only way, we can conceive of such a new type of relation between God and his creatures is if there are internal relations within the Godhead itself, as Rahner notes in the passage above. If there are such internal relations, then it may be possible for us to relate to God through some form of created participation of those internal relations. This would establish a new relation between God and the creature that in some sense imitates the intradivine relations.[10] The question then is: Do such internal relationships exist within God? And if so, what are they?

Of course, Christian belief in the Trinity provides such a structure of internal relations: of Father to Son (paternity) and Son to Father (filiation); of Father and Son to the Spirit (active spiration) and the Spirit to the Father and Son (passive spiration). Given these internal relations, we may conceive of the possibility of our participating in these relations as a genuine sharing in the divine life. The divine relations are the conditions for the possibility of a created imitation

---

10. Technically, this would be a form of exemplary causality whereby the intradivine relations form the basis of an analogous relationship between God and the creature, so that there is a real yet created participation in the divine life. See Neil Ormerod, "Addendum on the Grace–Nature Distinction." *Theological Studies* 75, no. 4 (2014): 890-98.

of these relations in the created order. So the notion of divine self-communication in this context implies that we participate in these internal relations, and by this participation we become partakers of the divine nature. In such circumstances, we can talk about the genuine entry of divine meaning and value into history, which is not achieved through some intermediary but constitutes a genuine sharing in the divine nature.[11]

The argument that a genuine divine self-communication requires internal divine relations brings us very close to the position of Barth and Rahner. For both these theologians, the doctrine of the Trinity was "in possession," that is, their reflections on revelation and its connection to the Trinity occurred within the framework of an established belief in the Trinity. Our position is slightly different in that we have not yet come to the point of affirming a doctrine of the Trinity and likewise our discussion of revelation prescinds from any claim to revelation having occurred. And so the relationship between a genuine divine self-communication and possible intradivine relationships must per force be more vague. As we can see, from the preceding paragraph, once we come to the point of making an affirmation of the doctrine of the Trinity, this can be made more precise and we can establish a more fully developed theology of revelation, not just foundations for such a theology.

While an affirmation of the existence of such internal relations takes us into the arena of doctrines rather than foundations, we can push our anticipatory exploration further through a consideration of the categories of meaning and value. Can we anticipate how such distinctions within the Godhead might arise? This would then constitute an anticipation of or foray not just into doctrines but also into systematics. We could argue as follows: God is the source

---

11. For a fuller exposition of this argument, see Ormerod, "Addendum on the Grace–Nature Distinction."

of all meaning and value, and is the most meaningful and valuable reality. As the fullness of meaning, God is both the source of meaning (meaning as intending) and the meaning expressed (meaning as intended). These are two different *modes* of meaning, which, given divine simplicity, cannot be distinct realities in God.[12] However, at the level of speculation or systematics these two modes might allow for an analogous grasp of how God can be both Speaker and Spoken, or as the biblical witness notes:[13] "In the beginning was the Word, and the Word was with God, and the Word was God" (John 1:1).

We could push this further to speak of the different modes that arise in relation to divine value, with God as the source of value and highest value, or the source of love and most lovable, so that together with our suggestions in relation to meaning, we can understand Rahner's argument that "the differentiation of the self-communication of God in history (of truth) and spirit (of love) must belong to God 'in himself'."[14] These observations can ground an approach to the Trinity known as the psychological analogy, first developed by Augustine in *De Trinitate*, and further refined by Aquinas in the *Summa Theologiae*. There, we find in the first question of the *Summa* to deal with the doctrine of the Trinity, Aquinas raising the question of whether there are processions in God (*ST* 1.27.1). He goes on to account for processions in terms of the formation of a concept from an act of understanding: "For whenever we understand, by the very fact of understanding there proceeds something within us, which is a conception of the object understood,

12. Famously, Karl Barth sought to replace the term "person" with "modes of being" (Barth, *Church Dogmatics*, 1/1:363) while Karl Rahner preferred the term "manners of subsisting" (Rahner, *The Trinity*, 42–45). Lonergan refers to the persons as "modes of being, but also subsistent" (Bernard J. F. Lonergan, "Christology Today: Methodological Reflections," in *A Third Collection*, ed. Frederick E. Crowe, [New York: Paulist, 1985], 74–99, esp. 93, also 99n45).

13. It should be noted that Thomas Aquinas refers to the Father as Speaker. See *ST* 1.34.1, especially ad 3.

14. Rahner, *The Trinity*, 99–100.

a conception issuing from our intellectual power and proceeding from our knowledge of that object."[15] This procession corresponds to what we have said above about meaning as intending and meaning as intended. He goes on to speak of this word as a "word of the heart," linking the word to the further act of value which relates to the procession of the Spirit.

None of this is an attempt to prove the doctrine of the Trinity or to preempt the distinctive roles of doctrines or systematics. It does, however, illustrate how the categories developed in the foundations of moral and intellectual conversion do anticipate Trinitarian doctrine and systematic theology. Doctrine can only arise out of judgments that occur in relation to actual events in revelation, not in terms of mere heuristic anticipations. *There can be no a priori basis to the actual doctrines, and without doctrines there can be no systematic understanding of those doctrines.* We shall discuss this further in chapter 10 when we discuss the eight distinctive functional specializations within theological method. On the other hand, the above example does illustrate perfectly the ways in which sound foundations provide helpful and suggestive categories both for doctrines and their systematic understanding.

The Revealed Revealer—A Searching Christology

In the previous chapter, we utilized the category of incarnate meaning as one way in which revelation may be carried into human history. We shall now expand on what this might mean. Given what we have written above we can easily conceive of a situation whereby someone who has experienced a participation in the divine life becomes themselves a carrier of divine meaning and value into human history. They become the medium through which these

---

15. Aquinas, *ST* 1.27.1.

meanings and values are expressed, in the incarnate meaning of their lives and expressed intersubjectively, artistically, symbolically and linguistically. The question remains: How would this participation in the divine life be manifest in those who carry this divine meaning and value? Would it be through some conceptual content that emerges within their minds or would it be that their very lives manifest the divine life through being the sort of persons they are or, better, have become through their participation in that life? Congruent with the approach adopted throughout this work we would argue that the primary way in which human beings manifest participation in the divine life is through the type of event we identified in chapter 2 as religious conversion.[16] This involves a transformation of human consciousness through the experience of God's love poured into our hearts, opening us up to the source of all meaning, truth, and goodness so that we begin to "see" the world through God's "eyes." However, such ocular metaphors can be misleading. Through our participation in the divine life, we not only grasp ("see") the meanings and appreciate the values present in our situations, with a consciousness more attuned to the divine presence, we also become a source of new divine meanings and values which manifest the divine presence, which are in fact God's response to our concrete situation.

We can witness this process most clearly in the lives of the saints, mystics, and Old Testament prophets. Many of the prophetic books describe the call of the prophet as a powerful religious encounter. For example, in the prophet Isaiah, we find the following encounter with the divine:

> In the year that King Uzziah died, I saw the Lord sitting on a throne, high and lofty; and the hem of his robe filled the temple. Seraphs were in

16. This is not to deny the possibility of conceptual content being communicated—what the tradition would call "infused knowledge"—but even such an event would be predicated on the type of experience we identify as religious conversion. Aquinas puts it thus: "Accordingly, inspiration is requisite for prophecy" *ST* 2-2.171.1 ad 4.

attendance above him; each had six wings: with two they covered their faces, and with two they covered their feet, and with two they flew. And one called to another and said:

'Holy, holy, holy is the Lord of hosts;
the whole earth is full of his glory.'

The pivots on the thresholds shook at the voices of those who called, and the house filled with smoke. And I said: 'Woe is me! I am lost, for I am a man of unclean lips, and I live among a people of unclean lips; yet my eyes have seen the King, the Lord of hosts!' (Isa. 6:1-5)

Out of this experience is a commissioning to speak God's word into the prophet's historical context:

Then I heard the voice of the Lord saying, 'Whom shall I send, and who will go for us?' And I said, 'Here am I; send me!' And he said, 'Go and say to this people:

"Keep listening, but do not comprehend;
keep looking, but do not understand."
Make the mind of this people dull,
and stop their ears,
and shut their eyes,
so that they may not look with their eyes,
and listen with their ears,
and comprehend with their minds,
and turn and be healed.' (Isa. 6:8-10)

Still, this word is not just a statement of cognitive meaning, saying what is or is not the case as God grasps it; it is more an effective meaning, one whose purpose is to transform the situation, to create a new reality, new meanings and values, not yet present:

For as the rain and the snow come down from heaven,
and do not return there until they have watered the earth,
making it bring forth and sprout,
giving seed to the sower and bread to the eater,
so shall my word be that goes out from my mouth;
it shall not return to me empty,

> but it shall accomplish that which I purpose,
> and succeed in the thing for which I sent it. (Isa. 55:10-11)

In the various prophetic writings, we find the prophets using different ways of communicating divine meaning and value, that is, meaning and value that surpasses the realm of natural knowledge for humans (and angels). And so the prophet Hosea marries a prostitute to symbolize God's covenant love of his bride, Israel, and Israel's continued infidelity to that covenant.

Of course, in dealing with the prophetic, one inevitably has to deal with the problem of false prophets. How does one tell the true from the false prophet? Furthermore, there is no external way of determining their authenticity. Pragmatically, the Old Testament simply notes that if what they say is true, or proves to be true, then they are true prophets. But even the prophetic gift itself is not permanent. The one who speaks God's word today, might not speak it tomorrow.[17] Not everything the prophet says is, strictly speaking, prophetic, and so we are left with an indeterminacy in relation to the prophetic gift. The prophetic gift is incomplete, partial, and transitory. Can we then anticipate something more, where the prophet does not merely speak God's word, but in some sense *is* God's Word? What might this mean?

Such a one would not simply be a carrier of revelation as with the prophets, such a one would *be* the full revelation of God into human history, the very entry of God into that history. Such a one would not simply participate in the divine life as other human beings might enjoy, but their participation in the divine life would *constitute* their identity, it would be *who* they are. This identity would not simply be another example of the creature-Creator relationship, but would be constituted as a personal participation in one of the

---

17. Again, as Aquinas would say, "prophecy is not a habit." *ST* 2-2.171.2.

intradivine relations, which we posit as a necessary condition for the possibility of a genuine divine self-communication. Such a one would *be* a divine "person," living as fully human in the conditions of human existence, as socially and historically conditioned, who would be God's revelation in history. The incarnate meaning of this one's life would be the definitive entry of divine meaning and value into human history, or, as Rahner states, such a one would be "the full and unsurpassable event of the historical objectification of God's self-communication to the world."[18] Further, as the entry of God into human history, such a one would be worthy of a love and devotion proper to God alone, to be loved unconditionally; and one to be trusted completely, for there can be no deception in the source of all meaning, truth, and goodness. We could say that we find in this person the Way, the Truth, and the Life, manifest in human history, the true teacher, the true prophet, the true judge.

Has such an event occurred? Do we actually find evidence in human history for such an entry of divine meaning and value? This would seem to be the experience of generations of Christians who have fallen in love with Jesus Christ, who have committed themselves to his life and teaching, and who have given up all to follow him in discipleship, humbly following their teacher even unto death. While our heuristic anticipation can envisage such a possibility, it is only the eye of love which discerns the realization of such a possibility in the poor carpenter from Nazareth who died, cursed on a cross, to be raised to new life by the Father. Indeed, for Christians their experience of religious conversion, the otherworldly falling in love with the source of all meaning, truth, and goodness, has been mediated to them precisely through their encounter with Jesus

18. Rahner, *Foundations*, 157.

Christ. However, to make such judgments moves us from foundations to doctrines and is beyond our present scope.

Our procedure here has similarities with that adopted by Rahner in his discussion of a "searching Christology"[19] and his notion of an "absolute savior."[20] Rahner posits a deep longing in the human heart for the one who will save us from our human plight, much as the Jewish people longed for a messiah. In both cases we find a strong anticipation of quite classical christological themes emerging out of foundational positions, to the extent that Rahner speaks of the "need for a closer unity between fundamental theology and dogmatic theology in Christology."[21] Whereas Rahner emphasizes the human longing for salvation, an "absolute savior," our focus has been on the possibility of an absolute revealer, though this component is also present in his approach.[22] Whereas Rahner builds his position on the basis of his transcendental methodology, our starting point has been religious, moral, intellectual, and psychic conversions, which one might suggest are to some extent presupposed by Rahner (at least in its religious and moral aspects), but not thematized as such.

Revelation, Salvation, and the Problem of Evil

In the previous chapter, we spoke about revelation without really speaking about the purpose of revelation. There our concern was more with the manner of revelation, in terms of the categories of meaning. We can now address the purpose of revelation by relating it to a theme that has been present throughout this work, that is, the problem of evil. We have clarified the nature of the problem of evil from the perspectives of moral, intellectual, and psychic conversions,

---

19. Ibid., 295.
20. Ibid., 211.
21. Ibid., 294.
22. For Rahner, the notions of revelation and salvation tend to merge. See ibid., chapter 5, "The History of Salvation and Revelation," 138–75.

while the experience of God's love flooding our hearts that initiates religious conversion assures us of God's loving concern for our human existence. Still the question remains: How does God respond to our human predicament, caught up in a history of sin and evil permeating the personal, cultural, and social dimensions of our existence? Lonergan notes, "Divine revelation is God's entry and his taking part in man's making of man. It is God's claim to have a say in the aims and purposes, the direction and development of human lives, human societies, human cultures, human history."[23] As such it functions not just cognitively, but effectively, constitutively, and communicatively, as God's response to the human condition. As we noted above in relation to Rahner's work, there is a close connection between revelation and salvation, or as the Vatican II Constitution on Divine Revelation, *Dei Verbum*, states: "This plan of revelation is realized by deeds and words having an inner unity: the deeds wrought by God in the history of salvation manifest and confirm the teaching and realities signified by the words, while the words proclaim the deeds and clarify the mystery contained in them. By this revelation then, the deepest truth about God and the salvation of man shines out for our sake in Christ, who is both the mediator and the fullness of all revelation."[24]

Through revelation, then, we encounter God's response to the problem of evil in human history, and that response has the purpose of saving us, freeing us from evil and its effects in our lives. Given our discussion of the problem of evil in the previous chapters, in light of moral, intellectual, and psychic conversions, we can conceive of evil as a privation, the choice of mere satisfaction over genuine value, a choice for which we can find no sufficient reason. It confronts us

---

23. Bernard J. F. Lonergan, "Theology in its New Context," in *Second Collection*, ed. William Ryan and Bernard Tyrrell (Philadelphia: Westminster, 1974), 55–68 (62).
24. *Dei Verbum*, n. 2.

with the unintelligible, the meaningless, in human history. Despite its power (*tremendum*) and attraction (*fascinans*), it must not be confused with the source of all meaning, truth, and goodness, which is its very antithesis. Still, if evil is the privation of meaning, truth, and goodness, it cannot be destroyed or corralled, leaving us pure and undefiled. The solution lies in creative acts of making meaning out of meaninglessness, acts of *creatio ex nihilo* (in a sense), the creation of new meaning out of the meaninglessness of evil. We overcome evil by transforming it into an opportunity to do something good: to forgive, to turn the other cheek, to go the extra mile for the other who has injured us. Not that doing good requires evil or makes evil somehow necessary, but love overcomes evil by absorbing its privation into the fullness of meaning, truth, and value. We can find such a transformation proclaimed and lived by Jesus and Gandhi. Both taught nonviolent resistance to evil.

The divine solution to the problem of evil is not a theory but a practice. It is a practice that takes the meaninglessness of evil and transforms it into an opportunity to create meaning and value. Often, such a practice will involve suffering, the suffering of resisting the urge to lash back, or to lash out at others, the suffering of resisting the forces of evil and not allowing them to crush or subvert us, or even enlist us in causing meaningless suffering for others. Still, this suffering we thus endure is not the meaningless suffering imposed on us by evil, but more like the suffering of giving birth, birth to new meaning and value in the face of the evil we confront. This suffering is truly redemptive. It is not the suffering that complies with or submits to the evil confronting us, but the suffering that can ask of the persecutors, "Why did you strike me?" (John 18:23), while still offering forgiveness to them from the cross.

On the basis of our foundational positions on conversion, we can resolve this notion of redemptive suffering into the elements that make it possible and sustainable.

First, I must experience myself as loved. Without being grounded in an unconditional love, a love which affirms me, then attempting to enter into a process of redemptive suffering will become a form of spiritual masochism. It will not be a form of self-transcendence, but of self-negation, confirmatory of one's own sense of worthlessness. This is not redemptive suffering but collusion in evil. In the terms of the present work, one must be grounded in a religious conversion, to know the love of God poured into our hearts, affirming us as loved and as loveable. In theological terms, one must be graced.

Second, I must learn to respond out of that experience of being loved to love others, not just those close to me, my friends and family, but even my enemies, those who do me wrong and persecute me. Through learning to love in this manner, I begin to bring God's love to a broken world, healing its hurts, righting its wrongs, through a willingness to suffer the evil that diminishes human existence, and through responding with prayer, forgiveness, and mercy. This is a most profound entry of divine meaning and value into human history as we incarnate the love of God who makes the sun to shine and the rain to fall on the good and evil alike. In theological terms, this responsiveness is the habit of charity.

These two aspects together (the experience of being loved and loving in return) constitute a most significant element in God's solution to the problem of evil in human history. Through religious conversion we can become incarnate carriers of divine meaning and value, creative agents of God's love in the world, working to build God's kingdom. However, these are not the only elements that we can anticipate. There are other elements that bolster and sustain us in the practice of redemptive suffering.

Third, I can cultivate a hope to sustain me through waves of despair that threaten to overwhelm me. To struggle against evil in all its manifestations is to run the risk of losing heart. The struggle may come at great personal cost, as evident in the life of Jesus or Gandhi. I need a hope that is more than an optimism that "things will work out in the end" because they have in the past. If salvation is God's work to overcome evil in the world, then we dare to hope in a more than human outcome, one that offers a fulfillment stronger than death. Even in the darkest moments, we can still cling to a hope that transcends our earthly existence.[25]

Fourth, my commitment can be bolstered through believing revealed truths (cognitive meaning) that affirm that God loves me; that God calls me to respond to that love by loving my neighbor, friend and foe alike; and that I can hope for a fulfillment so complete that it transcends this earthly existence. Faith schools me in these truths, which are then realized in my life through an ongoing religious conversion. Faith helps me identify and overcome the falsehoods of ideologies that distort our social and cultural orders, and the personal biases that arise from my own story of suffering and sin.

Taken together, these four elements are, in more traditional theological language, sanctifying grace, and the theological virtues of faith, hope, and charity. They form a comprehensive response to the problem of evil in human history by shifting our affective response to values, firing our imaginations and consolidating our minds in relation to that response. Further, if in fact our participation in God's response to the problem of evil involves a sharing in the divine nature (2 Pet. 1:5), then these four elements may themselves be different modes through which we share in the divine nature, and so relate us to the internal relatedness of God, whom through faith we know as Trinity. This takes us well beyond our foundational goals for the

25. On the theological virtue of hope, see Dominic Doyle, *The Promise of Christian Humanism: Thomas Aquinas on Hope* (New York: Herder & Herder, 2011).

present work, but does further our anticipation of the systematic coherence of Christian belief.[26]

The Ecclesial Nature of the Solution to the Problem of Evil

Such a divine solution to the problem of evil would be rendered ineffective if it were not carried in human history, and this communication would require communities of people for whom divinely revealed meanings and values are constitutive of their communal identities. Revelation can only be carried and hence rendered effective when it is incarnated in the hearts and minds of people, who, through their shared experiences, common understandings, judgments, and decisions, hand on that revelation of divine meanings and values from one generation to the next. In this way, the solution to the problem of evil becomes a historically effective means for addressing evil, not just now, or today and tomorrow, but in a sustainable way over centuries and even millennia.[27] The divine solution to the problem of evil elicits an *ecclesial* response; it creates a community whose divinely given responsibility is to:

- Mediate the experience of God's love flooding our hearts through

---

26. These suggestions find their inspiration in Robert M. Doran, *The Trinity in History: A Theology of the Divine Missions, Vol. 1: Missions and Processions* (Toronto: University of Toronto Press, 2012). See also Neil Ormerod, "The Metaphysics of Holiness: Created Participation in the Divine Nature," *Irish Theological Quarterly* 79, no. 1 (2014): 68–82.

27. Framing this in terms of the Kingdom of God, Pope John Paul II speaks of the church's mission in the following terms: "The Kingdom is the concern of everyone: individuals, society, and the world. Working for the Kingdom means acknowledging and promoting God's activity, which is present in human history and transforms it. Building the Kingdom means working for liberation from evil in all its forms. In a word, the Kingdom of God is the manifestation and the realization of God's plan of salvation in all its fullness." See the encyclical *Redemptoris missio, On the Permanent Validity of the Church's Missionary Mandate*, n. 15, accessed September 5, 2015 at: http:// w2.vatican.va / content / john-paul-ii / en / encyclicals / documents / hf_jp-ii_enc_07121990_redemptoris-missio.html.

the promotion of intersubjective, artistic, and symbolic carriers of meaning, which we find in prayer, liturgy, and sacraments;

- Promote through the contemplation of exemplary persons and through practices of spiritual self-discipline a life of generous and self-sacrificing love as the means for overcoming the effects of sin and evil and so building God's kingdom in the world, to love the world as God loves it;

- Model a living hope that the adversities of the present struggle with evil are not the last word in history, but that there is given to us a hope that goes beyond the present life, a hope for human flourishing grounded in God's love which can sustain us;

- Teach the truths (cognitive meanings) to be found in revelation so that not just hearts but also minds can be nourished and strengthened in the surety that we are loved, that God's love can be embodied to effectively deal with the problem of evil, and that we can hope for a future beyond that of our present travails.

Of course, such communities may arise around the memory of prophetic figures who have carried divine meaning and value into human history over the centuries. However, because the prophetic gift is transitory and partial, because of the difficulty of distinguishing between the divine meanings and values being conveyed and the merely human elements, both authentic and inauthentic, with which they are mixed, such communities will reflect only a fragmented grasp of the whole solution to the problem of evil.

And so we might anticipate the possibility of a community around one who not only speaks God's word, but who is God's word spoken into human history. As we indicated above, we can anticipate one whose incarnate meaning embodies completely divine meaning and value, who is the fullness of revelation in history, whose very identity is divine. The formation of a community of people, of disciples, around such a person, would not be a mere accident of history, an afterthought to the process, but an intrinsic element of the divine solution to the problem of evil. In this way, we can understand the repeated insistence within the tradition that Jesus "founded" the church, not in the sense of some juridical act, but in his own recognition that his mission needs to be continued into human history by the existence of such a community which promotes the solution to the problem of evil through the four elements identified above. Without some ongoing community, which of necessity includes its own institutional forms, the divine solution to the problem of evil would have been rendered historically ineffective.

Because the ongoing existence of a community that carries forward the divine solution to the problem of evil is itself part of the solution, and because it is God's solution and not just a human contrivance, the ongoing life of the community will be under the protection of divine providence. However, because divine providence elicits the cooperation of human freedom, such protection is not absolute but rather a shifting in the probability that:

- Members of the community will continue to experience the love of God mediated through the prayer, liturgy, and sacraments of the community;

- There will be members of the community who effectively live out that love to transform our present situation through the power of self-sacrificing love;

- There will be members of the community who manifest a living hope that the divine solution to the problem of evil will continue to be effective in history;

- The community will maintain itself in the cognitive meanings mediated in revelation as central to its identity.

Such a community will not be without its own structures of leadership and authority. These will be needed because there is a legitimate and religious duty to maintain the vitality of those elements that are constitutive of the community's identity. While the precise nature of these structures may vary in different times and places, if they are to represent a full response to the problem of evil as manifest in human history, they must then address that problem in all its dimensions. The problem of evil is initially and fundamentally a personal moral issue, a turning away from genuine values and toward the unintelligibility of sin. However, it impacts on the meanings and values of society as sin spreads to find support in alienating ideologies that seek to justify and normalize sin. And the most profound alienation is that from our fundamental orientation to meaning, truth, goodness, and beauty. Finally, sin becomes manifest in our social relations and institutions, which come to embody and institutionalize injustice, the maldistribution of power, of wealth, and of the basic necessities of life. The structures of leadership and authority will have a specific concern in each of these aspects of the life of the community.

Indeed, these observations spill over to the community as a whole. The community will have a specifically *religious* dimension that promotes the type of life we have identified above, of grace, charity, hope, and faith, as the entry of divine meaning and value into our human condition empowering us to address the problem of evil through the power of self-sacrificing love. This dimension will be fostered through prayer, liturgy, and sacraments whose purpose it is to mediate grace as foundational for the life of the community.[28]

28. It is for this reason that the document of Vatican II on the church, *Lumen gentium*, speaks of

These activities will be its primary focus and concern, to ensure the ongoing historical presence of a community grounded in the divine self-communication.

It will have a specifically *moral* dimension that seeks to promote moral conversion in its members, turning them away from evil and toward morally upright behavior. This is the first instance of grace's triumph over evil, that human hearts are converted away from sin, as moral fault, and toward human flourishing, authenticity, and genuine human values. The community is called to live qualitatively different lives as a consequence of their religious conversion. And a concern for human flourishing, authenticity, and genuine values implies a concern not just for oneself and one's own, but also for society as a whole, culturally, politically, economically and, increasingly, ecologically.[29] Where such a moral transformation is not evident, the community's claims to be a community grounded in divine grace must necessarily be suspect. On the other hand, while the moral life is theoretically possible without grace, continued sustained moral growth in a world impacted by sin is not possible. The weight of evil oppresses us all and grace is needed to liberate us from its effects.[30]

It will have a specifically *cultural* dimension, particularly as the life of the community extended over historical time frames. It will build up a body of religious writings, of theological reflection, doctrinal decisions, and moral teachings, all of which are debated and discussed by subsequent generations of the community. Some of these cultural products will become recognized classics, whose authority will

---

the Eucharistic liturgy as the "source and summit" of the Christian life. See *Lumen gentium*, Dogmatic Constitution on the Church, n. 11, accessed September 5, 2015 at: http:// www.vatican.va / archive / hist_councils / ii_vatican_council / documents / vat-ii_const _19641121_lumen-gentium_en.html.

29. We can find such concerns expressed in the body of Catholic social teaching, from *Rerum Novarum* to the latest encyclical by Pope Francis on the environment, *Laudato Si'.*

30. Such matters relate to the range of questions dealt with in Christian anthropology. See, for example, Ormerod, *Creation, Grace and Redemption.*

extend into the life of the community for centuries to come. Others will be more ephemeral, being of assistance in the short term within a particular context, but fading into insignificance with the passing of time. Nonetheless, the purpose of this cultural dimension is to provide a larger framework of meanings and values within which the religious and moral dimensions of the community are intelligibly expressed, communicated, defended, and propagated. In this way, the task of the cultural dimension of the community is to mediate between the religious (and moral) values of the community and the meanings and values to be found within the larger community in which they find themselves.[31]

Finally, it will have a specifically *social* dimension because the community of necessity has a social dimension. Liturgies do not organize themselves, buildings for community gatherings do not build themselves, and the religious, moral, and cultural dimensions require a supportive social infrastructure to ensure their ongoing viability. It is in the social dimension that people participate in the rites and liturgies, learn to pray together and individually, are challenged to grow in moral authenticity, and glean something of the cultural wisdom of the community. Children are raised and educated in the meanings and values of the community, especially those that arise from God's self-communication of the solution to the problem of evil in human history. The way in which the community as a whole lives out the divinely originated solution to the problem of evil is the most effective sign of the nature of that solution, and hence the

31. This encompasses what Paul VI called evangelization at depth, the transformation of cultures through the power of the Gospel. See *Evangelii Nuntiandi* n. 20: "All this could be expressed in the following words: what matters is to evangelize man's culture and cultures (not in a purely decorative way, as it were, by applying a thin veneer, but in a vital way, in depth and right to their very roots)" [Apostolic Exhortation, *Evangelii Nuntiandi*, n. 20, accessed September 5, 2015 at: http://w2.vatican.va/content/paul-vi/en/apost_exhortations/documents/hf_p-vi_exh_19751208_evangelii-nuntiandi.html].

most effective way in which it is communicated to those outside the community.

We can conceive of the relationship between these various dimensions in terms of a series of mediations, from the religious to the moral, from the moral to the cultural, and from the cultural to the social. Lonergan refers to this as the healing vector of grace operating in human history.[32] Grace is not just personally transformative, but also culturally and socially transformative as well. In more traditional language, these three mediations can be thought of as priestly (from religious to moral), prophetic (from religious and moral to cultural) and kingly (from cultural to social). While the internal mediations within the life of the community are the special responsibility of those who exercise leadership and authority within the community, the community as a whole has the divine mission to mediate divine meanings and values and their moral, cultural, and social implications into the whole human community.[33]

Again, what we find here is that the foundations we have laid in our earlier chapters, particularly chapter 3 on moral conversion, has provided us with a set of categories that allow us to anticipate classical ecclesial doctrines while providing a sound starting point for their systematic understanding. As with the Trinity and the Incarnation, our foundations are suggestive without being determinative. Does such a historical community (or communities) exist in response to the definitive entry of divine meaning and value revealing the divinely

---

32. Bernard J. F. Lonergan, "Healing and Creating in History," in *A Third Collection*, ed. Frederick E. Crowe (Mahwah, NY: Paulist Press, 1985), 100–109.

33. And so *Lumen gentium* speaks of the whole church participating in the priestly, prophetic, and pastoral ministry of Christ. See *Lumen gentium* n. 31: "These faithful are by baptism made one body with Christ and are constituted among the People of God; they are in their own way made sharers in the priestly, prophetical, and kingly functions of Christ; and they carry out for their own part the mission of the whole Christian people in the Church and in the world." For a fuller account of the mission of the church and its relationship to the church's ministry, see Neil Ormerod, *Re-Visioning the Church*.

originated solution to the problem of evil in human history? Foundations alone cannot answer such a question. They do, however, suggest the shape such a community will take and how it might understand its identity and mission to the world.

Conclusion

As we noted in chapter 1, the task of foundations as conceived in the present work is not to provide foundations for the whole of the theological enterprise, but rather to provide foundations for doctrines, systematics, and communications. While the full significance of this will be more evident in chapter 10 when we consider the question of theological method more fully, the purpose of this chapter has been to illustrate the value of sound foundations in anticipating the doctrinal judgments and systematic structures that the later theological tasks will generate. Again, to quote Rahner, "A keyhole forms an *a priori* law governing what key fits in, but it thereby discloses something about the key itself."[34] The keyhole of foundations discloses something about the key, the contents of the divine self-communication.

This still leaves the third element for which foundations is relevant, that of communications. Communications presupposes a context, and this is the issue we consider in the next chapter where we analyze our present context, not exhaustively, but in terms of both an increasing secularization, and a new and demanding encounter with the religious "other" through interreligious dialogue. Once more, our foundations do not seek to preempt the task of communications but at the same time sound foundations will shed new light onto our context that will assist in the communicative task.

---

34. Rahner, *Foundations*, 19.

9

The Communicative Context

Secularism and Religious Pluralism

In the previous chapter, we provided a heuristic anticipation of certain positions in relation to the church, its nature and mission. In this chapter, we move from those more abstract considerations to the present and more concrete context of the church's mission and communication, in a world of growing secularism on the one hand, and increasing exposure to religious pluralism on the other, while still drawing on the foundations developed in the first part of our work. Let us begin then with an ending: *Ite missa est*. These words express the dismissal declared at the end of the Roman Catholic liturgy. The phrase translates as "Go, you are sent," but the new translation of the Roman Missal gives a few options for this part, for example: "Go and announce the Gospel of the Lord," and "Go in peace, glorifying the Lord by your life." Each of these dismissals expresses the close connection between the experience of the Eucharistic liturgy and the responsibility to communicate an authentic Christian presence in the world.

Many recent ecclesial pronouncements emphasize this point. The very idea of evangelization for Pope John Paul II draws the activity of Christian mission back to the inner renewal of ongoing conversion in the Mystery of Christ.[1] And in *Evangelii Gaudium*, Pope Francis implores: "Throughout the world, let us be 'permanently in a state of mission.'"[2] He stresses the divine initiative in the liturgy and the dynamism of conversion: "The Church evangelizes and is herself evangelized through the beauty of the liturgy, which is both a celebration of the task of evangelization and the source of her renewed self-giving."[3]

Despite clear affirmations of the missionary nature of the church, the mandate for evangelization often makes Christians feel uncomfortable.[4] The idea of evangelization can conjure images of colonialism, reminding us of how religious conversion has functioned as a tool of cultural imperialism and the marginalization of indigenous peoples. It can also spark suspicions of hubris. The idea that we possess an existential truth that others somehow need seems to lose credibility once we abandon classicist pretensions to normativity and adopt an empirical concept of culture.[5] On doctrinal grounds, the affirmation of God's universal salvific will also seems to mitigate a zealous, evangelical attitude. And most Christians know people outside the church living what they consider morally virtuous

---

1. Encyclical, *Redemptoris missio*, On the Permanent Validity of the Church's Missionary Mandate, n. 2, accessed September 7, 2015 at: http://w2.vatican.va/content/john-paul-ii/en/encyclicals/documents/hf_jp-ii_enc_07121990_redemptoris-missio.html.
2. *Evangelii gaudium*, On the Proclamation of the Gospel in Today's World, n. 25, accessed September 7, 2015 at: http://w2.vatican.va/content/francesco/en/apost_exhortations/documents/papa-francesco_esortazione-ap_20131124_evangelii-gaudium.html.
3. Ibid., n. 24.
4. On the missionary nature of the church, see *Lumen Gentium* n. 5: "From this source [that is, Pentecost] the Church, equipped with the gifts of its Founder and faithfully guarding His precepts of charity, humility and self-sacrifice, receives the mission to proclaim and to spread among all peoples the Kingdom of Christ and of God and to be, on earth, the initial budding forth of that kingdom."
5. Lonergan distinguishes between a classicist notion of culture, grounded in the achievements of the past, and an empirical notion of culture that takes as its starting point the set of meanings and values present in a given culture. See Bernard J. F. Lonergan, "The Transition from a Classicist World-View to Historical Mindedness," in *A Second Collection*, ed. William F. Ryan and Bernard Tyrrell (Toronto: University of Toronto Press, 1996), 1–9. Kathryn Tanner notes the same transition (that is, from high culture to a modern view of culture) in her work: *Theories of Culture: a New Agenda for Theology* (Minneapolis: Fortress Press, 1997).

lives, and these are sometimes more exemplary than those of local believers. In fact, the church recognizes that Christians undermine the announcement of the gospel by the poor testimony of their moral failures.[6]

Christians must account for their hope (1 Peter 3:15), but often they do not know how to go about it. More pointedly, they do not know how they should behold their interlocutors. Are people outside the faith basically deficient, lacking in truth, or are they too gifts and mediators of grace for Christians? Of course, answers about others implicitly contain answers about self-understanding; the two are inseparable. The missionary obligation raises a powerful question about the very meaning of Christian identity.

The guiding themes of this chapter steer a course between the exclusivism that discounts the universal salvific activity of God and the no less mistaken relativism that approves of difference as a matter of principle. The first part of this chapter considers debates about the church's relation to the world and proposes a way forward in the midst of conflicting visions of Christian identity. The second part turns to the unique challenge that other religions pose to central Christian beliefs about salvation, Christ, and the church. The chapter explains how a methodical approach to theology reframes how we think about the church's relations to secular culture and to other religions, and how it then reorients the church to the responsibility of living out an authentic Christian presence in the world.

Disjunctions and Encounters in the People of God

Much of the discourse around the church's response to secularism

---

6. *Gaudium et spes* recognizes the role that religion can have in promoting atheism: "Hence believers can have more than a little to do with the birth of atheism. To the extent that they neglect their own training in the faith, or teach erroneous doctrine, or are deficient in their religious, moral or social life, they must be said to conceal rather than reveal the authentic face of God and religion" (*Gaudium et spes*, n. 19).

suffers from confusion about the meanings of the basic terms of the debates. How do we define the secular, the religious, and the sacred? How do we conceive the secular's relation to modernity, or the role of religion in modern society? These concepts are often unclear, and yet this lack of clarity does not prevent the assertion of strong and often heated positions about how we should view the church's relation to its secular context in the West. In fact, people within the church often feel deeply divided over this relation, and their struggle to grow in community signals the need for foundational criteria for understanding how the church changes in history.

The divisions are clearly discernible. On one side, voices cry out for the church to take up the fight against the forces of secularism and return to a Christendom that manifests the social significance of the gospel. Deploring these voices, others rush toward new proposals with little consideration of their opponent's concerns, often condemning what they perceive as bankrupt appeals to tradition that undermine the church's relevance. The 2014 Extraordinary Synod on the family elicited these divisions. When the media reported that early drafts of a document contained a markedly different, more "conciliatory" tone toward divorced Catholics and gay and lesbian Catholics, some who rejected any such shift railed against the media's misinformation, insisting that nothing had changed and that only strong moral boundaries can turn away "the cultural acids of modernity."[7] On the other side, Catholics who yearned for change began nodding to every whisper of a long overdue sea change in Catholic culture and morality. Many commentators, including bishops, declared that neither extreme grasped the reality of the synod, though few seemed especially surprised by the range of reactions.[8]

---

7. George Weigel, "An Extraordinary Synod, Indeed," *First Things* 22 (October 2014).

8. For a sample of these reactions, see "Reactions to the family synod range from concern

Beneath the surface of these reactions, we can identify basic attitudes that Charles Taylor describes as "seekers" and "dwellers."[9] Where seekers embrace the personal search for meaning and court change with hope for progress, dwellers reaffirm certain answers to life's basic questions and mine the depths of custom and institutional memory. Because these broader categories represent ideal types, they are not sealed against each other; people can adopt characteristics of both.[10] For Taylor, these categories portray the existential disjunction that besets religious identity in the climate of Western secularism. In other words, they describe distinct ways of living the faith in contemporary culture, and these ways often antagonize each other.

Such disjunction puts the church in a difficult situation, as Taylor notes. How does it speak to these diverse audiences? Of course, there are no simple answers, and Taylor offers little instruction beyond identifying aspirational goals. He says that respecting the tension between seekers and dwellers at least allows for the possibility of authentic communal growth.[11] If the church should bring these modes of religious living into a deeper sacramental union, it must promote mutual understanding and avoid taking sides in their rivalry. It should also bring about mutual sympathy, he says, for we can appreciate that most people lean toward a particular mode for serious reasons, even when we disagree with them or believe they neglect something essential in the faith.

Making an analytic distinction between seekers and dwellers softens the more extreme voices that continually insist on seeing

to elation," *National Catholic Reporter*, 10, November 2014, accessed November 25 2014, http://ncronline.org/news/vatican/reactions-family-synod-range-concern-elation.

9. Charles Taylor, "The Church Speaks—to Whom?," in *Church and People: Disjunctions in a Secular Age*, ed. Charles Taylor, Jose Casanova, and George F. McLean (Washington, DC: The Council for Research in Values and Philosophy, 2012), 17–24. The typology of seekers and dwellers is drawn from the work of Robert Wuthnow.

10. Ibid., 21.

11. Ibid.

the church's relation to modernity in confrontational terms, but the descriptive nature of the distinction stops short of explaining a way to facilitate the mutual respect and understanding sorely needed within the community. These categories express the existential divergence that many Christians experience, but if taken foundationally, they reify the disjunction. The project of growing in mutual understanding for these different ways of living the faith requires that our analysis of the existential meaning of religious identity move beyond the descriptive level.

The debates about the continuity or discontinuity of Vatican II exemplify the difficulty here. On the one hand, some readings of discontinuity underscore the "new beginnings" initiated by the Council; they represent a seeker attitude in accounting for how the Council fashioned a renewal of the church's engagement with the modern world.[12] On the other hand, more extreme readings of discontinuity emphasize change according to a staunchly dweller mode; they claim a "rupture" with the tradition rather than a new beginning or a genuine *aggiornamento*. Discontinuity for them translates into a lack of faithfulness to God's saving action in history.[13] Relatively recent papal assessments of these debates seek to avoid this latter reading by excluding or downplaying the possibility of discontinuity and switching to the language of reform. The insistence on continuity reveals a less extreme kind of dweller consciousness. In 2000, Pope John Paul II said that "to read the

---

12. See, for example, the multivolume work *History of Vatican II*, ed. Giuseppe Alberigo and Joseph A. Komonchak, trans. Matthew J. O'Connell, 5 vols. (Maryknoll, NY: Orbis, 1995); and for a condensed account: Giuseppe Alberigo, *A Brief History of Vatican II*, trans. Matthew Sherry (Maryknoll, NY: Orbis Books, 2006).

13. This is certainly a minority opinion, the clearest representative being Archbishop Lefebvre. John O'Malley says: "Nowhere in the Alberigo volumes is there the slightest suggestion that the 'new beginning' meant in any way a rupture in the faith of the Church. . . . The only person I know who believed and propagated that assessment was Archbishop Marcel Lefebvre" (John W. O'Malley, "Vatican II: Did Anything Happen?," *Theological Studies* 67, no. 1 [2006]: 3–33 (6)).

council as if it marked a break with the past . . . is decidedly unacceptable."[14]

Such debates painfully exhibit the church's struggle to deal adequately with the issue of development. If the different sides want to understand the reality of Vatican II and grow toward some sense of mutual appreciation, then they must move beyond merely descriptive categories that focus on the fact of change. The metaphor of continuity and discontinuity simply does not help explain the situation.[15] It cannot account for the complexities inherent in the broad cultural and social changes that occurred with Vatican II. Quite literally, the metaphor misses the point: the meanings and values which constitute the church as an intentional community are not measurable by any calculus or metric that would give the metaphor explanatory power. As the sociologist Roy Bhaskar has noted: "Meanings cannot be measured, only understood."[16] The metaphor of continuity and discontinuity thus misleads even for the purposes of description, because it contains an evaluation of concrete historical processes for which it can offer no account.

If we wish to understand the changes in meanings and values initiated by Vatican II, then we need to adopt a general theory of cultural and social change based on our foundations in moral conversion (chapter 3). And if this theory would link back to the question about the faithfulness of the changes to God's saving act in history, then we must also use our foundations in intellectual conversion to construct a metaphysic or ontology of meaning that can explain the "being of meaning" in historical communities

14. Cited in Ibid., 5.
15. Neil Ormerod, "Vatican II—Continuity or Discontinuity? Toward an Ontology of Meaning," *Theological Studies* 71, no. 3 (2010): 609–36. The discussion of Vatican II here follows this article. For a more comprehensive treatment of the foundational issues in ecclesiology, see *Re-Visioning the Church*.
16. Roy Bhaskar, "Societies," in *Critical Realism: Essential Readings*, ed. Margaret Archer, et al. (London: Routledge, 1998), 206–57 (226).

(chapter 4). On all counts, the metaphor of continuity and discontinuity fails to furnish adequate interpretive tools and effectively obscures our view of the real issues at stake.

On a methodical approach to theology, the fact of development requires an evaluation of concrete historical processes according to the foundational criteria of conversion (religious, moral, intellectual, psychic). This approach is not allergic to inevitable novelty in historical traditions. It avoids the anachronism that attributes to Scripture and the church Fathers an implicit grasp of what later theologians discovered. And it rejects the archaism that looks only to the plain meaning of biblical and patristic sources for genuine doctrine and condemns all else as corruption.

The methodical approach offers a third option. Of it, Lonergan wrote: "It would contend that there can be many kinds of developments and that, to know them, one has to study and analyze concrete historical processes while, to know their legitimacy, one has to turn to evaluational history and assign them their place in the dialectic of the presence and absence of intellectual, moral, and religious conversion."[17] Lonergan offered an analysis of meaning that contains a wealth of resources for understanding the fact of the church's development. It allows us to differentiate various carriers of meaning (intersubjective, artistic, symbolic, linguistic) and ask about changes in different functions of meaning (cognitive, constitutive, communicative, effective) as explored in chapter 4. And it enables us to apply with an explanatory control of meaning the criteria of authenticity to our reading of the history of the church.[18]

Returning to Vatican II, this means we need not insist on continuity as if nothing actually happened. Nor must we take sides in battles that reduce the complexities of development to a simplistic

17. Bernard J. F. Lonergan, *Method in Theology*, 312.
18. See Ormerod, *Re-Visioning the Church*, for an example of this over the history of the church.

opposition. Rather, we can focus on elements of authenticity and inauthenticity in the developments initiated or precipitated by the Council, for example: we can discuss the shift to the vernacular and the emphasis on full participation in the liturgy (*Sacrosanctum concilium*) as well as the perceived loss of the sacred in the Latin rites prior to the Council; and we can discuss the fuller understanding of the lay apostolate and increased appreciation of the laity's creative participation in the church's mission (*Apostolicam actuositatem*) as well as the correlative loss of esteem for the special place of ordained and religious life in the service and mission of the church.[19] If we affirm the authenticity of the orientation of each shift on the basis of a fourfold conversion, still we can also criticize the element of inauthenticity in the relatively predictable, secondary outcome. Most significantly, we can explain how these changes pertain more to the constitutive, effective, and communicative functions of meaning than to the cognitive; they indicate changes in what it means to belong, live out, and express the meaning of the community, not in what the community believes per se.

If the church should speak to both seekers and dwellers, then it needs criteria other than the descriptive standards of different modes of living the faith. It must speak with an adequate sense of its own development by making foundational the normative principles of history rather than deferring to felt or perceived needs for change or stability. The presence or absence of change simply does not imply the presence or absence of authenticity. Rather, the authentic orientation to meaning, truth, and value marks the horizon of genuine change in all historical communities. Once we identify the foundations of theology with the dynamics of conversion, we can

---

19. Ormerod, "Vatican II—Continuity or Discontinuity?," 634–35; see also Josef Pieper, *In Search of the Sacred: Contributions to an Answer*, trans. Lothar Krauth (San Francisco: Ignatius, 1991), 30.

explain how in the context of Western secularism seekers and dwellers can grow toward mutual understanding and collaboration.

The foundational reality of conversion cuts across the disjunctions with a dialectical analysis of authenticity and inauthenticity. It furnishes dialogic communication with the needed tools of interpretation, and envisions the further, most valuable step of an encounter of persons, each revealing to the other his or her native orientation to meaning, truth, value, beauty, and love. In sum, an adequate account of the church's growth over time anticipates the creativity of encounter among all the people of God.

Charting the Secular and the Sacred

Making conversion the foundational reality of theology shapes how we think about the role of religion in modern society and the meaning of secularization. Debates on these themes can go on rather endlessly, in part because the central concepts often mean different things to different people. The approach here does not seek to fix these meanings once and for all, but to give reference points for developing our thinking about what it means to live an authentic Christian presence in a secular world. If the last section discussed the importance of these criteria for understanding religious identity in relation to the church's development as a historical community, this section focuses more on the meanings of secularity, religion, and the sacred, which largely define the church's context in the West.

The commonsense meaning of the secular in contemporary culture implies the exclusion of religious authority from public discourse and the denial of the existence of transcendent being. It refers to what separates itself from religion, spirituality, and the church, to what fortifies the walls of government against their influence, and to what neutralizes religious conflict in the public arena. Somewhat ironically, it claims to protect the very thing it shuns in defining itself, that is, religion, through the promotion of religious freedom.

Interestingly enough, however, the word also has a Christian heritage. Only in the modern era did the secular undergo the more naturalistic connotations that we recognize today. The history of the word takes us back to the premodern church and the convention of distinguishing the priests of monastic and religious orders from the "secular" clergy of the diocese (a usage still found in the church). And the church Fathers used the Latin root of the word (*saeculum*) to describe the Christian view of the world. For them, *saeculum* designated the "transitory, provisional character of the present state of the world," opposing the Greek sense of *kosmos*, the beautiful, everlasting world order.[20]

We can trace more popular meanings of secularism to nineteenth-century debates about the role of religion in the moral education of society. Many Christians responded to rationalist attacks on Christianity by insisting on the necessity of faith for human morality. The early secularizers replied by arguing for nonreligious standards in the moral life and education of society, connecting the meaning of the "secular" to precisely these nonreligious standards.[21] Of course, the Christian tradition has always included strong voices recognizing the human capacity for apprehending moral principles without recourse to revelation, but the context tended toward an either/or disjunction between Christianity and natural morality: either the two are married and Christianity is necessary or they are distinct and we need not bother with religion. As Rémi Brague argues, the contemporary meaning of secularism grew out of "a false debate."[22]

The background assumptions of a culture or community often

20. Rémi Brague, "The Impossibility of Secular Society," *First Things* (October 2013): 27–31 (28).
21. Ibid. In his incisive reading of the historical context, Brague refers to the works of George Jacob Holyoake and John Stuart Mill.
22. Brague, "The Impossibility of Secular Society," 28.

shape the course of reflection on the meaning of faith and the role of religion in society in ways that go unnoticed.[23] The standard explanations of secularization illustrate this point by reading the fact of decline in religious belief and practice through the lens of naturalistic assumptions about religion and modernity, that is, assumptions that explanations of reality must exclude the supernatural. Most often, we end up with a subtraction story, as Taylor says, which defines modernity by its ability to shed the irrational, arcane, superstitious influence of religion.[24] Modern society no longer needs religion for making sense of the world, or giving moral direction to society, or comforting the fragile human psyche in an uncertain universe. The notion of the secular often carries a sense of self-assured rejection of religion rather than merely distancing or distinguishing a nonreligious space in political and public forums. The histories of nineteenth- and twentieth-century humanism and atheism in the United States offer striking examples of this belief in progressive secularism.[25]

Taylor takes a different approach to secularization. He offers a detailed historical analysis of the conditions in the modern era for an explosion of options in the spectrum of belief and unbelief. Secularity for him refers to this environment of options and their mutual contestation rather than merely the decline of religion or the separation from the public sphere.[26] If church attendance has declined and census data shows an increase of people with "no religion,"

23. Charles Taylor, *A Secular Age* (Cambridge, MA: Belknap Press, 2007), 427–28.
24. Ibid., 428–29.
25. The humanist movement predicted complete ascendancy over religions of the supernatural. The *Humanist Manifestos* of 1933 and 1973—"considered to be the charters of the organized humanist movement in the United States—both viewed secularism as ascending. *Humanist Manifesto II* predicted that the twenty-first century would be the 'humanist century,' as new strides in morals, ethics, and technology replaced older religious systems" (Richard Cimino and Christopher Smith, "Secular Humanism and Atheism Beyond Progressive Secularism," *Sociology of Religion* 68, no. 4 [2007]: 407–24 [412]).
26. Taylor, *A Secular Age*, 437.

still we can also recognize an anticipation of transcendence in a vast array of beliefs that shape the cultural landscape, ranging from evangelical megachurches to new age book shops and spirituality centers. Further, if we widen our sense of "religion" to match our foundation in religious conversion (chapter 2), then we interpret the situation differently still.[27] Of course, we can also recognize the varieties of unbelief, but we need not see the spectrum tilting in their favor by some inner mechanism of modernity. The options of belief and unbelief exist under the duress of contestation, developing according to shifts in meaning and value rather than naturalistic processes bent toward unbelief.[28]

The secular evokes different meanings and not all are merely descriptive, but when we turn to the notion of the sacred, we find a mixture of layers here as well. The popular meaning of the term may refer to religion or the holy, but it can also refer to whatever we value above all else. And thus it can include many different things in ordinary speech: love, freedom, family, even sport. The origins of the term are more specific, referring to something "set apart." As Joseph Pieper says: "The Latin verb *sancire*, the root of *sanctus* (holy, sacred), also means 'to fence off, to circumscribe.'"[29] The sacred stands in juxtaposition to what we experience as ordinary and commonplace. It contrasts with the profane, the original meaning of which refers to "the area in front of the temple (*fanum*), in front of its gates, 'outside.'"[30] In fact, Mircea Eliade defined these terms by their opposition: "The first possible definition of the sacred is that it is the opposite of the profane."[31]

---

27. Ibid., 427. Taylor does not disagree with the claim that secularization has resulted in a "decline of religion," but he understands the reasons and implications differently from the standard interpretations (Ibid., 436–37).
28. Ibid., 435.
29. Pieper, *In Search of the Sacred*, 13.
30. Ibid., 16.

For Eliade, the sacred refers to a dimension of human consciousness that disrupts our ordinary way of seeing the world and discloses a deeper reality. All religious living has at its core this power of the sacred, the manifestation of which Eliade referred to as a "hierophany."[32] "Every sacred space implies a hierophany, an irruption of the sacred that results in detaching a territory from the surrounding cosmic milieu and making it qualitatively different."[33] On this analysis, the desacralization of society represents a grave loss for the modern person. The dominance of the profane severely limits our existential possibilities.

René Girard, on the other hand, argues that sacralization can reveal a much grimmer reality, namely, violent sacrifice. Drawn into mimetic conflict and rivalry, people regularly experience caustic, relational tensions that threaten the stability of their community. Ordinarily, we resolve these rivalries by uniting with one another against third parties. Our common hatred for another brings us together and leads to violent acts of expulsion and lynching, the reconciling effect of which elicits our reverence and awe. The mechanism of scapegoating violence quite literally produces the sacred in the act of sacrifice: "Violence is the secret soul of the sacred."[34] For Girard, the gospels reveal the truth about the scapegoat mechanism, and their influence on modernity has had profound consequences. Such influence has enabled society to recognize the problem of sacrifice and institutionalize measures aimed at limiting it (such as modern law). Rather than an existential deficit, desacralization represents a modern achievement. And we can

31. Mircea Eliade, *The Sacred and the Profane*, trans. Willard R. Trask (New York: Harcourt Brace and Co, 1987), 10.
32. Ibid., 11.
33. Ibid., 26.
34. René Girard, *Violence and the Sacred* (Baltimore: Johns Hopkins University Press, 1977), 31.

ultimately attribute this achievement to the historical causality of revelation.

Different notions of the secular and the sacred crowd our assessments of religion in our modern, Western milieu, but these notions on their own do not offer a way of choosing among them. The issue of criteria returns to us. How do we normatively determine their contents? How should we identify the *authentically* sacred and *legitimately* secular while distinguishing them from counterfeit versions? Our approach in this book does not insist on ironclad definitions for these terms. Rather, it suggests that we use the heuristic content of a fourfold conversion to analyze the historical meanings and values at stake in our understandings of the secular and the sacred, and that we apply this analysis to our assessment of religion within our own context.

The foundational horizon of conversion allows us to embrace the flexibility of the categories. On the basis of moral conversion, for example, we can affirm a trajectory of secularizing in identifying nonreligious standards in the moral conduct of society (chapter 3). And yet we can disagree with naturalistic explanations of value and account for our moral apprehensions and aspirations with an adequate ontology of the good (for example, the normative scale of values) that leads to a needed sacralization.[35] The "false debate" that Brague recognizes in the context of early secularist thought illustrates for us how commonalities between the secular and religious can go unnoticed because of confusions and mistakes in the effective history of Christian theology.[36] Sorting out the dialectic of authentic

---

35. We examined this point in a discussion of models of God and moral conversion in chapter 6.
36. Noting the effective history of Christian faith and theology, Taylor recognizes "that there are clearly wrong versions of Christian faith" (Taylor, *A Secular Age*, 643). Still, he also does not think we can simply replace them with a single right version. The effective history of theology creates a kind of obscurity or lack of clarity that conditions all theological inquiry.

and unauthentic secularization requires a critical reading of Christian categories and their effects in the historical realities of modernity.

If we focus on conversion then, we can begin to attend to the different existential commitments of "secularizers" and "sacralizers," that is, people who argue for or against the withdrawal or extension of religious feeling and belief over particular orders of human activity. No doubt their mutual antagonism often signals a deeper existential divergence, but we would make a critical mistake in thinking of their mutual opposition according to a simple correspondence with the presence or absence of religious conversion. Almost invariably, the other modes of conversion are at stake as well and no particular group has an exclusive or invulnerable claim to any of them.

Most significantly, religious conversion is not restricted to sacralizers and the religious. The dynamic reality encompasses the data on an ongoing process of personal (and communal) growth in relation to the total (inchoate) fulfillment of human consciousness. The phenomenological analysis that underpins this notion allows us to explain how religious conversion does not coincide with religious belief and most often precedes moral, intellectual, and psychic conversions. Consequently, at the existential level, we can recognize an authentic orientation to many of the more strident criticisms of religion. Consider, for example, the postmodern, existentialist, feminist, and economic critiques of how certain images of God strengthen ideologies of inequality and the abuse of power.[37] Here, with the proper hermeneutic, we can find prophetic voices (perhaps inadvertently) calling a religious community back to faithfulness. The most devastating critiques of religion may arise from the presence of religious and moral conversion on the part of the critic.[38] The fourfold heuristic allows us then to move from the limited viewpoint

---

37. As found for example in liberation, feminist, ecological, and postcolonial discourses.

of an authentic critique to the more comprehensive viewpoint that provides a more authentic understanding of religion.

Since genuine religious experience fulfills the exigencies of human consciousness for meaning, truth, and value, it provides criteria for affirming a sacred that does not suffer from the aberrations of sacrificial violence.[39] If we then affirm the authentic sacred on the horizon of religious consciousness, still we also recognize the distinction between the religious horizon and belief. But what does this imply for the authentic sacred in symbol and sacrament? How do we make sense of the outward expression of the sacred as "set apart"? Here, we can appreciate the anthropological and social value of the religious tradition. The setting apart of the sacred in architecture and liturgy celebrates the mystery of love and awe that we experience within us, and promotes our attentiveness to it in ways that immerse us in the history of the community. No doubt we can affirm the sacredness of all things on the basis of God's universal gift of unrestricted love, but we limit our appropriation of religious consciousness if we fail to acknowledge and celebrate its own distinctive quality.[40]

Taylor's definition of secularity opposes naturalistic conceptions and reflects his belief in the cultural value of a transcendent horizon.[41] His approach agrees with ours on this point. His analysis goes on to show how the competing options of belief and unbelief confront

---

38. Christopher Hitchens's critiques of religion clearly have some bases in his own moral conversion: *God is not Great*.
39. Girard's analysis of the nonsacrificial reading of the gospels complements our notion of authentic religious experience and illustrates the precariousness of conversion within the church.
40. The qualitative difference does not negate the interaction of the sacred and profane within a common and comprehensive reality. Pieper criticizes analyses (for example, Eliade's) that separate the sacred and profane too completely. He sees the distinction as critical, especially for resisting naïve, totalizing calls for desacralization, but he also sympathizes with attacks on pseudosacredness; see Pieper, *In Search of the Sacred*, 20–22. The question then becomes a matter of conceiving adequately the notion of the "authentically sacred."
41. Taylor, *A Secular Age*, 437.

common dilemmas in our contemporary context and must demonstrate their value by dealing with these dilemmas honestly and persuasively.[42] More than anything, Taylor wants a conversation among the competing options. He wants exclusive humanists and orthodox believers to overcome simplistic, often demonizing, caricatures and dismissals of one another. He wants all seekers and dwellers to meet at a common table.

Making conversion the foundational reality of theology brings Christians to this dialogue with the interpretive skills for discerning authenticity and inauthenticity (albeit precariously and over time) on each side of the table. The ongoing process of religious development places all sides in the context of communal growth. It helps Christians to give an account of their hope without presupposing all the answers or some deficit on the part of another. More constructively, the scale of values allows Christians to imagine a political community that esteems religious value without insisting on the hegemony of belief as in Christendom.[43] If religious value marks a critical component of the structure of the human good, then cultivating religion within society ideally strengthens a collective commitment to the critical exigencies for meaning, truth, value, and collaborative action. But this happens only if Christians surrender rivalries and caricatures, if they pray for truth and authenticity more than institutional custom or change, if they refuse to assume the outcome of dialogue and stay open to the mystery of redemptive love in historical communities.

The foundational reality of conversion anticipates an authentic Christian presence that brings sympathetic discernment to our secular world. And thus it makes one, very important presupposition: "That every good Christian is more ready to put a good interpretation on another's statement than to condemn it as false."[44]

---

42. See, for example, Taylor's definition of the "maximal demand" (Ibid., 639–40).
43. See, for example, Neil Ormerod, *A Public God?*, especially chapter 6.

Being Christian in a World of Many Religions

The fact of religious pluralism in our era raises questions about the meanings of central Christian doctrines, and in the environment of secularity these questions often spark various levels of uncertainty and defensiveness about the truth of Christian faith. The typical reactions to pluralism fit with the mainline positions in the theologies of religions: exclusivists demand the necessity of faith in Christ for salvation; pluralists embrace many religious pathways to ultimate reality; and inclusivists attempt to strike some balance by simultaneously recognizing the universality of grace and the truth of the Christian mysteries. The different theologies of religions attempt to use the biblical and theological resources of the tradition to explain Christianity's relationship to other religions. The trajectory of the project often creates a very difficult tension between faithfulness to Christian tradition and openness to the wisdom of other religious ways. In fact, many people disagree with the entire endeavor, finding it dissatisfying no matter which position one happens to choose.[45]

The rest of this chapter explains how our approach to theological foundations envisions a new direction for handling the question of religious pluralism. When we make conversion the foundational reality of theology, we can take history seriously in theology and recognize the shifts in meaning and value at stake in the growth of the religious community over time. Christian doctrine answers specific questions at key moments in the history of the community,

---

44. St. Ignatius of Loyola, *The Spiritual Exercises of St. Ignatius: Based on Studies in the Language of the Autograph*, trans. Louis J. Puhl (Chicago: Loyola Press, 1951), n. 22. The presupposition of the spiritual exercises is instructive because it includes dialectic and the need for correcting errors within the interpersonal context of mutual generosity and a collaborative commitment to truth.

45. For example, some comparative theologians criticize the theologies of religions for making judgments about the religions without ever engaging their distinct worldviews. See James Fredericks, "A Universal Religious Experience? Comparative Theology as an Alternative to a Theology of Religions," *Horizons* 22, no. 1 (1995): 67–87.

but it does not answer each and every question for all times and places. The consequences are significant for our understanding of religious pluralism: no longer can we simply make sense of plurality by appealing to an overarching metaphysical or doctrinal framework. The question of Christianity's final relationship to other religions does not allow us to step outside our current context of religious living in our search for an answer not yet present. In what follows, we begin with a brief discussion of representative positions in the theology of religions and illustrate how their foundations generate closed horizons. The last part of the chapter explains how our foundations avoid this problem of closure and emphasize attentiveness to the contingencies of the religions in history.

The Closed Horizon of Theologies of Religions

We now consider examples of different positions within the theologies of religions, including pluralist, exclusivist, inclusivist, and postliberal. Our concern is not classification, however. Here, we aim only to illustrate how these different theologies rely on foundational positions that overly determine the final relationship of Christianity to other religions.

John Hick's work most notably represents the pluralist position in the theologies of religions. He suggests that each of the religions has salvific value and that no single religion has an exclusive claim to ultimate truth. Once we define salvation according to criteria of spiritual transformation rather than creedal assent or formal initiation, then we can (inductively) affirm that in each of the world's religions we find people who express the "fruits of the Spirit" and deserve our admiration. Hick says this leads to pluralism: "It therefore seems logical to me to conclude that not only Christianity, but also these other world faiths, are human responses to the Ultimate. They see the Divine/Sacred/Ultimate through different human conceptual 'lenses,' and they experience the divine/sacred/ultimate presence through their different spiritual practices in correspondingly different forms of religious experience. But they seem to constitute more or less equally authentic human awarenesses of and response to the Ultimate, the Real, the final ground and source of everything."[46]

Hick's position appeals to a modern sensibility that recoils at exclusive claims to truth. Drawing heavily on Kant's epistemology, he explains why we can observe spiritual "fruits" in each of the religions and why it makes sense to surrender exclusive claims.[47] The fundamental distinction between reality in itself (*an sich*) and the phenomenal manifestation or humanly perception of reality applies to religious experience and knowledge as well.[48] Each of the religions has a unique and spiritually fruitful perspective on ultimate reality, and each must therefore surrender any claim to superiority.

Hick thus proposes a Copernican revolution in Christian theology. The traditional doctrines that imply exclusive claims to truth must undergo a radical revision in accordance with the basic insight of pluralism. He says of the Incarnation, Trinity, and Atonement: "The three pillars of traditional orthodoxy inevitably come under criticism in any attempt to develop our theology in the light of the realization that Christianity is not the one and only salvific path, but is one among others."[49] Hick's epistemological foundation leads him to a clear answer to the question of religious pluralism: the world's

46. John Hick, "A Pluralist View," in *More Than One Way? Four Views on Salvation in a Pluralistic World*, ed. Dennis L. Okholm and Timothy R. Phillips (Grand Rapids: Zondervan, 1995), 27–59 (44–45).
47. Hick writes: "I am suggesting applying this [Kantian] insight to our awareness of the Real, by distinguishing between the noumenal Real, the Real *an sich*, and the Real as humanly perceived in different ways as a range of divine phenomena" (*A Christian Theology of Religions: the Rainbow of Faiths*, 1st American ed. [Louisville, KY: Westminster John Knox Press, 1995], 29).
48. "A Pluralist View," 46–51. Hick also refers to Aquinas's dictum: the thing known is in the knower according to the mode of the knower. But he interprets this dictum according to Kantian suppositions and in a way that misrepresents the meaning of Aquinas. See Aquinas, *ST* 1.12.4.
49. Ibid., 52.

religions express more or less equally valid and valuable perspectives on relating to reality in a salvific way.

Karl Barth's approach opposes Hick's revolutionary proposal. Many people label Barth an exclusivist because of his emphasis on the absolute necessity of special revelation for salvation.[50] "In revelation," Barth writes, "God tells man that he is God, and that as such he is his Lord. In telling him this, revelation tells him something utterly new, something which apart from revelation he does not know and cannot tell either himself or others."[51] If we restrict genuine knowledge of God to revelation as communicated in the gospel, then we possess no criteria for expecting true knowledge of God outside faith in Christ. In chapter 6, we discussed how Barth rejects the possibility of natural theology and apologetics because of the postlapsarian helplessness of the human condition, and how he emphasizes the absolute primacy of God's mercy in bridging the gap between God and humanity. For Barth, true and saving knowledge depends entirely on divine revelation. In a way, he flips around Hick's universalist application of Kant. God bridges the impossible divide between divine being and human cognition: Jesus (the noumenal) makes reality truly known to us in faith. And this perspective results in a resounding rejection of religion. "Religion is unbelief. . . . From the standpoint of revelation, religion is clearly seen to be a human attempt to anticipate what God in His revelation wills to do and does do. It is the attempted replacement of the divine work by a human manufacture. The divine

---

50. Barth never developed a theology of religions and the complexities of his thought leave room for debate on his precise position. Joseph Di Noia emphasizes this point in Joseph Di Noia, "Religion and the Religions," in *The Cambridge Companion to Karl Barth*, ed. John Webster (Cambridge UK: Cambridge University), 243–57 (243–45). Most importantly, the trajectory of Barth's reflections on religion and revelation illustrates our point about the significance of theological foundations.

51. Karl Barth, *Church Dogmatics*, 1/2:301; cited in Paul F. Knitter, *No Other Name?: A Critical Survey of Christian Attitudes toward the World Religions* (Maryknoll, NY: Orbis Books, 1985), 82.

reality offered and manifested to us in revelation is replaced by a concept of God arbitrarily and willfully evolved by man."[52]

Not even Christianity escapes Barth's condemnation. All religions exhibit idolatry and self-righteousness because of human sinfulness.[53] If God alone justifies us, then we are lost in the absence of the reality of divine grace. None of the positive and human elements in the religions anticipate the disruptive, saving power of the gospel. Christianity's uniqueness rests strictly in the gratuity of this knowledge. In other words, the truth of Christianity owes nothing to its status or quality as a religion and everything to God's self-revealing gift in the Incarnation. When we turn to Christianity's relation to the religions, we see that Barth's way of opposing religion to revelation largely determines the issue: if all religions stand in the darkness of their humanity and absolute need for grace, still the saving light of revelation shines on those who bear the name of Christ.[54]

Karl Rahner has a more positive view of the religions and the possibility of salvation outside Christian faith. Significantly influential at Vatican II, his work contributed to Catholic theology's shift to thinking about salvation primarily on the basis of God's universal salvific will rather than the need for baptism. If we begin with God's desire for friendship with the whole human family, then we tend to think optimistically about the fate of people outside the church. Rhetorically, Rahner asks: "But can the Christian believe even for

52. Barth, *Church Dogmatics*, 1/2:299–300; cited in Knitter, *No Other Name?*, 84.

53. Di Noia argues that *Unglaube* is better translated as "faithlessness" rather than "unbelief," and emphasizes that Barth strictly opposes this term to revelation and not other religions: "It is crucial to observe that, for Barth, the judgment that all religion is unfaith is strictly a divine judgment rendered by revelation itself and knowable only by the grace of faith. This judgment is emphatically not one that is pronounced upon the world of non-Christian religions by Christianity nor its representatives" (Di Noia, "Religion and the Religions," 250).

54. It should be noted that Barth is at times more nuanced than he seems on this question. See Paul Chung, "Karl Barth's Theology of Reconciliation in Dialogue with a Theology of Religions," *Mission Studies* 25, no. 2 (2008): 211–28.

a moment that the overwhelming mass of his brothers [who are not explicitly Christian] . . . are unquestionably and in principle excluded from the fulfillment of their lives and condemned to eternal meaninglessness? He must reject any suggestion, and his faith is itself in agreement with his doing so. For the Scriptures tell him expressly that God wants everyone to be saved" (1 Tim. 2:4).[55]

Rahner's emphasis on God's universal salvific will has become characteristic of the Catholic approach, but his view of salvation outside the church depends on his specific way of conceiving the relation between human nature and divine grace. For Rahner, the human person has an infinite openness to receiving supernatural grace, and the unconditional ordination of this openness expresses the very effect of the divine gift operating within human consciousness. He calls this mediating principle the "supernatural existential," and this forms the basis of his famous theory of the "anonymous Christian."[56]

The title of the "anonymous Christian" points to the truth about the reality of salvation. The universality of grace implies that whenever people freely embrace the dynamic orientation of their horizons toward transcendence in faith, hope, and love, they live in "the state of Christ's grace," even if they lack "explicit knowledge" of it. The saving presence of God in all times and places has a deeply christological meaning, because the event of the Incarnation imparts to human history its deepest existential truth. "Such a 'presence' of Jesus Christ," Rahner writes, "throughout the whole history of salvation and in relation to all people cannot be denied or overlooked

---

55. Karl Rahner, "Anonymous Christians," in *Theological Investigations*, trans. Karl-H. and Boniface Kruger, 6:390–98 (391). New York: Seabury, 1974.

56. For an explicit reference to the "supernatural existential," see ibid. 393. Rahner elaborates: "This means positively that man in experiencing his transcendence, his limitless openness—no matter how implicit and incomprehensible it always is—also already experiences the offer of grace—not necessarily expressly as grace, as distinctly supernatural calling, but experiences the reality of its content" (Ibid., 394).

by Christians if they believe in Jesus Christ as the salvation of *all* people, and do not think that the salvation of non-Christians is brought about by God and his mercy independently of Jesus Christ."[57]

Rahner's appreciation of history in the economy of salvation leads him to affirm the value of the world's religions in mediating the free acceptance of the graced horizon of human experience.[58] Relative to their positive, supernaturally influenced elements, the religions can contribute to the salvation of those outside the church and thus anticipate the gospel (*preparatio evangelica*).[59] Still, Rahner left no doubt about the truth of Christianity. He argued that our transcendental experience has an inner drive toward becoming explicit in Christian faith and practice, and that Christianity makes visible the supernatural reality that other religions more dimly reflect: "the Church will not so much regard herself today as the exclusive community of those who have a claim to salvation but rather as the historically tangible vanguard and the historically and socially constituted explicit expression of what the Christian hopes is present as a hidden reality even outside the visible Church."[60] Rahner's theory relates Christianity to the world's religions according to his foundational position of the supernatural existential: the universality of God's self-gift permeates human history and orients all people toward the fullness of salvation in Christ and his body, the church.[61]

---

57. Karl Rahner, *Foundations of Christian Faith*, 312.
58. Rahner rejects the idea that non-Christian religions are in principle excluded from contributing positively to the salvation of their adherents. He deems such a view "ahistorical and asocial"; see ibid., 314.
59. For Rahner's affirmation of supernatural elements of non-Christian religions and how he applies his notion of a "lawful religion," a religion that we can regard as a positive means for attaining salvation, see "Christianity and the Non-Christian Religions," in *Theological Investigations*, 5:115–34 (125–31).
60. Ibid., 133; cited in Knitter, *No Other Name?*, 129–30.
61. The givenness of the content of grace signals the traces of idealism in Rahner's position. Revelation makes an *a priori* claim on the structures of consciousness. For example: "The expressly Christian revelation becomes the explicit statement of the revelation of grace which

The approach of postliberal theology attempts to find a way out of this common typology in the theology of religions. George Lindbeck's influential book, *The Nature of Doctrine*, focuses on the cultural-linguistic meaning of doctrine and its formative value for Christian faith and practice. He contends that doctrine functions for Christians as an authoritative set of linguistic rules that shape "discourse, attitude, and action."[62] He considers what he calls the "experiential-expressivist" supposition that (religious) experience precedes and informs belief and assumes the opposite: belief shapes experience. Christians interiorize a set of skills through practice and training within the context of community and essentially grow into their experience through the formative influence of their religious language.

The idea of salvation has a precise meaning within the Christian community, and we cannot answer questions about how this meaning applies to those outside the linguistic system of Christianity. Lindbeck rejects the idea of a common ground for the religions or a universal experience of grace. He insists rather on their incommensurability. The religions are too different and specific in their cultural-linguistic meanings to assume an anonymous unity.[63] The absence of neutral criteria leaves us in a situation of plurality that escapes our adjudications. And this ultimately leads to exclusivist criteria: "There is no damnation—just as there is no salvation—outside the church. One must, in other words, learn the language of faith before one can know enough about its message knowingly to reject it and thus be lost."[64] For Lindbeck, the salvation of all people depends

man always experiences implicitly in the depths of his being" (Rahner, "Anonymous Christians," 394).

62. George A. Lindbeck, *The Nature of Doctrine*, 18.

63. For a strong, theological affirmation of religious diversity as grounded in the reality of God, see S. Mark Heim, *The Depth of the Riches: A Trinitarian Theology of Religious Ends* (Grand Rapids: Eerdmans, 2001).

64. Lindbeck, *Nature of Doctrine*, 59.

on their confrontation with the gospel, for only then does it become a meaningful possibility for them. If people never hear the gospel in this life, then we can trust that in the next they will meet Christ and the singular meaning of their redemption. The cultural-linguistic approach imagines a postmortem solution to the problem of salvation for people who never hear the gospel. It defines Christianity's relationship to the religions according to the grammar of its linguistic field.

Each of the theologies of religions discussed in this section incorporates foundational positions that determine Christianity's relationship to the religions. All of the approaches assume that we need to figure out that relationship if we want to explain the truth of Christian faith in the context of religious pluralism. The next section suggests that our foundational positions anticipate a different direction in the theology of religions. Rather than connecting the truth of Christianity to the ultimate meaning of religious pluralism, our approach recognizes the importance of human history both for discerning that meaning and for appropriating the truth of Christian faith.

The Open Horizon of Religious Conversion

In chapter 2, we explained how the heuristic notion of religious experience orients us to the historical data of the religions. Rather than specifying conceptual content or religious belief, the category of religious experience allows us to recognize within the histories of religions a principle of authentic expression in the existential reality of their adherents. It allows us to appreciate the normative influence of religious authenticity within the particularities of distinct traditions' beliefs, symbols, and rituals. It does not commit the religions to an overarching relativism (pluralism), or a dogmatic absolutism (exclusivism), or suggest a hierarchy of truth and value among them (inclusivism), or enclose the religions within mutually exclusive cultural-linguistic borders (postliberalism). Rather, the heuristic notion of religious experience gives us a verifiable base for our interpretive explorations of religious expressions and their development over time. It enables us to move toward creative and redemptive possibilities for interreligious dialogue and collaboration.

Here, we arrive at a key idea: the heuristic nature of this category. It implies several critical points for our understanding of the foundations of Christian theology. Most importantly, it implies that theology's foundational reality (as defined) is not exclusive to the Christian tradition. The category of religious experience refers to the transcultural reality of the fulfillment of human consciousness. And we project no conceptual content on this conscious state. Its terms and relations are implicitly defined according to an analysis of interiority. In other words, we arrive at the definition by attending to our experienced fulfillment of our conscious desire for meaning, truth, value, beauty, and love. The heuristic definition allows us to talk about religious experience in a way that focuses strictly on the structure of consciousness. It does not imply the idea of a common essence for all religious experience or the assumption of inner unity for the various symbolic, linguistic systems of diverse religious traditions. The supposed prelinguistic content of essentialist conceptions of religious experience is impossible to verify. Rather, the heuristic notion recognizes that appropriations of religious experience invariably draw on the resources of tradition and belief, and that questions about cross-cultural or interreligious commonality are satisfied only by correct judgment rather than appeals to supposedly common experience.

If the foundations of Christian theology are not exclusive to Christianity, then we cannot logically determine Christian theological concepts from our foundations. The contingencies of history are critical to deriving special theological categories. The history of the religious tradition informs the appropriation and formulation of religious experience as well as further sets of categories (such as God, revelation, church). Here, for example, and throughout this book, we describe a dynamic state of being-in-love unrestrictedly, but even this formulation reflects a culturally specific matrix of meaning. References to "being-in-love" may not quite express the reality for some people, and may miss it altogether for others.[65] If different communities or traditions speak about religious experience in various terms, we ought not to assume the negligibility of these differences, for they mediate the effective history of the community in both its relative authenticity and inauthenticity. The Christian community, for example, has reasons for using the language of love (1 John 4:8), but a lengthier discussion of a specific usage of the term may reveal a creeping sentimentalism that cannot cope theologically with the mystery of the cross. And we could uncover this inadequacy with a more attentive, critical analysis of religious interiority. Our analysis also allows us to recognize the principle of religious authenticity in different carriers of meaning (artistic, symbolic, intersubjective), including the symbol of the cross, and not focus entirely on differences of cognitive meaning.[66]

When we ask about Christianity's final relationship to the religions, we move beyond foundations and into Christian doctrine. The question anticipates our consideration of the content of Christian faith, but the key to the resolution belongs to how we

---

65. The referent of "the reality" in this sentence is possible to attain because of our implicitly defined understanding of the structure of consciousness. The definition marks a heuristic limit and enables us to interpret the meaning of our experience concretely in approximation to that limit.

66. Arguably, this perspective complements the project of comparative theology. For a more detailed explanation of Lonergan's notion of religion and how it disposes theology for comparative encounters, see Christiaan Jacobs-Vandegeer, "Method, Meaning, and the Theologies of Religions," *Irish Theological Quarterly* 80, no. 1 (2015): 30–55.

approach that content. Our foundational categories determine the horizon within which we understand the meaning of doctrine and approach the question of religious pluralism. Many differences in the theologies of religions primarily betray diverging foundational positions in relation to the various conversions rather than doctrinal commitments. The foundational reality of theology that we propose does not settle Christianity's final relationship to the religions by appealing to overarching metaphysical and doctrinal frameworks. It anticipates an analysis of religious meaning and value within historical communities that in many instances develop more or less authentically over relatively long intervals of time.

Christianity and the Religions

How then should we consider the uniqueness of Christianity? Let us begin by saying that our approach does not prefigure a pluralist revolution of doctrine, as we have seen in the previous chapter. Nor does it anticipate a logical deduction of doctrinal truths and their implications. Such readings of doctrine betray mistaken views on theological foundations. If we identify the foundational reality of theology with the ongoing (personal and communal) conversion of the theologian, then we can recognize that in church doctrine the community affirms in faith the true meaning of its religious experience. And religious experience always unfolds within a community's history. Concretely, the two are inseparable. Doctrine affirms a truth that strikes to the heart of the historical community's search for the meaning, truth and value, and the implications of its religious experience.[67] Most importantly, then, grasping the

67. Lonergan refers to Voegelin: "Indeed, as Eric Voegelin has claimed, nothing can be achieved by pitting right doctrine against wrong doctrine, for that only intensifies preoccupation with doctrine. What is needed, he urges, is the restoration of the search for the meaning of life." (Bernard J. F. Lonergan, "Theology and Praxis," in *A Third Collection*, ed. Frederick E. Crowe, [New York: Paulist, 1985], 184–201 [188–89]).

meanings of Christian doctrine entails grasping their limitations. And these limitations bring us always back to the history of the community, to its many and diverse questions, to its problems and difficulties, to its desires and values, and to its biases and scotoma. The limitations of Christian doctrine narrate the historical (and dialectical) development of the community of faith.

Still, these limits in no way obscure our attainment in faith of transcendent realities. The Christian mysteries expressed in dogma outstrip the proportion of our natural knowing and are attained in contemplation only by the infused light of faith. And the horizon of our contemplation of the mysteries of faith extends indefinitely, in concert with our potential for existential growth. The limits of Christian dogma mark thresholds for religious development within the narratives of personal and communal history. Our limitations and growth are thoroughly historical, and this implies that our understanding of dogma allows for endless deepening.

Again, what does this say about the uniqueness of Christianity? It says that we need not expect the received doctrinal tradition to answer each and every question that arises within the community.[68] Such an expectation in fact betrays a misunderstanding of doctrine, the meaning of which pertains to specific judgments. No doubt the limitations define the achievements of the community over time, but if a theologian expects Christian doctrine to solve all problems and answer all questions for all times and places, then the limitation of doctrine must seem like a problem to overcome. And this problem is nothing more than the problem of history. Once theology makes

---

68. Of course, this point is rather straightforward Catholic teaching: "Yet even if Revelation is already complete, it has not been made completely explicit; it remains for Christian faith gradually to grasp its full significance over the course of the centuries" (*Catechism of the Catholic Church*, 66, accessed September 7, 2015 at: http://www.vatican.va/archive/ENG0015/_PH.HTM). If, however, intellectual conversion is lacking, then references to the completeness of revelation will seem to logically imply the exclusion of all apparently alternative claims to truth.

meaning rather than logic foundational, it makes history integral to its collaborative task of mediating between religion and culture.

The meanings of all the religions develop over time, and the analysis of meaning based in interiority allows us to expand our (Christian) understanding of the way divine meaning transforms human history. Once we recognize different carriers and functions of meaning, then we can see how religious experience flourishes in various cultures in different, complicated, and dialectical ways (such as artistically, symbolically, linguistically, intersubjectively, constitutively, effectively, cognitively, and communicatively; see chapters 3 and 7).[69] Such an analysis of meaning complements comparative theologians' engagements with particular religious traditions and their efforts to learn from them. It also allows us to continue with the theologies of religions, but in a way that chooses a different starting point. Rather than presaging the final relationship of Christianity to the religions, this approach offers us the tools for recognizing the ongoing development of that relationship in history.

The foundational realities of religious and intellectual conversion offer correctives to the Kantian commitments of the pluralist hypothesis as well as inclusivism's idealist tendency to decide about the inner content of all the religions in the economy of salvation. The same foundations enable us to discern the distinctiveness of religious ways and particularities without suspending judgment indefinitely about the presence or absence of authenticity in their concrete expressions. Rather than retreating into linguistic provincialism, our

---

69. The foundations that we propose prepare theology to discern the relationship of Christianity to the religions in history. Such a theological task is consistent with the perspective in *Dominus Iesus*, which, affirming the uniqueness and centrality of the Paschal Mystery in relation to the universal salvific will of God, says: "Bearing in mind this article of faith, theology today, in its reflection on the existence of other religious experiences and on their meaning in God's salvific plan, is invited to explore if and in what way the historical figures and positive elements of these religions may fall within the divine plan of salvation" (Congregation for the Doctrine of the Faith, *Dominus Iesus*, On the Unicity and Salvific Universality of Jesus Christ and the Church, n. 14, accessed September 7, 2015).

approach opens theology toward dialectical and dialogical interreligious encounters and enables us to imagine mutual growth, collaboration, and transformation as a result. It allows us to fully embrace the meaning and truth of church doctrine, and to appreciate its formative value, without presupposing that doctrine must logically account for each and every question that arises within the community of faith. Rather, we can explain how the church appropriates the truth of the faith in the historical reality of its ongoing, holistic conversion. And that historical reality of personal and communal existential growth brings together in various ways all the seekers, dwellers, unbelievers, and believers of many religious ways.

Conclusion

Discussions about secularism and religious pluralism too often evoke defensive attitudes and betray a sense that Christian faith encounters other viewpoints and ways of living as threats. Such a sense need not define the church. The path to overcoming this problem begins with the adoption of a different perspective on what it means to appropriate the meaning of Christian faith. If the meaning of faith entails a closed horizon, then the presence of difference invariably poses a threat. If the meaning of Christian faith unfolds on the open horizon of our ongoing conversion, then we can embrace others according to the very criteria that orient our growth in faith. The foundational reality of conversion places theology always in contexts of collaboration and reciprocal learning. The goal is not to carve out a Christian space in the world, but rather to communicate the meaning of the gospel in the deepest possible way. And this cannot happen without attending to the complex patterns of authenticity and inauthenticity in society, culture, and the church. The task of living an authentic Christian presence in the world begins most radically with this attentiveness. Only by listening can we ever hope to encounter the grace that always already meets us first, moving us to say: "Thanks be to God."

10

Theological Method

The overall aim of this book has been the development of theological foundations, a task conceived as a specialization or stage within a functionally differentiated and collaborative theological method. However, to this point, we have said little to explain the nature of that theological method, though it has functioned throughout this book. Elements of this method appear in (later) chapters where we distinguish the task of foundations from doctrines and systematics. Now it is time to make that method more explicit. Our method distinguishes eight interrelated theological tasks, each of which makes a distinct contribution to the theological project. Following the terminology of Bernard Lonergan, we call these tasks *functional specialties*.[1] The tasks are *functional*, that is, they break the overall project of theology into distinctive steps or stages; and so the *specialties* do not divide up theology into themes or subject areas, or sources and resources, but into a series of interlocking stages that move theology from data to results to the communication of those results. Developing theological foundations marks a distinct stage or specialty within this process.

---

1. See Lonergan, *Method*.

As we have emphasized from the beginning, our theological foundations are grounded in conversion, as religious, moral, intellectual, and psychic. These conversions tell us something about the subjectivity of the theologian. This, in turn, will help us lay out the theological method implicit in our foundations.

Conversion and the Transcendental Imperatives

We begin with *religious conversion*. We spoke in chapter 2 of this in terms of falling in love unrestrictedly so that we see the world through the eyes of love. We noted how St. Paul spoke of God's love poured into our hearts through the Holy Spirit given to us (Rom. 5:5), and described the Spirit's residence in us by pointing to the fruits: love, joy, peace, patience, kindness, goodness, gentleness, faithfulness, and self-control (Gal. 5:22). These expressions capture something of the reality we mean by religious conversion and its impact on our lives. The transcendental imperative that expresses this conversion is "Be in love." We are called to "Be in Love" at the natural level of family, friends, and lovers, but even more so with the One who is the source of everything that is, of all meaning, truth, and goodness in our lives. However, as with all fallings in love, it is not so much an achievement as a gift and invitation; not something we generate ourselves, rather something that overtakes us, seduces us, envelops us.

Moral conversion entails a shift in our decision making from mere satisfactions to genuine values. In chapter 3 we recalled the story of St. Ignatius of Loyola who learned through his own experience of reading the lives of the saints how to discriminate between fleeting satisfactions and genuine values and then committed himself to those values. Similarly, St. Augustine, while converted religiously, struggled with his moral conversion to sexual continence, eventually to embrace this as well. The transcendental imperative that expresses this conversion is "Be responsible." We are all called to "Be responsible," to act responsibly by basing our decisions on genuine values, to take responsibility for our own moral living, not to just flow with the crowd, but to take responsibility for ourselves, for others, and for the world, in promoting genuine flourishing in human history.

More difficult and less common is *intellectual conversion*. This has a twofold aspect: the appropriation of our own knowing processes grounded in intelligence and reason; and the alignment of our criteria for reality with our processes of knowing. Again, in chapter 4, we illustrated this process of conversion in the life of St. Augustine as he turned from thinking about God as somehow extended in space and time to thinking of God as "Truth." Intellectual conversion means rejecting the persistent myth that reality is "already-out-there-now," to be apprehended by taking a good look. It means rather that we think of the real as the objective of intelligent and reasonable questioning. We are called to bring intelligence and reason to bear in grasping reality, to persist in asking the basic questions, "What is it?" (questions for intelligence) and "Is it so?" (questions for reasonable judgment) until we address all the relevant questions and thus attain reality, truth, and being. The imperatives that express this conversion are: "Be intelligent" and "Be reasonable."

Finally, most difficult and perhaps least common is *psychic conversion*. Psychic conversion asks us to attend to what attracts us and holds out attention. It asks us to attend to beauty. Are we attracted to the beauty of genuine meaning, truth, and goodness, or are we distracted with "many things"? The imperative that expresses this is "Be attentive," attentive to the object of our attention, to the data, but also to our own attentiveness, to ask to what it is that we are attracted, what holds our attention, so that we might better align ourselves to meaning, truth, and genuine value.

These imperatives, Be attentive, Be intelligent, Be reasonable, Be responsible, and Be in love, provide us with the structure of the basic operations and orientations of human consciousness. We begin with the data to which we attend; we ask questions for intelligence, "What is it?," so as to discover the meaning of the data. We then have an insight, formulate an hypothesis, and this raises the critical question, "Is it so?," with its demand for reasons, so that we can come to an informed judgment about the meaning of the data. Finally the questions arise, "What are we to do?" "What decisions flow from this judgment and how are we to respond properly, to be responsible in the current situation?" The movement from data to decision entails a cumulative process structured by questions and answers. This process relies on and reveals our inner orientation to meaning, truth, and goodness. The final imperative, Be in love, discloses our deepest and most fundamental orientation, the wellspring of all our other conscious processes, the *apex animae* (the peak of the soul). Do our questions and answers come from a place of hardness of heart, of self-reliance and self-assertion? Or do they come from a heart of flesh, of graciously receiving our lives, our existence, as gift from the source of all meaning, truth, and goodness? This basic orientation has a profound effect on all our conscious operations.

How then does this structure relate to the theological task? We might begin by reflecting on more traditional approaches at least within a Catholic context. A student in the preconciliar church would begin theological preparation with courses in philosophy, which may (or may not) catalyze some type of intellectual conversion. Religious and moral conversion were more or less taken for granted, perhaps an issue for spiritual formation rather than theological formulation and explication, so the student moved on, after a course in fundamental theology/apologetics, to a study of the basic religious and moral doctrines that were part of the church's heritage. If lucky, the student may have studied not only the doctrines (proven by reason, Scripture, and authority), but what doctrines might mean and how they might systematically relate to one another, before hitting courses concerned with their pastoral implementation and communication, preaching, catechesis, moral guidance and pastoral care, according to the mind of the church.

We might roughly align these with the imperatives as follows. Courses in fundamental theology/apologetics are in some sense taking *responsibility* for the further theological tasks to come, laying out foundations through a consideration of sources (scripture, tradition, authority, reason) and their relative authority in preparation for the religious and moral doctrines which form the church's heritage. The study of doctrines presents the tradition's *reasoned* judgments of religious and moral truths while systematics sought to *intelligently* understand the meaning of these doctrines and their relationship to one another, always aware that in dealing with religious mysteries, such understanding could never be exhausted. Finally, in considering the pastoral implementation and communication of the church's doctrines and their meanings, one must be *attentive* to the concrete particularities of the recipients, as they are not abstractions but living, breathing human beings, who live in a particular social and cultural setting. While this might seem somewhat forced, this approach basically describes the type of theological education that occurred within Catholic tradition prior to Vatican II.[2]

The other thing to note here is that the movement through the theological disciplines is the opposite to that of the natural movement

---

2. Of course, much of this structure was put aside post-Vatican II when courses began to incorporate aspects of historical consciousness into theological studies.

we posited above, from attention to intelligence, reasonableness, and then responsibility. This raises the obvious question, how did we get to that level of responsibility in the first place? More concretely, this question was posed in terms of the emergence of historical consciousness and the historical development of doctrine. If doctrines have histories, which we can trace in detail through all their tortuous debates, in what sense do they hold our allegiance? The traditional approach started, after a foray into apologetics, with what is ontologically prior (*priora quoad se*), in the basic judgments of Christian revelation, rather than what we first encounter, the *intersubjective, artistic, symbolic* carriers of revelatory meanings experienced as data. With the emergence of historical consciousness, theological scholars began to read the traditional sources of theology not as authoritative documents carrying meanings and values of the tradition, but simply as historical documents to be read and understood as products of their place and time. Theology discovered *critical historical method.* In itself, this was a theological revolution that threatened to relativize what had always been taken as absolute. It created a theological problem because it appeared to involve two sources of truth, one known through historical investigation, the other through revelation and the articles of faith, where the two sources may or may not coincide.

Much of the history of twentieth century theology has been about the encounter of traditional theological approaches with modern critical historical method. Its impact was first felt in relation to Scriptural studies, then to patristic and doctrinal studies. Joseph Ratzinger has identified as a central problem for theology the need to find "a better synthesis between historical and theological methods, between higher criticism and church doctrine." Further, "a truly pervasive understanding of this whole problem has yet to be found which takes into account both the undeniable insights uncovered by historical method, while at the same time overcoming its limitations."[3] Following the work of Lonergan, what we propose in terms of theological method is one way of seeking to address this challenge.

Transcendental Imperatives and Functional Specialties

We have noted above the ways in which a more traditional approach to theology incorporates the transcendental imperatives (be responsible, be reasonable, be intelligent, and be attentive) by moving from fundamental theology to doctrines, systematics, and then finally to concrete applications to the life of the church. However, we can also envisage a reversal of the imperatives as applied to the data of revelation entering into and shaping human history. Taken together, these processes give us an eightfold differentiation of theological tasks. Following Lonergan, we call these tasks "functional specialties." The following table best illustrates these:

Imperatives	Positive phase	Normative phase
Be responsible	Dialectics	Foundations
Be reasonable	History	Doctrines
Be intelligent	Interpretation	Systematics
Be attentive	Research	Communications

Traditional theology was very strong in relation to what we call the normative phase of theology, with a strong emphasis on doctrine,

---

3. Joseph Ratzinger, "Foundations and Approaches of Biblical Exegesis," *Origins* 17, no. 35 (1988): 593, 595–602 (596). For Ratzinger, the limitations of critical historical method lay in its neglect of the dogmatic tradition, as exercising some control as to its outcomes. Similarly Lonergan commented: "the whole problem in modern theology, Protestant and Catholic, is the introduction of historical scholarship." Quoted in Frederick E. Crowe, *Developing the Lonergan Legacy: Historical, Theoretical and Existential Themes*, ed. Michael Vertin (Toronto: University of Toronto, 2004), 79.

its understanding, and applications. The first, positive phase, which arises with autonomy in relation to the normative phase, encompasses the movement from attending to the original data (research), intelligently reading it in context (interpretation), and constructing an historical narrative that accounts for its meaning and significance (history). Such historical narratives often disagree, and do so in quite fundamental ways, so theologians must sort out and adjudicate the differences (dialectics). This process then establishes a background and launching pad for the normative phase. In fact, we used this strategy in chapter 1 where we identified dialectical differences among various theological writings and the need to resolve them. Now, we shall consider each of the specialties in more detail and how they relate to one another and to the theologian's ongoing conversion.

Research

Research is the starting point for any theological task, but here the term has a more precise delineation. It is concerned with our attentiveness to the data. This most basic form of research is concerned with the accuracy of the data, the sort of work we find in Scripture studies where scholars seek to ensure that we have an accurate manuscript for the Bible, usually referred to as textual criticism. Of course, this extends to all other texts, patristic, medieval, and modern. Have we got an accurate text?[4] Are we starting with accurate data?[5] This is often meticulous and detailed work requiring

---

4. Here, we focus on texts as it is the most common issue for theology, but we could include archaeology, numismatics (coins), monuments, ancient cartography, and so on, as data of interest for their historical implications.

5. As Paul Maas notes, "We have no autograph manuscripts of the Greek and Roman classical writers and no copies which have been collated with the originals; the manuscripts we possess derive from the originals through an unknown number of intermediate copies, and are consequently of questionable trustworthiness. The business of textual criticism is to produce

specialized knowledge of ancient manuscripts, their production, reproduction, and storage methods, and so on. A good example of this type of work would be the efforts to decide on the accuracy of the text of John's account of the adulterous woman (John 7:53–8:11), which occurs in some manuscripts but not others. Generally, scholars who work in this field develop a kitbag of methods for making decisions about which text is accurate. Such *lectio difficilior*, a more difficult reading, is preferred because a scribe is more likely to smooth out difficulties than introduce them.[6] All this is very familiar territory for scholars working in the field. Most historical and systematic theologians, however, take this work for granted as part of the scholarly background for their overall projects.

While the focus above has been on texts, the same issues arise in relation to various fields of data. These fields may include archaeology, numismatics (coins), monuments, ancient cartography, or data about social practices, both ancient and modern, or even data on religious experiences. In each case, the functional specialty of research raises questions about the accuracy of the data. While theology has traditionally been concerned with this aspect in relation to traditional sources such as Scripture, church documents, and the texts of major figures from the past, increasingly other data, particularly in relation to the social sciences, are becoming important in theological studies.

However, as we have noted, to be attentive is also to focus on our own attentiveness. Why do we choose this data over all other available data? What is it about this data that captures and holds our attention? What draws us into this particular study? This can be taken broadly—Why do I study Christian history and tradition rather than

a text as close as possible to the original (*constitutio textus*)." Maas, *Textual Criticism* (Oxford: Clarendon, 1958), 1.

6. See, for example, Bruce M. Metzger and Bart D. Ehrman, *The Text of the New Testament: Its Transmission, Corruption, and Restoration* (Oxford: Oxford University, 2005).

Buddhism?—or it may be taken more narrowly—Why do I study St. Paul rather than the Gospels, Augustine rather than Gregory of Nyssa, Aquinas rather than Bonaventure, Luther rather than Calvin? Are my choices themselves part of my own responsiveness to God's call mediated through the tradition's many carriers of meaning (such as texts and persons)? This may not be the place to address such questions at length, but inevitably, wherever we start, such questions—related as they are to our psychic, religious, moral, and intellectual conversion—are important to our theological engagement.

Interpretation

Of course, accurate texts are important, but without the active engagement of a skilled interpreter, they remain just "black marks on white paper." *Interpretation* asks about the meaning of the text as intended by the author and as heard by the intended audience. To do so accurately requires asking various questions. What is the literary form of the text? Is the text poetic, mythic, legendary? To misread the literary form will be to misread the text, as when some people read Genesis as if it were a scientific treatise. What rhetorical tropes does the author deploy, that may have been familiar to the audience, but are no longer familiar to us? If the text is an historical narrative, how has the author constructed that narrative, what sources have been utilized, what message is conveyed through the author's structuring of the narrative, and so on? All these are the familiar approaches of modern Scripture scholarship—form criticism, narrative criticism, rhetorical criticism, and so on. They require detailed knowledge of the languages of the text, the culture and literature of the era in which it was written, the literary sources available to the author, and so on. And the technique will differ with the literary form involved. More technical texts such as the *Summa Theologiae* or documents produced by church councils require a different approach than what exegetes use for the literary forms of the New Testament.

The task of interpretation orients us to the text's meaning as intended by the author and as heard by the intended audience.[7] This is a relatively delineated task leading to the not uncommon criticism that biblical scholars are "good at telling us what the text meant, but not what it means for us today." Of course, this is a valid and important issue, but addressing it requires further work. One must take into account the way in which the text has been received within the tradition, how the tradition has found in the text divine meaning and value, and expressed that meaning and value in its teachings (doctrines, systematics). Then one must make the transition through a reading of the contemporary setting in all its present complexity, in an attempt to bring the text into dialogue with that setting. This is a profoundly creative and even artistic task. It may be quite premature to think one can move directly from the original meaning of the text to the meaning the text now has for us, without these intervening tasks. On the other hand, these questions highlight that the theological task is not complete with interpretations of the text in its original context, but we must move on to the next task which links texts and their authors into a historical narrative.

We can see the emergence of this specialty in the shifting approaches to reading the Gospels. In a precritical worldview, people tend to read the Gospels as if they offer diaries of the life of Jesus, telling us what Jesus did on a day-to-day basis. One of the first aims of modern biblical criticism was to ask, What really happened?, and a large amount of scholarly activity aimed at getting to the

---

7. For a defense of this stance from a biblical scholar, see Ben F. Meyer, *Reality and Illusion in New Testament Scholarship: A Primer in Critical Realist Hermeneutics* (Collegeville, MN: Liturgical, 1994).

history *behind* the narrative.[8] This was the dominance of historical criticism. However, biblical scholars began to consider a question that precedes the historical question, which is the literary question. And so now exegetes focus more on narrative criticism, treating the Gospel as a literary construct where the author shapes the narrative with particular ends in mind. Of course, this does not devalue the historical question, but rather seeks the answer to that question through the mediation of interpreting the text as a literary unit.

History

We can view texts as complete units with their own formal meaning, as constructed by their authors and then the task is one of interpretation. However, we can also view a text as part of a historical flow of texts, persons, and events. Then, the text becomes an historical marker, part of the dynamic process of *history*. Texts refer to this process in two possible ways: as records of events within the process of history, and as themselves elements within that process. The specialty of history constructs a narrative of the events recorded and of the texts that record those events. It seeks to uncover the dynamics of the process of history. It does not find immediate access to events in past records, but must steer its way through multiple accounts and sources in order to shed light on those events, to uncover what is moving forward in history. It is *critical* history.

We have already discussed one application of the specialty of history, that is, as witnessed in the quest for the historical Jesus. While the initial attempts tended to bypass the literary question, the most recent efforts take the literary issue into their full consideration. Still, the aim is the same, namely, to recreate, through the events

---

8. This was particularly evident in the various quests for the historical Jesus. See, for example, Gregory W. Dawes, *The Historical Jesus Quest: Landmarks in the Search for the Jesus of History* (Louisville: Westminster John Knox, 2000).

as narrated, something of the actual history of Jesus. One notable attempt is the multivolume work by John Meier, *A Marginal Jew*. As with the work of text criticism, those who undertake this reconstruction have developed a kitbag of tools, or criteria of authenticity, in attempts to locate the genuineness of sayings and events as narrated in the Gospel.[9] Of course, different authors develop different criteria and even when they use the same criteria, they may come up with quite different answers. The question then arises, how do we give an account of these divergent positions? Is it just that some are better at this type of work than others? Or perhaps the type of objectivity being sought is a myth? To address these questions a further task in the theological project needs to be undertaken. However, before we do that we should note other possible examples of the specialty of history:

- There can be a developing movement within the history of the church, such as the consolidation of certain doctrinal positions. For example, the early church's thinking on the divinity of Jesus underwent significant development from the creation of the New Testament texts to the councils of Nicaea and Constantinople.[10] Certain attitudes and ways of speaking and acting were "moving forward" in this process. Some positions were abandoned; others were refined or highlighted, until a stable point was reached and a conclusion was eventually consolidated. Such processes are more conflictual than linear, and since the historian may have an interest

---

9. See, for example, the criteria developed in Meier, *A Marginal Jew: Rethinking the Historical Jesus*, 1, 167–95. Also Meyer, *The Aims of Jesus*, 76–94.
10. See, for example, the accounts in the following works: Bernard J. F. Lonergan, *The Way to Nicea: the Dialectical Development of Trinitarian Theology*, trans. Conn O'Donovan (London: Darton, Longman, and Todd, 1976); John Behr, *The Way to Nicaea* (Crestwood, NY: St. Vladimir's Seminary, 2001); and the magisterial Lewis Ayres, *Nicaea and its Legacy: An Approach to Fourth-Century Trinitarian Theology* (Oxford: Oxford University, 2004), for the history of reception and consolidation.

in the conflict, the narrative of the process becomes an evaluation: Is this development good or bad? Is it progress or decline? Again, the inquiry anticipates a further step.

- Development may also occur in the thinking of a particular individual, and historians may consider this as a subset of the above process. On a complex issue, such as the interrelationship of grace and human freedom, there may be a trajectory of thought within the work of a particular thinker.[11] Earlier insights give way to later ones, while dead ends are left behind as new pathways open up for development. It would then be wrong to try to interpret later writings within the framework of earlier positions, which have been superseded. To do such an account well requires not only a thorough knowledge of the thinker, but also of the issue that occupies his or her attention.[12]

Coda on Critical Historical Method

The three specialties of research, interpretation, and history taken together constitute what theologians generally refer to as *critical historical method*. As a method, it is not specific to theology and could be applied to any received text in, say, literature, history, science or philosophy. What then makes these tasks theological? An easy answer would be that what makes these tasks theological is the subject matter. So instead of applying these tasks to Homer's *Iliad*, we use them to understand Mark's Gospel. However, more than this is at issue. These steps concern the use of our natural human reasoning in dealing with data, any data, even that of a religious tradition.

---

11. See, for example, Bernard J. F. Lonergan, *Grace and Freedom: Operative Grace in the Thought of St. Thomas Aquinas*, ed. Frederick E. Crowe and Robert M. Doran, vol. 1, Collected Works of Bernard Lonergan (Toronto: University of Toronto, 2000).
12. Just as to write a history of mathematics one should be a pretty good mathematician oneself. Otherwise one cannot appreciate the nature and significance of the developments that occur.

To exclude them from theology would be to exclude reason itself, seeking refuge in some faith-filled but unthinking fideistic realm. These steps do not presuppose faith in the one undertaking them, but neither do they exclude faith; nor should they be viewed as hostile to faith. Does faith then make any difference to the process and to the outcomes? Raising such a question may lead us to consider questions of objectivity. Does the faith stance of the theologian make them any the less objective than a "detached" nonreligious enquirer? Or does faith open the investigator up to realities that the nonreligious enquirer is closed off to? Indeed, if the data is about the inbreaking of divine meaning and value into human history, then nonreligious researchers may find themselves "tone deaf" to the religious depths of the material, to its divine meanings and values. In the terms of the present work, religious conversion provides a more profound orientation to meaning, truth, and goodness because it opens up the enquirer to the religious depths of the data. On the other hand, if one systematically rejects the very possibility of such an inbreaking of divine meaning and value, one may be cutting oneself off from truth. The only guarantor of objectivity is one's fidelity to the precepts: Be attentive, Be intelligent, Be reasonable, Be attentive, and Be in love.

Dialectics

We have already noted that the outcomes of critical historical method are not uniform. This is very evident when we turn to critical historical studies of the life of Jesus. Many of the divergences in outcomes lie not in the data, but in the presuppositions of the researchers attending to the data. Of course, some differences in the outcomes of critical history may be complementary, the result of differing perspectives in the investigators or the inclusion of new data shedding light on the question. This provides us with a fuller account and can be welcomed. However, some differences are dialectical oppositions, emerging from opposed horizons; what one says is true, the other says is false; what one says is good, the other finds wicked; what one judges to be from God, the other finds merely human or worse, evidence for the devil.[13] The researcher may have assumptions about how or whether God acts in history, or have notions of objectivity as "taking a good look," and so on. The presence or absence of religious, moral, intellectual, and psychic conversions forms part of the background of the researcher and affects the way the data is handled. However, the first task is to attend to the divergent outcomes provided by critical historical method, to identify the patterns that may be present within this divergence, and so raise the question as to the sources of this divergence within the subject. This brings us to the next specialty, *dialectics*.

The specialty of dialectics is most clearly in evidence in the work of liberation and feminist theology. Both these approaches remind us that the theologian's horizon influences the outcome of theology. If a theologian enjoys some of the privileges of power and wealth, then this can introduce unintended distortions or scotomas into their readings of the documents and traditions of the past. What is required is a preferential option for the poor and marginalized to read history from the underside, from the perspective of history's victims.[14] Feminist theologians remind us that patriarchy becomes a lens through which we read Christian tradition. Sexism is a sin from which we require a conversion in order to deal more adequately with both the documents of the past and the present institutional context.[15] Both these theological approaches not only highlight the significance of dialectically divergent horizons operating with the theologian, they also point to the resolution of this divergence in a process of

13. For example, the Pharisees found in Jesus' miracles signs of the devil. See Mark 3:20-30.
14. See the seminal work in liberation theology, Gutiérrez, *A Theology of Liberation*.
15. See works such as Elisabeth Schüssler Fiorenza, *But She Said: Feminist Practices of Biblical Interpretation* (Boston: Beacon, 1992); Ruether, *Sexism and God-Talk*.

conversion within the theologian. In this instance, one could well argue that the underlying issue is one of moral conversion, or at least a dimension of moral conversion. Both involve a movement from mere satisfactions offered by power and privilege toward genuine value, the genuine value of the other, either the poor or women systematically excluded from power and privilege.

Dialectics then asks a question of the theologian: Where do I stand? In the face of these dialectically opposed horizons that emerge in our dialectical analysis of the outcomes of the first three functional specialties, where do I stand? To which horizon will I hitch my wagon? Is my present horizon challenged to enlarge, or perhaps be radically restructured on fundamental questions of truth, meaning, value, beauty and even God? Dialectics raises the question of *conversion* in its various modalities: religious, moral, intellectual, and psychic. This in fact takes us back to chapter 1 where we raised issues of divergence within theological stances, the significance of those divergences and the ways they might be resolved. This then leads us to the functional specialty of the present work.

Foundations

If dialectics raises the question of conversion, *foundations* thematizes conversion as the horizon for the second, normative phase of theology. With foundations, the theologian becomes the object of theological concern. Am I converted toward the source of all meaning, truth, and goodness (religious conversion)? Do I make my decisions on the basis of genuine values or mere satisfactions (moral conversion)? Have I overcome, or even recognized the existence of, the persistent myth that knowing is a matter of taking a good look, that reality is already out there now to be seen, and objectivity consists in seeing what is there to be seen and not seeing what is not there to be seen (intellectual conversion)? Am I oriented toward beauty as a participation in the truly meaningful, the truly real, the truly good, and truly holy (psychic conversion)?

Of course, people can engage in theology without attending to these questions, but to that extent their theology is likely to fall short of the demands to be attentive, intelligent, reasonable, responsible, and in love with God. These demands are constitutive of human authenticity, and all that the conversions identified above do is to make these demands explicit and foundational for the theological task. Nonetheless, we all fall short of these demands to some extent as Lonergan reminds us: authenticity is ever a withdrawal from inauthenticity.[16] However, the transcendental precepts and the conversions that thematize them present an account of "faith and reason" as at the heart of the theological project, with no diminution of faith, nor any truncation of reason.

Of course, many postmodern voices insist on anti-foundationalist strategies that reject any conception of foundations as misleading and even violent. There is only an ongoing task of building and knocking down and starting over again, doing the best we can as authentically as we can. While the postmodern emphasis on authenticity is to be welcomed, its rejection of foundations and the possibility of objectivity in theology is itself the product of mistaken positions on knowing, objectivity, and reality.[17] On the foundations developed above, objectivity is itself the fruit of authenticity, conceived as fidelity to the transcendental precepts.[18] Any attempt to deny the authenticity of such precepts will inevitably call us to be *attentive*

---

16. Lonergan, *Method*, 110.
17. See the thorough discussion in Frederick G. Lawrence, "The Fragility of Consciousness: Lonergan and the Postmodern Concern for the Other," *Theological Studies* 54 no. 1 (1993): 55–94. Also on the importance of the emergence of authenticity in the present era see Taylor, *A Secular Age*.
18. Lonergan, *Method*, 292.

to certain data, to understand it *intelligently*, to come to a *reasonable* judgment concerning that data and our understanding of it, and to then act *responsibly* in the light of that judgment. Such an argument would be performatively self-refuting.

The other task of foundations is to provide us with a language with which to undertake theology, that is, a set of categories for raising and answering theological questions, where the meaning of those categories is set by the horizon of the converted theologian. Of course, theologians may speak of meaning, truth, goodness, and beauty, but the horizons from which they operate may or may not be morally, intellectually and psychically converted. To that extent, while they are using the same words, the meanings these words have within those horizons will be very different. For example, Tertullian, Origen, and Athanasius all spoke of the Father and the Son as being of one substance/*homoousios*. However, for Tertullian substance meant "material stuff," shaped by his adherence to Stoic materialism; for Origen substance meant some sort of Platonic idea; while for Athanasius it meant "what is true of the Father is true of the Son, except the Father is not the Son." For Athanasius the real (substance) is aligned with true judgment, marking the beginnings of intellectual conversion. And so in the present work, the conversions have established the meaning of categories such as God, value, a hierarchical and normative scale of values, being, real, truth, objectivity, and beauty. This is of course only the beginning of the foundational task, but it helps establish the basic horizon that will generate all genuine categories for future theological work.

Doctrines

If foundations seek to be responsible in explicating the horizon of the theologian, the functional specialty of *doctrines* seeks to be reasonable in making judgments of truth and value that emerge from those foundations. Primary among these will be judgments of religious truth that emerge from religious conversion in interaction with the data of the religious tradition, though the manner of their expression will be shaped by the presence or absence of moral, intellectual, and psychic conversion in those who formulated them. Religious conversions normally occur within the context of a particular religious tradition, which itself is constituted by its adherence to a set of judgments of truth (doctrines as cognitional meaning) made in the past that establish its identity as an historical community (doctrines as constitutive meaning). Immediately then, the theologian may be confronted with a tension between her own personal judgments made on the basis of her own theological foundations, and those of the historical community which has mediated the experience of religious conversion to her. This raises the question not only of the authenticity of the theologian, but also of the authenticity of the tradition the theologian has received. Such a question pushes us back to issues of dialectics (Can she discern a pattern in the differences?) and foundations (Where does she stand?). It may be that the theologian's conversion is incomplete, that her authenticity is still a work in progress. Or it may be that the religious judgment of the tradition is expressed inadequately because couched in inadequate moral, intellectual or psychic conversions. The theologian may then have the task of expressing either a different (and thus corrective) religious truth or the same religious truth in a way that harmonizes more with moral, intellectual, and psychic conversions. A third possibility is that of the inauthenticity of the tradition itself, that its religious judgments are flawed and in need of correction. Then the task of the theologian is the reforming of the tradition itself.[19]

In the Christian tradition, the major religious judgments of the

19. We need look no further than the Reformation for an instance where some theologians, notably

tradition have been on God as Trinity,[20] the person of Christ,[21] and on grace and sin.[22] These judgments focus on the way in which the events of the New Testament, the mission, death, and resurrection of Jesus, have mediated a profound religious conversion in those who knew him and in the ongoing life of the church.[23] A second level of judgments deals with the ongoing life of the community itself, its sacramental and moral life, its canonical writings, its institutions and structures.[24] A third level of judgments deals with the ways in which the church constitutes itself through this process of making such judgments, when it begins to reflect on its own performance as an historical community making substantive judgments on doctrinal matters.[25] This presents us with a doctrinal hierarchy, not of truth but of importance or centrality to the core of revelation.[26] Significantly, over history, the more we move through these levels, the more likely disputation will occur, leading to schism within the broader church.

We have already discussed in chapter 7 on revelation questions concerning the permanency of doctrines and doctrinal development. Here we shall simply repeat that one of the greatest challenges facing

Luther and Calvin, questioned the authenticity of the judgments of the Christian tradition as then received, particularly on questions of sin and grace.

20. The Councils of Nicaea (325 CE) and Constantinople (381 CE), in particular.
21. The Councils of Ephesus (431 CE) and Chalcedon (451 CE), in particular.
22. More so in the West than in the East, with the Councils of Carthage and Orange. These were subject to further debate and disputation in the Reformation and Counter-Reformation.
23. As is often pointed out we have no formally declared doctrines on this most foundational event itself. It is so foundational that to question it immediately marks a break with the tradition itself.
24. Most evidently at the Council of Trent, though it was also concerned with ongoing issues on grace and sin as raised by the Reformers.
25. Most evident at Vatican I on papal infallibility and Vatican II's attempts to nuance Vatican I in *Lumen Gentium*.
26. Hence Vatican II talks of a hierarchy of truths within the context of ecumenism: "When comparing doctrines with one another, they [theologians] should remember that in Catholic doctrine there exists a 'hierarchy' of truths, since they vary in their relation to the fundamental Christian faith" (*Unitatis Redintegratio*, n. 11). Second Vatican Council Decree on Ecumenism, Unitatis Redintegratio, n. 11, available at http://www.vatican.va/archive/hist_councils/ii_vatican_council/documents/vat-ii_decree_19641121_unitatis-redintegratio_en.html (accessed October 2, 2014).

the whole notion of doctrine at the moment is finding a way through the tensions of a permanently valid truth affirmed in doctrines and the impact of historical consciousness on our understanding of doctrinal development. Many of these tensions arise out of questions of intellectual conversion, over questions of truth and objectivity. Without a firm grounding in intellectual conversion, the distinction between doctrines and systematics breaks down, doctrines appear as just one theological option among many, and the distinctive roles of theologians and church authorities become lost. As A. N. Williams notes of contemporary theological work, for example, "the terms 'systematic theology', 'Christian doctrine' and 'dogmatics' have no uniformly established usage and a preference for one or the other is often arbitrary."[27] Similarly, Nicholas Healy refers to "official systematic theology" as "the form of theological inquiry and production that has some authority over other forms, or . . . at least claims or assumes that authority."[28] This stands in contrast with what he calls "professional systematic theology" carried out in the academy or university, which "is necessarily diverse in its methods, starting points and agendas, and should not be restricted by the method, starting point and agenda of official theology."[29] Our position, however, which emerges out of intellectual conversion, draws a sharp distinction between the task of doctrines and that of systematics, to which we now turn.

Systematics

The functional specialty of *systematics* is best expressed by the classical ideal of "faith seeking understanding." As an activity that draws

27. A. N. Williams, "What Is Systematic Theology?," *International Journal of Systematic Theology* 11, no. 1 (2009): 40–55 (41).
28. Nicholas M. Healy, "What is Systematic Theology?," *International Journal of Systematic Theology* 11, no. 1 (2009): 24–39 (27).
29. Ibid., 38.

upon and is grounded in faith, systematics presumes the outcomes of both foundations and doctrines as its basic normative content. The judgments of doctrines are true, but remain judgments concerning divine meaning and value, and hence beyond human comprehension. They are mysteries in the sense, not of being unintelligible, but of being so full of meaning as to be inexhaustible for human understanding. There is a richness of meaning present in these doctrines that we can never cease to better understand. The task of systematics is to work toward an understanding of these mysteries in a coherent and comprehensive way, bringing the whole into a unified intelligible framework.

However, given that we are not able to fully understand the mysteries of faith, how shall we go about this task? Here the teaching of Vatican I is instructive:

> Now reason, if it is enlightened by faith, does indeed when it seeks persistently, piously and soberly, achieve by God's gift, some understanding, and that most profitable, of the mysteries, whether by analogy from what it knows naturally, or from the connexion of these mysteries with one another and with the final end of humanity; but reason is never rendered capable of penetrating these mysteries in the way in which it penetrates those truths which form its proper object. For the divine mysteries, by their very nature, so surpass the created understanding that, even when a revelation has been given and accepted by faith, they remain covered by the veil of that same faith and wrapped as it were, in a certain obscurity, as long as in this mortal life 'we are away from the Lord, for we walk by faith, and not by sight' [2 Cor. 5:6f].[30]

Here, the council puts forward two paths for reaching some level of understanding of the mysteries expressed in doctrines. The first is through an "analogy from what it knows naturally." We can witness

---

30. Vatican I Dogmatic Constitution, *Dei Filius*, chapter 4, translation from Norman P. Tanner, *Decrees of the Ecumenical Councils*, 2 vols. (London/Washington, DC: Sheed & Ward/ Georgetown University, 1990), 2:808.

this at work in the *Summa Theologiae* 1.27.1 where Aquinas asks whether there are processions in God. This is a question calling for a judgment, a yes or a no. As such, Aquinas settles the matter in the affirmative by drawing on the authority of Scripture and church doctrines. However, he does not leave the matter there because, though the question has been answered, without some understanding, the mind would not be properly nourished; without understanding, however limited, the doctrine will appear as just an arbitrary fact about God to be assented to, but unrelated to anything else and hence in the end will appear meaningless. Hence, he immediately seeks out an analogy for the divine procession, based on the procession within the human mind of a concept from an act of understanding. This procession can be naturally known, though not without difficulty. Of course, there are dissimilarities involved as well, because the procession of a concept from an act of understanding in us does not produce a distinct person, but there is enough of a similarity for us to get some handle on what a procession might mean in God. This is a paradigmatic example of the use of analogy.

While analogy attempts to provide us with some understanding of a mystery of faith, the council proposed the second approach of uncovering "the connexion of these mysteries with one another and with the final end of humanity." In more contemporary parlance, this task concerns the internal coherence of Christian faith. It seeks the intelligible connections among the different beliefs Christians hold as true. This is a more architectonic project to be found, for example, not in the individual questions of the *Summa*, but in its overall construction as Aquinas moves from God to questions of Trinity, to creation, to a focus on human beings, their virtues and vices, to their redemption through grace, the theological virtues and their relationship to the other virtues, finally to the specifics of redemption in the incarnation and the sacramental life of the church.

Underlying this overall construction is the connection between belief in the Trinity, the Trinitarian processions and their extensions into the created order, the divine missions of the Son (incarnation) and the Spirit (grace). We can see current reflections of this process in the work of current theologians seeking connections between the doctrine of the Trinity and incarnation, creation, church, the moral life, and so on.[31] Given the explosion of scholarship today and the breadth of material needed to be dealt with, it is doubtful that any one theologian would be able to achieve at the level of our times what Aquinas achieved at the level of his times. Even the task of systematics is inevitably collaborative.

While the goal of such a project is to demonstrate the coherence of Christian faith, at least internally, such coherence does not establish the truth of the beliefs involved.[32] Incoherence establishes dissonance and falsehood, but things could be relatively coherent and still false. To seek to demonstrate truth through coherence is to invert the relationship between doctrines and systematics. Doctrines are held as true not because of their coherence but because of a complex set of judgments of truth—what God reveals is true; these doctrines have been revealed by God, through the mediation of the Christian tradition and the authority of the church; these judgments concur with my foundational commitments to religious conversion mediated to me by that same church; I hold these doctrines as true. Systematics proceeds on the basis of this affirmation of truth. This is not just a theological observation, but also in some sense a psychological norm. As Augustine regularly noted, "Unless you believe, you will not understand." Without the conviction of faith, doctrines appear more like nonsense and unworthy of investigation. In the conviction of

31. See, for example, Anne Hunt, *Trinity: Nexus of the Mysteries of Christian Faith* (Maryknoll, NY: Orbis Books, 2005).
32. For example, Wolfhart Pannenberg places great stress on the question of the coherence of Christian faith.

faith one is willing to spend the time to seek "persistently, piously and soberly" for that limited understanding that systematics might offer us.

Communications

Of its very nature systematics is a technical task. It is not content with a merely descriptive approach but seeks explanatory knowledge, limited but real, through analogies and the interconnection of different beliefs. We have noted previously the different realms of meaning and systematics tends to find expression in a theoretic control of meaning (such as metaphysics), or perhaps more securely in interiority, where one's basic terms and relations are grounded in an interiorly differentiated consciousness. Neither of these realms may be readily accessible to the proverbial person on the street. A further theological task is then to be found in the specialty of *communications*. This involves the transposition of meaning from the technical language of systematic theology into the commonsense language of a particular culture. Such a task requires an attentiveness to and creativity within the interpersonal, symbolic, and artistic carriers of meaning that effectively mediate this form of communication. This specialty takes theology out of the realm of the academy and into the concerns of pastoral care, preaching, catechesis, and community building in the life of the church. It marks a return to the lived experience of the church from which all theology must emerge.

Of course, there is always the temptation to short-circuit the process in an attempt to move directly into communications from various other components in a theological task. We noted earlier the criticism often made of critical historical methods that they are very good at telling us what the text meant in its original historical context, but not as good at telling us what the text means for us today. It is often tempting to think that the outcomes of earlier phases must have some immediate applicability to the contemporary life of the church. However, this temptation has inherent difficulties. Often as not it is an attempt to bypass the intermediary normative phase of theology, creating unnecessary tensions between the work of positive scholarship in the first phase and the claims of the tradition mediated in the normative phase. This was very evident in the first quest for the historical Jesus, which pitted the Jesus of history against the Christ of faith, using historical outcomes in an attempt to rid the church of the dogmatic figure of Christ.[33] We can now look back at this and recognize the necessity of sound dialectics and foundations to address these outcomes prior to their communication to the church. In this normative phase the theologian takes on responsibility for handing on the tradition in all its fullness and depth, its variety and range, in a way which communicates divine meanings and values into the concrete circumstances of people's lives, in all their social and cultural complexity.

Of course, there is no automated process by which such a transposition can be undertaken. Often, it is a topic taken up in missiology, under the heading of enculturation, but within contemporary culture with its rapidly changing cultural assumptions and the growing impact of globalization, the task of such a transposition is ongoing, never complete and always subject to possible revision. New and creative expressions of the faith are needed to communicate the divine meanings and values carried in revelation; however, each such attempt carries a rightful anxiety that this new expression faithfully captures the divine intent. In the face of this anxiety, some would seek refuge in past formulations and

---

33. See the classical work, Albert Schweitzer, *The Quest of the Historical Jesus* (Minneapolis: Fortress Press, 2001).

315

pious practices scorning attempts at "innovation," but in the end the outcome of such an approach is to make faith look quaint and somewhat out of touch with the present situation. In the very attempt at being faithful, a different message is conveyed: to be faithful to God means living in the past, not the present. In seeking to avoid risk, they create their own set of risks: "If you make a mistake, you get up and go forward: that is the way. Those who do not walk in order not to err, make a more serious mistake."[34]

Conclusion: Theology as a Collaborative Project

Any academic enterprise is of necessity a collaborative cultural project. Scholars organize conferences to share ideas, they publish in peer-reviewed journals in order to communicate their work, they collaborate with colleagues in designing curricula for their students, and so on. In all of these labors, a process of self-correction operates within the discipline. The most egregious errors are weeded out: sources overlooked or misquoted, logical errors in theological reasoning, and exaggerated or unbalanced claims. This type of self-correcting process is present in all academic disciplines, including theology. In many disciplines, particularly those with minimal value-dimensions (such as mathematics or physics), this self-correcting process is enough to ensure that over time significant progress is made, error is eliminated, and new horizons for research and study can build on what has been securely established in the past.

Once value elements become integral to the discipline as a whole, be it the human meanings and values that fall under the aegis of the human sciences, or the divine meanings and values proper to theological disciplines, things become more complicated. The

34. From a homily of Pope Francis, 8 May 2013 for Mass in the Chapel of the *Domus Sanctae Marthae* residence in the Vatican, accessed August 7, 2015, http://www.catholicismusa.com/christians-are-people-of-bridges-not-walls-seek-victims-of-idolatry-and-worldliness/.

discipline automatically becomes more conflictual as the impact of the presence or absence of religious, moral, intellectual, and psychic conversions becomes more prominent. Without a method that thematizes conflict and points toward its resolution, these disciplines become fragmented into approaches with different methodologies leading to diverse, often opposed conclusions. Under such circumstances, the idea that a discipline might make progress becomes more difficult to maintain; debates are often at cross-purposes and what some regard as an advance, others reject as a retrograde step. Genuine progress, if it is acknowledged at all, is more haphazard and fragmentary and so ever precarious.

Is this then the fate of theology for the future? Can it no longer be a discipline which can securely build on the past, but must ever start anew to rebuild itself from scratch, reproducing all the debates of the past, following up all the previous dead ends, lest there be something there worth retrieving? One of the advantages of the method described above and enunciated by Bernard Lonergan is that it thematizes such conflict in the functional specialty of dialectics and finds some resolution through the specialty of foundations grounded in conversion. However, in order to implement such a proposal, a deeper sense of collaboration needs to emerge, more than the types of collaboration we outlined above. What is needed is a *methodological* collaboration which goes beyond a mere *de facto* resignation to a theological pluralism toward a more unified vision of theology as a collaborative project based on eight distinct but intimately related functional specialties each of which makes its own vital contribution to the theological task of mediating the past into the present for the sake of the future. Our hope is that the present work acts as an invitation to such a collaborative vision.

Bibliography

Adams, Marilyn McCord. *Horrendous Evils and the Goodness of God.* Ithaca, NY: Cornell University Press, 1999.

Alberigo, Giuseppe. *A Brief History of Vatican II.* Translated by Matthew Sherry. Maryknoll, NY: Orbis Books, 2006.

Asad, Talal. *Genealogies of Religion: Discipline and Reasons of Power in Christianity and Islam.* Baltimore: Johns Hopkins University, 1993.

Augustine. *The Confessions.* Translated by Maria Boulding. New York: Vintage Books, 1998.

————. *The Trinity.* Translated by Edmund Hill. Edited by John E. Rotelle, OSA. Brooklyn, NY: New City Press, 1991.

Aulén, Gustaf. *Christus Victor: An Historical Study of the Three Main Types of the Idea of the Atonement.* London: SPCK, 1970.

Ayres, Lewis. *Nicaea and Its Legacy: An Approach to Fourth-Century Trinitarian Theology.* Oxford: Oxford University, 2004.

Balthasar, Hans Urs von. *The Glory of the Lord: A Theological Aesthetics.* Vol. 1, *Seeing the Form.* Translated by Erasmo Leiva-Merikakis. New York: Ignatius Press, 1983.

Baptism, Eucharist and Ministry. Faith and Order Papers. Vol. 10, Geneva: World Council of Churches, 1982.

Barth, Karl. *Anselm, Fides Quaerens Intellectum: Anselm's Proof of the Existence of God in the Context of His Theological Scheme.* Pittsburgh Reprint Series. 1st English ed. Pittsburgh: Pickwick Press, 1975.

————. *Church Dogmatics*. Translated by G. T. Thomson. Edited by Geoffrey William Bromiley and Thomas Forsyth Torrance. 4 vols. Edinburgh: T.& T. Clark, 1936–1962.

————. *The Epistle to the Romans*. Translated by Edwyn Clement Hoskyns. London: Oxford University Press, 1933.

Barth, Karl, and Emil Brunner. *Natural Theology*. London: Geoffrey Bles, 1946.

Behr, John. *The Way to Nicaea*. Crestwood, NY: St. Vladimir's Seminary, 2001.

Bernstein, Richard J. *Beyond Objectivism and Relativism: Science, Hermeneutics, and Praxis*. Oxford: Blackwell, 1983.

Bhaskar, Roy. "Societies." In *Critical Realism: Essential Readings*. Edited by Margaret Archer, Roy Bhaskar, Andrew Collier, Tony Lawson, and Alan Norrie. 206–57. London: Routledge, 1998.

Boff, Clodovis. *Theology and Praxis: Epistemological Foundations*. Maryknoll, NY: Orbis Books, 1987.

Boff, Leonardo. *Ecology & Liberation: A New Paradigm*. Maryknoll, NY: Orbis Books, 1995.

Boff, Leonardo, and Clodovis Boff. *Introducing Liberation Theology*. Maryknoll, NY: Orbis Books, 1987.

Borg, Marcus J. *Jesus, A New Vision: Spirit, Culture, and the Life of Discipleship*. 1st ed. San Francisco: Harper & Row, 1987.

Brague, Rémi. "The Impossibility of Secular Society." *First Things* (October 2013): 27–31.

Buber, Martin. *Eclipse of God: Studies in the Relation of Religion and Philosophy*. Westport, CT: Greenwood Press, 1977.

Caputo, John D. *The Prayers and Tears of Jacques Derrida: Religion without Religion*. Bloomington: Indiana University Press, 1997.

Caussade, Jean-Pierre de. *Abandonment to Divine Providence*. Notre Dame: Christian Classics, 2010.

Chung, Paul. "Karl Barth's Theology of Reconciliation in Dialogue with a Theology of Religions." *Mission Studies* 25, 2 (2008): 211–28.

Cimino, Richard, and Christopher Smith. "Secular Humanism and Atheism

Beyond Progressive Secularism." *Sociology of Religion* 68, 4 (2007): 407–24.

Clark, Francis. "'Bleeding Hosts' and Eucharistic Theology." *The Heythrop Journal* 1, 3 (1960): 214–28.

Cole, John R. *Pascal: The Man and His Two Loves.* New York: NYU Press, 1995.

Commission, International Theological. "The Interpretation of Dogma." *Irish Theological Quarterly* 56, 4 (1990): 251–77.

Cone, James H. *A Black Theology of Liberation.* 40th Anniversary Edition. Maryknoll NY: Orbis Books, 2010.

————. *God of the Oppressed.* Rev. ed. Maryknoll, NY: Orbis Books, 1997.

Crossan, John Dominic. *The Historical Jesus: The Life of a Mediterranean Jewish Peasant.* 1st ed. San Francisco: HarperSanFrancisco, 1992.

Crowe, Frederick E. *Developing the Lonergan Legacy: Historical, Theoretical and Existential Themes.* Edited by Michael Vertin. Toronto: University of Toronto, 2004.

Cullmann, Oscar. *Salvation in History.* New York: Harper & Row, 1967.

Curnow, Rohan Michael. *The Preferential Option for the Poor: A Short History and a Reading Based on the Thought of Bernard Lonergan.* Marquette Studies in Theology. Milwaukee: Marquette University Press, 2012.

Dadosky, John D. *The Eclipse and Recovery of Beauty: A Lonergan Approach.* Toronto: University of Toronto Press, 2014.

Daly, Robert J. *Sacrifice Unveiled: The True Meaning of Christian Sacrifice.* London: T & T Clark, 2009.

Davies, Paul. "Now Is the Reason for Our Discontent." *Sydney Morning Herald*, 1 January 2003.

Dawes, Gregory W. *The Historical Jesus Quest: Landmarks in the Search for the Jesus of History.* Louisville, KY: Westminster John Knox, 2000.

Dawkins, Richard. *The God Delusion.* London: Bantam, 2006.

Derrida, Jacques. *On Cosmopolitanism and Forgiveness.* Thinking in Action. New York: Routledge, 2001.

Di Noia, Joseph. "Religion and the Religions." In *The Cambridge Companion* to Karl Barth. Edited by John Webster. 243–57. Cambridge, UK: Cambridge University.

Dobell, Brian. *Augustine's Intellectual Conversion: The Journey from Platonism to Christianity.* Cambridge: Cambridge University Press, 2009.

Dodd, C. H. *The Apostolic Preaching and Its Developments.* New York: Harper & Brothers, 1936.

Doran, Robert M. "Imitating the Divine Relations: A Theological Contribution to Mimetic Theory." *Method: Journal of Lonergan Studies* 23, 2 (2005): 149–86.

————. *Psychic Conversion and Theological Foundations: Toward a Reorientation of the Human Sciences.* Chico, CA: Scholars Press, 1981.

————. *Subject and Psyche.* Marquette Studies in Theology 3. 2nd ed. Milwaukee: Marquette University Press, 1994.

————. *Theological Foundations.* 2 vols. Marquette Studies in Theology. Milwaukee: Marquette University Press, 1995.

————. *Theology and the Dialectics of History.* Toronto: University of Toronto Press, 1990.

————. *The Trinity in History: A Theology of the Divine Missions.* Vol. 1, *Missions and Processions.* Toronto: University of Toronto Press, 2012.

Doyle, Dominic. *The Promise of Christian Humanism: Thomas Aquinas on Hope.* New York: Herder & Herder, 2011.

Dulles, Avery. *Models of Revelation.* Maryknoll, NY: Orbis Books, 1992.

————. "Two Languages of Salvation: The Lutheran-Catholic Joint Declaration." *First Things* 98, December (1999): 25–30.

Dunn, Geoffrey D. *Tertullian.* New York: Routledge, 2004.

Durkheim, Emile. *The Elementary Forms of the Religious Life.* Translated by Joseph Ward Swain. New York: Free Press, 1965.

————. *The Rules of Sociological Method.* Translated by Sarah A. Solovay and John H. Mueller. Edited by George E. G. Catlin. 8th ed. Chicago: The University of Chicago, 1938.

Edwards, Denis. *Earth Revealing—Earth Healing: Ecology and Christian Theology.* Collegeville, MN: Liturgical Press, 2001.

Eliade, Mircea. *The Sacred and the Profane.* Translated by Willard R. Trask. New York: Harcourt, Brace, and Co., 1987.

Emery, Gilles. Translated by Matthew Levering. *Trinity in Aquinas.* Ypsilanti, MI: Sapientia Press of Ave Maria College, 2003.

Fleming, Chris. *René Girard: Violence and Mimesis.* Cambridge, UK; Malden, MA: Polity Press, 2004.

Fredericks, James. "A Universal Religious Experience? Comparative Theology as an Alternative to a Theology of Religions." *Horizons* 22, 1 (1995): 67–87.

Fulmer, J. Burton. "Anselm and the Apophatic: 'Something Greater than Can Be Thought'" *New Blackfriars* 9, 1020 (2008): 177–93.

Girard, René. *Deceit, Desire, and the Novel: Self and Other in Literary Structure.* Baltimore: Johns Hopkins Press, 1965.

————. *The Scapegoat.* Baltimore: Johns Hopkins University Press, 1986.

————. *Violence and the Sacred.* Baltimore: Johns Hopkins University Press, 1977.

Girard, René, and James G. Williams. *The Girard Reader.* New York: Crossroad, 1996.

Greene, Brian. *The Elegant Universe: Superstrings, Hidden Dimensions, and the Quest for the Ultimate Theory.* London: Jonathan Cape, 1999.

Gutierrez, Gustavo. *A Theology of Liberation: History, Politics, and Salvation.* Translated by Sister Caridad Inda and John Eagleson. Maryknoll, NY: Orbis Books, 1973.

Haldane, Richard. *The Pathway to Reality.* London: Dutton, 1905.

Harnack, Adolf von. *Outlines of the History of Dogma.* Translated by Edwin Mitchell. London: Hodder and Stoughton, 1893.

Harris, Sam. *The End of Faith: Religion, Terror, and the Future of Reason.* New York: Norton, 2004.

Healy, Nicholas M. "What Is Systematic Theology?" *International Journal of Systematic Theology* 11, 1 (2009): 24–39.

Heim, S. Mark. *The Depth of the Riches: A Trinitarian Theology of Religious Ends.* Grand Rapids: Eerdmans, 2001.

Hennessy, Jayme M. "The Beauty and Brutality of the Pietà." In *She Who*

Imagines: Feminist Theological Aesthetics. Edited by Laurie M. Cassidy and Maureen H. O'Connell. 37–52. Collegeville, MN: Liturgical, 2012.

Hick, John. *A Christian Theology of Religions: The Rainbow of Faiths*. 1st American ed. Louisville, KY: Westminster John Knox Press, 1995.

————. "A Pluralist View." In *More Than One Way? Four Views on Salvation in a Pluralistic World*. Edited by Dennis L. Okholm and Timothy R. Phillips. 27–59. Grand Rapids: Zondervan, 1995.

Himes, Brian. "Lonergan's Position on the Natural Desire to See God and Aquinas's Metaphysical Theology of Creation and Participation." *The Heythrop Journal* 54, 5 (2013): 767–83.

History of Vatican II. Translated by Matthew J. O'Connell. Edited by Giuseppe Alberigo and Joseph A. Komonchak. 5 vols. Maryknoll, NY: Orbis, 1995.

Hitchens, Christopher. *God Is Not Great: How Religion Poisons Everything*. 1st ed. New York: Twelve, 2007.

Hunsinger, George. *Eucharist and Ecumenism: Let Us Keep the Feast*. Cambridge: Cambridge University Press, 2008.

Hunt, Anne. *Trinity: Nexus of the Mysteries of Christian Faith*. Maryknoll, NY: Orbis Books, 2005.

Jacobs-Vandegeer, Christiaan. "Sanctifying Grace in a 'Methodical Theology.'" *Theological Studies* 68, 1 (2007): 52–76.

Jaspers, Karl. *The Origin and Goal of History*. New Haven: Yale University Press, 1953.

Johnson, Elizabeth A. *She Who Is: The Mystery of God in Feminist Theological Discourse*. New York: Crossroad, 1992.

Kant, Immanuel. *Critique of Pure Reason*. Translated by Norman Kemp Smith. Unabridged ed. New York: St. Martin's Press, 1965.

Katz, Steven. "Language, Epistemology, and Mysticism." In *Mysticism and Philosophical Analysis*. Ed. Steven Katz, 22–74. London: Oxford University, 1978.

Kerr, Fergus. "Knowing God by Reason Alone: What Vatican I Never Said." *New Blackfriars* 91, 1033 (2010): 215–28.

Knitter, Paul F. *No Other Name?: A Critical Survey of Christian Attitudes toward the World Religions.* Maryknoll, NY: Orbis Books, 1985.

Krauss, Lawrence. *A Universe from Nothing: Why There Is Something Rather Than Nothing.* New York: Free Press, 2012.

Lawrence, Frederick G. "The Fragility of Consciousness: Lonergan and the Postmodern Concern for the Other." *Theological Studies* 54, 1 (1993): 55–94.

Lindbeck, George A. *The Nature of Doctrine: Religion and Theology in a Postliberal Age.* Philadelphia: Westminster Press, 1984.

Lonergan, Bernard J. F. "Christology Today: Methodological Reflections." In *A Third Collection.* Edited by Frederick E. Crowe. 74–99. New York: Paulist, 1985.

_____. *The Collected Works of Bernard Lonergan.* Edited by Frederick E. Crowe and Robert M. Doran. 20 vols. Toronto: University of Toronto Press, 1988–.

_____. "Doctrinal Pluralism." In *Collected Works of Bernard Lonergan: Philosophical and Theological Papers: 1965–1980.* Edited by Robert Croken and R. M. Doran, 17:70–106. Toronto: University of Toronto Press, 2004.

_____. *Grace and Freedom: Operative Grace in the Thought of St. Thomas Aquinas.* Vol. 1 of *Collected Works of Bernard Lonergan.* Edited by Frederick E. Crowe and Robert M. Doran. Toronto: University of Toronto, 2000.

_____. "Healing and Creating in History." In *A Third Collection.* Edited by Frederick E. Crowe, 100–109. Mahwah, NY: Paulist Press, 1985.

_____. *Insight: A Study of Human Understanding.* Vol. 3 of *Collected Works of Bernard Lonergan.* Edited by Frederick E. Crowe and Robert M. Doran. Toronto: University of Toronto Press, 1992.

_____. *Method in Theology.* London: Darton, Longman, and Todd, 1972.

_____. "Natural Knowledge of God." In *A Second Collection.* Edited by William Ryan and Bernard Tyrrell, 117–33. Philadelphia: Westminster Press, 1974.

_____. "Theology in Its New Context." In *Second Collection.* Edited by

William Ryan and Bernard Tyrrell, 55–68. Philadelphia: Westminster, 1974.

_____. "Theology and Praxis." In *A Third Collection*. Edited by Frederick E. Crowe, 184–201. New York: Paulist, 1985.

_____. "The Transition from a Classicist World-View to Historical Mindedness." In *A Second Collection*. Vol. 13 of *Collected Works of Bernard Lonergan*. Edited by William F. Ryan and Bernard Tyrrell, 1–9. Toronto: University of Toronto Press, 1996.

_____. *Understanding and Being: The Halifax Lectures on Insight*. Vol. 5 of *Collected Works of Bernard Lonergan*. Edited by Elizabeth A. Morelli, Mark D. Morelli and Frederick E. Crowe. 2nd ed. Toronto: University of Toronto Press, 1990.

_____. *The Way to Nicea: The Dialectical Development of Trinitarian Theology*. Translated by Conn O'Donovan. London: Darton, Longman, and Todd, 1976.

Loyola, Ignatius of. *The Spiritual Exercises of St. Ignatius: Based on Studies in the Language of the Autograph*. Translated by Louis J. Puhl. Chicago: Loyola Press, 1951.

Maas, Paul. *Textual Criticism*. Oxford: Clarendon, 1958.

McFague, Sallie. *Metaphorical Theology: Models of God in Religious Language*. Philadelphia: Fortress Press, 1982.

MacIntyre, Alasdair. *After Virtue: A Study in Moral Theory*. 2nd ed. Notre Dame, IN: University of Notre Dame, 1984.

_____. *Whose Justice? Which Rationality?* Notre Dame, IN: University of Notre Dame, 1988.

May, Gerald. *Addiction and Grace*. San Francisco: Harper and Row, 1988.

_____. *The Awakened Heart: Living Beyond Addiction*. 1st ed. San Francisco: HarperSanFrancisco, 1991.

McCabe, Herbert. *God Matters*. London; New York: Continuum, 2005.

McCormick, Patrick T. *God's Beauty: A Call to Justice*. Liturgical Press, 2012.

McDonagh, Sean. *To Care for the Earth: A Call to a New Theology*. 1st U.S. ed. Santa Fe: Bear & Co, 1987.

McFague, Sallie. *Metaphorical Theology: Models of God in Religious Language.* Philadelphia: Fortress Press, 1982.

McInerny, Ralph. *Dante and the Blessed Virgin.* Notre Dame, IN: University of Notre Dame, 2010.

Meier, John P. *A Marginal Jew: Rethinking the Historical Jesus.* 3 vols. New York: Doubleday, 1994.

Merton, Thomas. *Love and Living.* New York: Harcourt Trade Publishers, 2002.

_____. *Conjectures of a Guilty Bystander.* Garden City, NY: Doubleday, 1966.

Metzger, Bruce M., and Bart D. Ehrman. *The Text of the New Testament: Its Transmission, Corruption, and Restoration.* 4th ed. Oxford: Oxford University, 2005.

Meyer, Ben F. *The Aims of Jesus.* London: SCM, 1979.

_____. *Reality and Illusion in New Testament Scholarship: A Primer in Critical Realist Hermeneutics.* Collegeville, MN: Liturgical, 1994.

Milbank, John. *Theology and Social Theory: Beyond Secular Reason.* Cambridge, MA: Blackwell, 1991.

Moore, Andrew. "Should Christians Do Natural Theology?" *Scottish Journal of Theology* 63, 2 (2010): 127–45.

Moreland, J. P. "The Argument from Consciousness." In *The Blackwell Companion to Natural Theology.* Edited by William Lane Craig and J. P. Moreland. Oxford: Blackwells, 2009.

Mudd, Joseph C. *Eucharist as Meaning: Critical Metaphysics and Contemporary Sacramental Theology.* Collegeville, Minnesota: Liturgical Press, 2014.

Newman, John Henry. *Conscience, Consensus, and the Development of Doctrine.* Edited by James Gaffney. 1st ed. New York: Image Books, 1992.

_____. *On Consulting the Faithful in Matters of Doctrine.* London: G. Chapman, 1961.

O'Collins, Gerald. "The Pope's Theology." *The Tablet,* June 27, 1992: 246.

_____. *Rethinking Fundamental Theology.* Oxford: Oxford University Press, 2011.

O'Malley, John W. "Vatican II: Did Anything Happen?" *Theological Studies* 67, 1 (2006): 3–33.

O'Malley, John W, Neil Ormerod, Stephen Schloesser, and Joseph Komonchak. *Vatican II: Did Anything Happen?* Edited by David G. Schultenover. New York: Continuum, 2007.

Ormerod, Neil. "Augustine's *De Trinitate* and Lonergan's Realms of Meaning." *Theological Studies* 64, 4 (2003): 773–94.

_____. "Bernard Lonergan and the Recovery of a Metaphysical Frame." *Theological Studies* 74, 4 (2013): 960–82.

_____. *Creation, Grace and Redemption.* Maryknoll, NY: Orbis, 2007.

_____. "Desire and the Origins of Culture: Lonergan and Girard in Conversation." *Heythrop Journal* 54, 5 (2013): 784–95.

_____. "A Dialectic Engagement with the Social Sciences in an Ecclesiological Context." *Theological Studies* 66, 4 (2005): 815–40.

_____. "The Dual Language of Sacrifice." *Pacifica* 17, 2 (2004): 159–69.

_____. "Addendum on the Grace–Nature Distinction." *Theological Studies* 75, no. 4 (2014): 890–98.

_____. "The Metaphysics of Holiness: Created Participation in the Divine Nature." *Irish Theological Quarterly* 79, 1 (2014): 68–82.

_____. *A Public God: Natural Theology Reconsidered.* Minneapolis: Fortress Press, 2015.

_____. *Re-Visioning the Church: An Experiment in Systematic-Historical Ecclesiology.* Minneapolis: Fortress Press, 2014.

_____. "The Transcultural Significance of the Council of Chalcedon." *Australasian Catholic Record* LXX (1993): 322–32.

_____. *A Trinitarian Primer.* Collegeville/Strathfield: Liturgical Press/St. Pauls, 2011.

_____. "Vatican II—Continuity or Discontinuity? Toward an Ontology of Meaning." *Theological Studies* 71, 3 (2010): 609–36.

Ormerod, Neil J. and Shane Clifton. *Globalization and the Mission of the Church.* Ecclesiological Investigations. Edited by Gerard Mannion. London: T&T Clark, 2009.

Otto, Rudolf. *The Idea of the Holy: An Inquiry into the Non-Rational Factor in the Idea of the Divine and Its Relation to the Rational.* 2d ed. New York: Oxford University Press, 1950.

Pannenberg, Wolfhart, Rolf Rendtorff, Trutz Rendtorff, and Ulrich Wilkens. *Revelation as History.* New York: Macmillan, 1968.

Pascal, Blaise. *Pensées.* New York: E. P. Dutton, 1958.

Pieper, Josef. *In Search of the Sacred: Contributions to an Answer.* Translated by Lothar Krauth. San Francisco: Ignatius, 1991.

Pelikan, Jaroslav Jan. *The Emergence of the Catholic Tradition (100–600).* Chicago: University of Chicago Press, 1971.

Plantinga, Alvin. *God, Freedom, and Evil.* New York: Harper & Row, 1974.

Plato. *Symposium.* Translated by Alexander Nehamas and Paul Woodruff. Indianapolis: Hackett, 1989.

Price, James. "The Objectivity of Mystical Truth Claims." *Thomist* 46, 1 (1985): 81–98.

_____. "Typologies and the Cross-Cultural Analysis of Mysticism: A Critique." In *Religion and Culture: Essays in Honor of Bernard Lonergan, SJ.* Edited by Timothy P. Fallon and Philip Boo Riley. Albany: SUNY, 1987.

Rahner, Karl. "Anonymous Christians." Translated by Karl-H. Kruger and Boniface Kruger. In *Theological Investigations.* Vol. 6, 390–98. New York: Seabury, 1974.

_____. "Christianity and the Non-Christian Religions." Translated by Karl-H. Kruger. In *Theological Investigations.* Vol. 5, 115–34. Baltimore: Helicon, 1966.

_____. *The Dynamic Element in the Church.* New York: Herder and Herder, 1964.

_____. *Foundations of Christian Faith: An Introduction to the Idea of Christianity.* Translated by William V. Dych. New York: Crossroad, 1982.

_____. "The Theological Concept of Concupiscentia." Translated by Cornelius Ernst. In *Theological Investigations.* Vol. 1, 347–82. London: Darton, Longman, and Todd, 1961.

_____. "Theology as Engaged in an Interdisciplinary Dialogue with the Sciences." Translated by David Bourke. In *Theological Investigations.* Vol. 13, 80–93. New York: Seabury, 1975.

_____. *The Trinity*. New York: Crossroad, 1997.

Ratzinger, Joseph. "Foundations and Approaches of Biblical Exegesis." *Origins* 17/35 (11 February 1988): 593, 95–602.

Ricœur, Paul. *The Symbolism of Evil*. New York: Harper & Row, 1967.

Ruether, Rosemary Radford. *Gaia & God: An Ecofeminist Theology of Earth Healing*. 1st ed. San Francisco: HarperSanFrancisco, 1992.

_____. *Sexism and God-Talk: Toward a Feminist Theology*. 10th anniversary ed. Boston: Beacon, 1993.

Rush, Ormond. *The Eyes of Faith: The Sense of the Faithful and the Church's Reception of Revelation*. Washington, DC: Catholic University of America, 2009.

Saint Justin Martyr: The Fathers of the Church, a New Translation. Translated by Thomas B. Falls. New York: Christian Heritage, 1948.

Scarry, Elaine. *On Beauty and Being Just*. Princeton University Press, 2013.

Schillebeeckx, Edward. *Christ: the Christian Experience in the Modern World*. Translated by John Bowden. London: SCM Press, 1980.

_____. *Church: The Human Story of God*. Translated by John Bowden. New York: Crossroad, 1990.

_____. *The Eucharist*. New York: Sheed and Ward, 1968.

Schüssler Fiorenza, Elisabeth. *But She Said: Feminist Practices of Biblical Interpretation*. Boston: Beacon, 1992.

Schwager, Raymund. *Jesus in the Drama of Salvation: Toward a Biblical Doctrine of Redemption*. New York: Crossroad, 1999.

_____. *Must There Be Scapegoats?: Violence and Redemption in the Bible*. 1st ed. San Francisco: Harper & Row, 1987.

Schweitzer, Albert. *The Quest of the Historical Jesus*. Minneapolis: Fortress Press, 2001.

Sherman, Jacob H. "Metaphysics and the Redemption of Sacrifice: On René Girard and Charles Williams." *Heythrop Journal* 51, 1 (2010): 45–59.

Tanner, Kathryn. *God and Creation in Christian Theology: Tyranny and Empowerment?* Minneapolis: Fortress Press, 2004.

_____. *Theories of Culture: A New Agenda for Theology*. Minneapolis: Fortress Press, 1997.

Tanner, Norman P. *Decrees of the Ecumenical Councils*. 2 vols. London/ Washington, DC: Sheed & Ward/Georgetown University, 1990.

Taylor, Charles. "The Church Speaks—To Whom?" In *Church and People: Disjunctions in a Secular Age*. Edited by Charles Taylor, Jose Casanova and George F. McLean. 17–24. Washington, DC: The Council for Research in Values and Philosophy, 2012.

_____. *A Secular Age*. Cambridge, MA: Belknap Press, 2007.

Tillich, Paul. *The Courage to Be*. The Terry Lectures. New Haven: Yale University Press, 1952.

Turner, Denys. *Faith, Reason, and the Existence of God*. Cambridge: Cambridge University, 2004.

Voegelin, Eric. *The New Science of Politics, an Introduction*. Chicago: University of Chicago Press, 1952.

Weber, Max. *The Protestant Ethic and the Spirit of Capitalism*. Translated by Talcott Parsons. Dover Publications, 2003.

Weigel, George. "An Extraordinary Synod, Indeed." *First Things*, 22 October 2014.

Whitehead, Alfred North. *Process and Reality: An Essay in Cosmology*. Edited by David Griffin and Donald W. Sherburne New York: Free Press, 1978.

Wilkins, Jeremy. "Grace and Growth: Aquinas, Lonergan and the Problematic of Habitual Grace." *Theological Studies* 72, 4 (2011): 723–49.

Williams, A. N. "What Is Systematic Theology?" *International Journal of Systematic Theology* 11, 1 (2009): 40–55.

Williams, Rowan. *Teresa of Avila*. London: Continuum, 2003.

Wink, Walter. *The Powers That Be: Theology for a New Millennium*. New York: Doubleday, 1998.

Wright, N. T. *Jesus and the Victory of God*. Minneapolis: Fortress Press, 1996.

Zizioulas, John. *Being as Communion: Studies in Personhood and the Church*. Crestwood, NY: St. Vladimir's Seminary Press, 1985.

Zizioulas, John, and Paul McPartlan. *Communion and Otherness: Further Studies in Personhood and the Church*. New York: T & T Clark, 2006.

Index

self-communication and, 235;
intradivine relations and,
235–36
divinization, 247–48
Dobell, Brian, 93n8
Docetism, 208n17
doctrinal stances: foundations of
theology and, 229
doctrine: conversion and, 285;
development of, 224–28;
hierarchy of, 309; history and,
285; limitations of, 285;
meaning and, 225, 284n67;
postmodernism and, 210;
religious, 112–13; religious
experience and, 285;
resurrection of Jesus and, 309;
revelation and, 195, 202,
207–12; theologies of religions
and, 284; of Trinity, 231–37
doctrines (functional specialty),
309–10; authenticity and, 310;
foundational theology and,
166; truth and, 309–10
Dodd, C. H., 220n32
Dominus Iesus (Congregation for
the Doctrine of the Faith),
286n69
Doran, Robert M., xii, 7n11, 66n4,
72n16, 143n41, 144n42,
247n26; on aesthetics, 129; on
conversion types, 129–30; on
Jung and good and evil,
148n52; on the psyche, 128

Dostoyevsky, Fyodor: *Idiot, The,*
187–88
Doyle, Dominic, 87n34, 246n25
Dulles, Avery, 15n27, 41n21,
114n32; *Models of Revelation,*
53–54, 195–96; on
propositions and revelation,
200; on revelation as
symbolically mediated, 198
Dunn, Geoffrey D., 155n4
Dunn, James, 18
Durkheim, Emile, 44; on
sociology, 11
dwellers and seekers, 260, 263–64

Easter Triduum, 138; mystery of
salvation and, 198
ecological theologies, 68
ecumenical dialogue, 53–54
Edwards, Denis, 68n8
effective meaning, 113–14, 292;
cognitive meaning and, 218;
communicative meaning and,
220; revelation and, 212–14,
224
Ehrman, D., 297n6
Eliade, Mircea: on the sacred and
the profane, 267–68
Emery, Gilles, 2n4
empirical data, 40n19
empiricism, 115; knowledge of
God and, 179
enculturation, 315–16
Ende, Michael, 149n55